Developing Projects Using
Visual Basic® 5.0/6.0

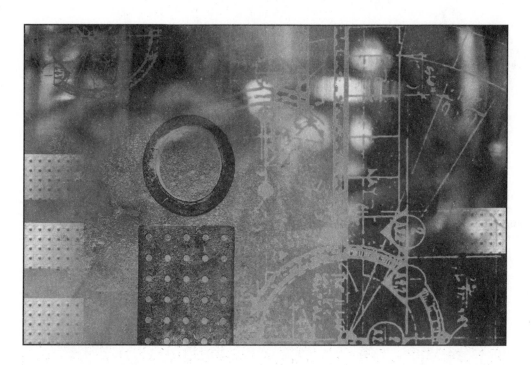

Debbie Tesch
Roy Boggs

COURSE
TECHNOLOGY

ONE MAIN STREET, CAMBRIDGE, MA

an International Thomson Publishing company I T P®

Cambridge • Albany • Bonn • Boston • Cincinnati • London • Madrid • Melbourne • Mexico City
New York • Paris • San Francisco • Singapore • Tokyo • Toronto • Washington

Developing Projects Using Visual Basic 5.0/6.0 is published by Course Technology.

Managing Editor	Kristen Duerr
Product Manager	Cheryl Ouellette
Production Editor	Ellina Beletsky
Developmental Editor	Jessica Evans
Text Designer	Kim Munsell
Cover Designer	Efrat Reis

©1999 by Course Technology— I(T)P®

For more information contact:

Course Technology
One Main Street
Cambridge, MA 02142

International Thomson Editores
Seneca, 53
Colonia Polanco
11560 Mexico D.F. Mexico

ITP Europe
Berkshire House 168-173
High Holborn
London WCIV 7AA
England

ITP GmbH
Königswinterer Strasse 418
53227 Bonn
Germany

Nelson ITP, Australia
102 Dodds Street
South Melbourne, 3205
Victoria, Australia

ITP Asia
60 Albert Street, #15-01
Albert Complex
Singapore 189969

ITP Nelson Canada
1120 Birchmount Road
Scarborough, Ontario
Canada M1K 5G4

ITP Japan
Hirakawacho Kyowa Building, 3F
2-2-1 Hirakawacho
Chiyoda-ku, Tokyo 102
Japan

Trademarks
Course Technology and the Open Book logo are registered trademarks and CourseKits is a trademark of Course Technology. Custom Editions and the ITP logo are registered trademarks of International Thomson Publishing Inc.

I(T)P® ITP logo is a registered trademark of International Thomson Publishing.

Microsoft, Visual Basic, and Windows are registered trademarks of Microsoft Corporation.

Some of the product names and company names used in this book have been used for identification purposes only and may be trademarks or registered trademarks of their respective manufacturers and sellers.

Disclaimer
Course Technology reserves the right to revise this publication and make changes from time to time in its content without notice.

ISBN 0-7600-5855-5

Printed in the United States of America

1 2 3 4 5 6 7 8 9 10 BM 02 01 00 99

Preface

Developing Projects Using Visual Basic 5.0/6.0 is designed to provide students with an opportunity to follow the development of a real-life programming project from its design to its delivery to the client. Throughout the book, students will create a complete Visual Basic application for a temporary employment service agency. You can use this book to supplement any class where Visual Basic 5.0 or 6.0 is available as a course programming language. This book assumes that students will learn basic programming concepts from an introductory textbook or from the instructor. The goal of this book is to support a course where the instructor wants students to experience the real-life application of Visual Basic concepts.

Organization and Coverage

Developing Projects Using Visual Basic 5.0/6.0 contains an introductory chapter that explains, from a systems analysis view, the continuing project (Shely Services, Inc.) and the three progressive (continuing) projects that students will develop on their own as they complete the book. In Chapters 2 through 8, students will see how an application is developed. In Chapter 9, students will deliver the application to the client.

When students complete this book, they will have experienced the development of a project from design to delivery. Students will learn how to organize and program a project in Visual Basic; how to develop and manage data files, including sequential, random, and Access files; and how to generate detail, summary, and control break reports. This book emphasizes project development considerations and data management processes in a real-life environment.

Approach

Developing Projects Using Visual Basic 5.0/6.0 distinguishes itself from other Visual Basic books because of its project-based approach. Students are introduced to the skills needed by programmer/analysts. The book's concentration on data management and user interaction with the data gives students the necessary skills to begin a career in information-related fields. Through the actual process of programming a complete project from design to delivery, the student experiences the patience and discipline required during a project's development. A model project is developed step by step, throughout the textbook, and students use the project as a guide to develop their own project development skills using Visual Basic. Students can use any of the three progressive (continuing) projects, along with the material in each chapter, to develop their own projects. After completing the book, students will have prepared a project that will provide tangible evidence of their programming accomplishments.

Features

Developing Projects Using Visual Basic 5.0/6.0 is a unique and exceptional textbook because it includes the following features:

■ **"Read This Before You Begin" Page** This page is consistent with Course Technology's unequaled commitment to helping instructors introduce technology into the classroom. Technical considerations and assumptions about hardware, software, and default settings are listed in one place to help instructors better serve their students.

- **Project Approach** The textbook uses a project-based approach to lead the student from a project's design to its completion and delivery. Students experience the development of a project by performing programming functions similar to those of the programmer/analyst.
- **Exercises** are included for each major section of the book. Exercises focus students on developing new applications or functionality, modifying an existing program, or debugging an existing program.
- **Examples** from the Shely Services application appear throughout each chapter to help the student understand the material better and to serve as guides for developing independent projects.
- **Summaries** Following each chapter is a Summary that recaps the programming concepts and Visual Basic code covered in the chapter.
- **Progressive Projects** Each chapter concludes with three progressive (continuing) projects that students develop using the skills learned in the chapter. These progressive projects result in complete applications. The projects are designed to allow students to experience, organize, and program a project in Visual Basic; to develop and manage data files, including sequential, random, and Access files; and to generate detail, summary, and control break reports.
- **Independent Projects** Each chapter includes three independent, stand-alone projects that are designed to allow students to create smaller applications to solve less significant problems.

Visual Basic Software

This textbook uses the Professional Edition of the Visual Basic 5.0 or 6.0 programming language.

The Supplements

Supplements for this textbook are provided on a CD-ROM, which is available only to text adopters. The CD-ROM includes the following files:

- **Student Data Files**, containing all of the data and programs that students will use for the chapter exercises and projects, are provided on the CD-ROM. See the "Read This Before You Begin" page before Chapter 1 for more information on Student Files.
- **Solution Files**, containing solutions to all of the exercises and projects and for each step of the Shely application, are available on the CD-ROM.

Acknowledgements

We would like to thank all the people who helped make this textbook a reality, especially Jessica Evans, our Development Editor, and Kristen Duerr, Managing Editor, and her staff. We are grateful for the many reviewers who provided helpful and insightful comments during the development of this textbook, including Rick Wilkerson, Dyersburg State Community College; Raymond Major, Virginia Polytechnic Institute and State University; and Mark Shellman, Gaston College. Finally, we dedicate this book to our families: wife Judy, husband Bob, and Mommy's Melanie for the many hours they have endured without our company during the life of this project.

Debbie Tesch
Roy Boggs

Contents

Read This Before You Begin

To the Student

Student Disks

To complete the chapters, exercises, and projects in this textbook, you need Student Disks. Your instructor will provide you with Student Disks or ask you to make your own.

   If you need to make your own Student Disks, you will need seven blank, formatted, high-density disks. You will need to copy a single folder to a single disk — one each for Chapters 2 through 8 — from a file server or stand-alone computer. Your instructor will tell you which computer, drive letter, and folder contain the files you need. The programs in this book require you to save any data files in the root directory of drive A.

Using Your Own Computer

If you are using your own computer, you must contact your instructor to get the Student Files for this book. In addition, you must have a computer running Windows 95/98 or Windows NT operating system, 500 MB of free disk space, and a minimum of 32 MB of memory (64 MB is recommended for Windows NT). You will need to install the Visual Basic software, version 5.0 or 6.0.

File Designations

The programs in this textbook always assume the lowest level file designation for data files (for example, A:\CHCust.mdb). If you store your Student Files in numbered chapter folders on floppy disks, you must either relocate the data files to the root directory of drive A, or change the file location in the code (for example, A:\Chapter6\CHCust.mdb if the files are in the Chapter6 folder). If you store your Student Files on a hard drive, then you will need to use that drive's designation and the designation of any folder(s) you establish (for example: C:\Chapter6\CHCust.mdb if the files are in the Chapter6 folder on drive C). If you do not move the data files into the root directory of your disk, then you will have to change the file locations in the code, or your programs will not compile correctly.

To the Instructor

To complete the chapters in this book, your students must use a set of Student Files. You must be a registered adopter of this book to receive these files. Follow the instructions in the Help file to copy the student files to your server or stand-alone computer. You can view the Help file using a text editor such as WordPad or Notepad.

   Once the files are copied, you can make Student Disks for the students yourself, or tell students where to find the files so they can make their own Student Disks. Make sure the files are copied correctly onto the Student Disks by following the instructions in the Student Disks section, which will ensure that students have enough disk space to complete all of the chapters and assignments in this textbook.

Course Technology Student Files

You are granted a license to copy the student files to any computer or computer network used by students who have purchased this book.

The Visual Basic 5.0/6.0 Development Environment

Introduction ▶ Experienced professionals and beginning Windows programmers can use the Visual Basic toolset to simplify rapid application development. In Visual Basic, you build the Windows application graphical user interface (GUI) using prebuilt objects, called controls, and a drag-and-drop approach to design the appearance and location of interface elements. An **object** is an item in the GUI environment, such as the OK button, that you can manipulate and program to perform tasks. Visual Basic, which is an adaptation of the BASIC language, contains statements, functions, and keywords related to the GUI interface to accomplish application objectives. The result is a powerful programming language used *on* the Windows desktop to develop applications *for* the Windows desktop. After studying Chapter 1, you will be able to describe concepts unique to Visual Basic applications development.

Visual Basic Concepts

To program in the Windows environment, you must understand the concepts of windows, events, and messages. A **window** is a rectangular object with its own boundaries. Common window examples include document windows within word processing programs, the Visual Basic application itself as a window on the desktop, and dialog boxes. Other window examples, which Visual Basic actually perceives as objects, include command buttons, icons, text boxes, option buttons, and menu bars.

The Windows operating environment monitors all windows for **events**, or signs of activity. Events occur as a result of user actions (such as clicking a mouse button or pressing a key), program control, or other application window actions (such as changing data in a text box or giving a control the focus).

When an event occurs, the event sends a message to the operating system for processing. The system processes the message and broadcasts it to the other windows. Each window takes the appropriate action based on its instructions for dealing with that particular message. For example, when a window is uncovered by another window, it repaints itself. The Visual Basic programmer deals only with messages that Visual Basic can't handle automatically. These messages are presented to the programmer as Event procedures. **Event procedures** are the code windows associated with events that the programmer can use to manipulate objects.

The Event-Driven Model

Traditional, or procedural, applications control code execution and sequence. Program execution begins with the first line of code and continues along a predefined path. Visual Basic is an event-driven programming language. In the event-driven model, Event procedures (or sections of code) are executed in response to events. It is the sequence of events that determines the sequence in which code executes. Events can be triggered by user actions, messages from the operating system or other applications, or by the application code itself.

Interactive Development

Procedural applications development follows a process of writing, compiling, and testing code. Generally each step is completed before moving on to subsequent steps. The Visual Basic approach to development is interactive. Visual Basic interprets the code as the programmer enters it, so the compiler can report syntax and spelling errors immediately. In addition, the compiler partially compiles code as it is entered, which eliminates much of the delay between entering code and testing the application. The interactive nature of Visual Basic permits running an application as it is built. This interactive nature also allows the programmer to test the effects of current code quickly and easily.

Objects, Properties, Methods, and Functions

In addition to being event-driven, Visual Basic also is an object-oriented programming language because the programmer uses objects to perform tasks. Interface elements located on a **form** (the Visual Basic term for "window" during the design phase of development) represent objects, called **controls** in Visual Basic, that the programmer can use to perform tasks, which include the complete set of events associated with an object. For example, a command button, such as the OK or Cancel button in a dialog box, can respond to a mouse click, the pressing of a key on the keyboard, or many other events.

Each object has a default set of characteristics associated with it called properties and a predefined set of actions called methods. **Properties** control the appearance and behavior of the object. A programmer can use the Visual Basic development environment to change these default settings. **Methods** expedite rapid application development for common actions performed on objects. For example, the PrintForm method initiates all system actions required to print a copy of the form to the printer.

In addition to methods, Visual Basic retains **functions** as predefined procedures that result in values. You might be familiar with functions in other applications—for example, the SUM function in Microsoft Excel is used to compute the total of a row or column of numbers.

The Integrated Development Environment

The Visual Basic **integrated development environment** (**IDE**) consists of elements organized as distinct windows within the application. Use the element descriptions in this section and in Figure 1-1 to familiarize yourself with the IDE. (Your startup screen might look different.)

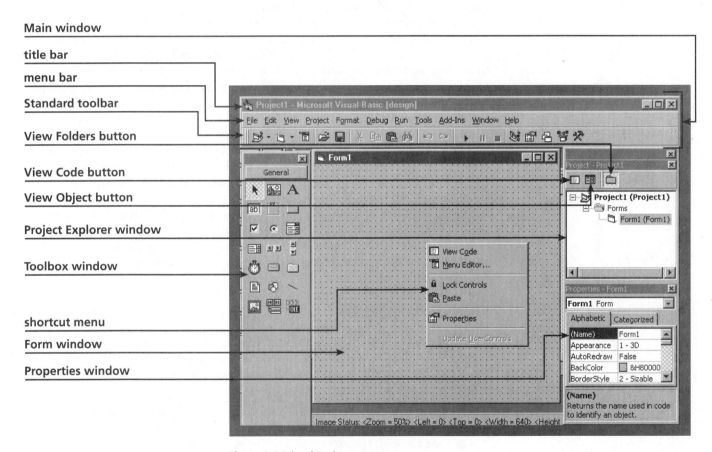

Figure 1-1: Visual Basic startup screen

The **Main window** in Visual Basic contains the title bar, menu bar, and the Standard toolbar. The **title bar** contains the name of the program (Microsoft Visual Basic) and the name of the current saved project or "Project#" for unsaved projects. The title bar also indicates the current status of the Visual Basic application: **design** indicates that the application currently is under development, and **run** indicates that the application currently is being executed.

The **menu bar** contains commands that are used to work with Visual Basic. Menus provide access to programming specific functions, such as Project, Format, or Debug. The **Standard toolbar** contains buttons that represent shortcuts for executing menu commands. For example, you can click the Save button instead of clicking File on the menu bar and then clicking Save.

The **Form window** appears in the center of the screen. You use this window to create the application interface. Each form in the application has its own Form window.

The **Toolbox window** contains the toolset that you use at design time to place objects on a form. You can customize the default toolbox using the Add Tab command on the shortcut menu to add additional controls to the window.

The **Project Explorer window** lists the forms and projects in the current project. The list is displayed as a hierarchy of the projects included in the application and each item contained in each project. The Project Explorer window contains three buttons—View Code, View Object, and Toggle Folders—that you can use to display the hierarchy in different ways. The **View Code button** displays the program code associated with the selected file. The **View Object button** displays the object associated with the selected file. The **Toggle Folders button** controls the display of folders in the List window. Clicking the Toggle Folders button causes only the items contained in the folders to be displayed.

The **Properties window** lists the current property settings for the selected form or control. Only properties that can be set at design time appear in the Properties window.

Shortcut menus have become a Windows standard for providing shortcuts to frequently performed actions in Windows applications. When you right-click any object on the screen, the shortcut menu that appears depends on the current position of the mouse pointer.

The **Object Browser**, which is available only at design time, allows the programmer to inspect objects, such as intrinsic constants, that are available for use in the project. The programmer uses the Object Browser to search for available objects, to find methods and properties available for those objects, and to paste code procedures into an application. You will learn about the use of intrinsic constants and the Object Browser in Chapter 4.

Additional IDE elements available in Visual Basic include the Code Editor window, Form Layout window, and windows provided for use in debugging your application (Immediate, Locals, and Watch windows). You will learn about each of these elements when you use them during the application development process.

Project Management

Visual Basic uses projects to manage the files that make up an application. A **project** is the collection of files that make up the application. You use the Project Explorer window to manage the components that make up a project. A project consists of the following elements:

- A project file with the extension .vbp that keeps track of all application components
- One file with the extension .frm for each form
- One binary data file with the extension .frx for each form containing data for properties of controls on the form; these files are generated automatically for any .frm file that contains binary properties
- One file with the extension .cls for each class module, if any exist
- One file with the extension .bas for a standard module that contains only basic code, if any exist

- One or more files with the extension .ocx that contain ActiveX controls, if any exist
- A single resource file with the extension .res, if necessary

Creating, Opening, and Saving Projects

From within the IDE, the File menu allows the programmer to create, open, and save projects. The **New Project** command closes the current project (and prompts the programmer to save any files that have changed) and opens the New Project dialog box from which a type of project can be selected.

The **Open Project** command closes the current project (and prompts the programmer to save any files that have changed). Visual Basic then opens the requested project including the forms, modules, and ActiveX controls listed in the project file.

The **Save Project** command updates the project file of the current project, including all of its form, standard, and class modules. The Save Project As command allows the programmer to specify a new filename for the project. The programmer is prompted to save any forms or modules that have changed. Alternatively, you can save a new project by using the Save <*filename*> As and the Save Project As commands on the File menu. When you use this alternative, you must save the form before saving the project.

Creating and Running an Executable File

Completed Visual Basic projects are distributed to the user via the use of an executable file with the file extension .exe. An **executable file** consists of compiled code in a file that can run outside the Visual Basic environment on any computer running Microsoft Windows. The executable file contains the machine code version of an application. Use the File menu's Make <*projectname.exe*> command to create the executable file.

To run an executable file, the user needs a copy of the .exe file, a copy of the Visual Basic run-time files, and copies of any data files associated with the application, as well as the run-time files associated with the data files. Microsoft allows the distribution of this file with applications. To run the application on a computer without Visual Basic installed, use the Run command on the Start menu to run the .exe file.

The Visual Basic Application Development Process

The emphasis with object-oriented/event-driven (OOED) languages, such as Visual Basic, is on the objects included in the user interface and on the events that occur through those objects. Consequently, the procedure-oriented approach to the programming solution of step-by-step, top-to-bottom development is inappropriate. The goal of the Visual Basic programmer is to develop an interface that gives the user as much control as possible, while guarding against application errors.

The programming process in Visual Basic consists of a five-step process: plan the application, build the user interface, code the application, test and debug the application, and deliver the application (which includes project documentation). The application plan culminates in an identification of tasks the application needs to perform, the objects needed to accomplish these tasks, and the events required to trigger an object to perform its task.

The interactive nature of the development environment allows the programmer to continue refinements and development of the user interface while involved in the coding process. You can test event code immediately as each event process is completed. Delivering the application involves gathering all documentation for delivery with the executable file. This text will emphasize the build, code, and test processes of application development.

In the next section, the Visual Basic development process is presented as a copyright screen is developed. The copyright screen ultimately might be displayed through the development of an About menu item in the Help menu or a **splash screen**, which is an image that appears while the application is loaded into memory.

Building the User Interface

Figure 1-2 shows a sketch of the user interface based on the design plan. Using this sketch, the programmer places the appropriate controls on the form and sets the applicable properties of those controls. The Toolbox window is used to select the appropriate controls and the Properties window is used to make any adjustments to default property settings.

Figure 1-2: Sketch of Shely Services, Inc. copyright screen

While giving the user as much control over the interface as possible, you should remember that the interface should not distract the user from the task at hand. De facto Windows GUI design guidelines provide suggestions for placing and sizing controls, including the use of graphics and appropriate font styles and sizes. Experience with Windows application interfaces is perhaps your best teacher. Figure 1-3 shows the completed user interface for Shely Services, Inc.

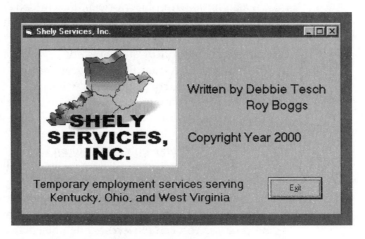

Figure 1-3: Shely Services, Inc. copyright screen

Coding the Application

Coding the application involves writing Visual Basic instructions that tell the objects on the Visual Basic interface how to respond to events. The application plan identifies events associated with objects, which often is described as accomplishing the application's tasks. The only event associated with the copyright screen at this point is the Click event, which is associated with the Exit button. When the user clicks the Exit button, the application should terminate. The End statement tells Visual Basic to terminate the application. Figure 1-4 shows the Click event procedure for the Exit button. You double-click the Exit object button to view the screen shown in Figure 1-4.

Figure 1-4: Click event procedure for the Exit command button

Testing and Debugging the Application

You test an application by running it to see if it accomplishes its required tasks. You must test applications that require data entry by using valid and invalid data. If errors are located in the application, the process of **debugging** is used to locate and remove those errors.

Delivering the Application

Programmers deliver the completed application to users as an executable file only after thorough testing and removal of application errors. The simplicity of the copyright screen application has been used to describe the application development process. You will learn more about the development process throughout this book.

Using Online Help

Access to online Help in Visual Basic is available by pressing the F1 key or using the Help menu. Help topics in the Help menus are available via the Index, Contents, and Find tabs. The Index tab is used most frequently to search for information on a specific topic. You use the Index tab by typing a topic to search for in an alphabetical list of keywords. Selecting a topic from the list or typing the first few letters of the topic accesses a particular topic.

Pressing the F1 key in the application provides access to context-sensitive Help. **Context-sensitive Help** displays a Help window for the currently selected feature.

The Help menu also provides access to the Microsoft Visual Basic Books Online program. The Books Online program provides electronic access to a library of programmers' reference materials. These materials provide coverage of all levels of Visual Basic topics, from introductory to advanced.

The Shely Services, Inc. Project

Over the course of the term, you will construct a Visual Basic application for Shely Services, Inc. The project that you will create is described next.

Project Name and Purpose

The project name is the Temporary Employee Management System (TEMS). The project purpose is to create a system for managing data about Shely Services temporary employees, who currently are assigned to a job or who are available for work assignments.

TEMS Description

Shely Services provides temporary employees for businesses located in Kentucky, Ohio, and West Virginia. Employees are available for secretarial, clerical, light industrial, and marketing positions.

When Shely Services reaches an agreement with a temporary employee (or client), data about the client or about the particulars of the agreement—including the job's ID and title—are entered into a database table. Shely Services usually contracts between 50 and 100 jobs at any one time.

Before the beginning date of the agreement, Shely Services assigns the job to a supervisor, who contacts temporary employees and assigns employees to the job. When the job ends, the employees are reassigned or released, and the job is deleted from the assigned list. A temporary employee can be assigned to only one job at a time. Shely Services can support a maximum of 400 temporary employees.

TEMS Project Parameters

Shely Services requires a program written in Visual Basic that will permit interactive maintenance of the temporary employees' data. The program also must produce printed reports from the database and a backup utility to back up the data to disk.

The Shely Services Database

The basic data for Shely Service's temporary employees are stored in an Access database. The database name is ShelyTemps.m2b. Data with information about current jobs are stored in the same database.

The key field for the job ID joins the two tables. In order to simplify program development, employee IDs are numbered from 100 to 499. Job IDs also are numbered from 100 to 499. A job must exist in the CurrentJobs table before Shely Services can assign it to an employee.

The TemporaryEmployees table contains data about an employee. Figure 1-5 describes the fields in the table.

Field Name	Field Type	Field Length	Description
EmployeeID	Text	3	Primary key, required, no zero length, no duplicates
LastName	Text	30	
FirstName	Text	25	
Address	Text	50	
City	Text	15	
State	Text	2	Must be KY, OH, or WV
Zip	Text	5	
Phone	Text	14	(###) ###-####
Listed	Yes/No		
Shift	Text	16	
Secretarial	Yes/No		Secretarial position
Clerical	Yes/No		Clerical position
Industrial	Yes/No		Light industrial position
Marketing	Yes/No		Marketing position
Typing	Number		Integer, speed in words per minute
OptValues	Text	1	Storage for Option Button Values (1 – 4)
Notes	Memo		256 characters
JobID	Text	3	Foreign key, "000" is unassigned

Figure 1-5: TemporaryEmployees table description

The CurrentJobs table contains data about current jobs. Figure 1-6 describes the fields in the table.

Field Name	Field Type	Field Length	Description
JobID	Text	3	Primary key, job identification number
JobTitle	Text	30	Job title

Figure 1-6: CurrentJobs table description

Figure 1-7 shows the relationships that exist between the tables in the Shely Services database.

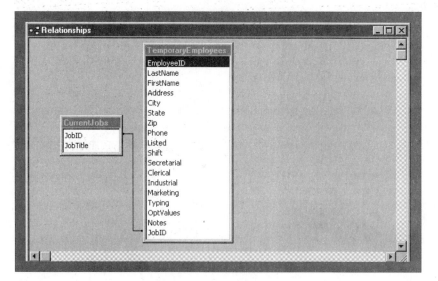

Figure 1-7: Shely Services database relationships

The Main Screen

Figure 1-8 shows the main screen that you will generate as part of the program. Access to the data must be password protected.

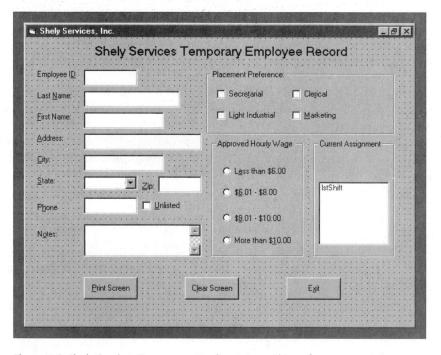

Figure 1-8: Shely Services Temporary Employee Record interface

Password Protection

Access to the SHURES program must be password protected with three levels of access. Passwords and permission levels exist in a random file. The filename is SSicher.txt, its access is random, and its record length is 256 characters. The word *Sicher* is German for "security"—it is best to avoid using obvious filenames for files that contain security data, such as passwords and access codes. Figure 1-9 describes how data are stored in the random file.

Data Description	Location in SSicher.txt
Other Data 1	1
Employee ID	2 – 4
Employee Last Name	5 – 34
Other Data 2	35 – 248
Access Code	249 – 250 (2 = read; 4 = read, add, update; 8 = full)
Password	251 – 256

Figure 1-9: Random file storage

Reports

Shely Services requires three printed reports. Any employee with access rights to the TemporaryEmployees table can generate every report. All reports contain a header showing the date the report was generated, the page number, the company's name, and the report title. All reports also contain a footer that indicates that the report was completed successfully.

The first report is a master list of all temporary employees. For each employee, it contains the employee's ID, last and first names, complete address, and phone number (if listed). Employee records are sorted alphabetically by last name.

The second report lists those temporary employees who are unassigned and available for assignment. Shely Services assumes that a temporary employee who is unassigned is available and can be contacted about an assignment. The report contains each employee's ID, last and first names, areas for which he or she is available, and if applicable, the employee's typing speed in words per minute. Employee records are sorted alphabetically by last name.

The third report lists all current jobs and the employees assigned to each job. Employees are sorted by job and by last name. Standard control break subtotals and totals occur for each job and for all jobs combined. Jobs are listed by job number and job title. Employees are listed by employee ID, and last and first names.

Delivering the Project

Completed projects must be delivered as proprietary executable code only. The source version, accessed by the Visual Basic application, should be unavailable to the client.

S U M M A R Y

As you complete the chapters in this book, you will develop the complete Shely Services, Inc. system for managing temporary employees. The TEMS program uses the power of Visual Basic and the Windows 95/98 operating environment to provide a desktop application that is rapidly developed and easily modified. Small companies, such as Shely Services, as well as large corporate entities are discovering the value of rapid development in the Visual Basic environment. You will be on your way to becoming a productive part of this development environment after you complete this book.

PROGRESSIVE PROJECTS

The following progressive (cumulative) projects are similar in design, but each project contains a different challenge. The first project requires an intersection table to associate two existing tables with each other based on different foreign keys. This project will use multiple SQL calls. The second project requires more interactions to display user requests. This project will focus largely on generating multiple forms for user access. The third project contains more opportunities to develop forms for data display.

There is a lot of room for creativity and programmer ingenuity in each of the projects. Your project should be user-friendly, professional in design and execution, and well documented. The best project will be well defined. The project assignment in each chapter will set parameters for the project, and then it is your job to complete the project within the parameters.

Top priority in each project is to manage the data in the database. There must be no way in which a user can corrupt data in the database or interrupt a carefully planned execution of events related to the data. A project might look great, but if it isn't useable, it is a waste of time and effort. Always remember to protect the data.

1. Bean County Plumbing Inventory System (BCPIS)

Project Name and Purpose: The project name is Bean County Plumbing Inventory System (BCPIS). The project purpose is to develop a system for managing the parts inventory of the Plumbing Division of the Water Distribution Section of bean county.

BCPIS Description: The Distribution Section of the Bean County Water Department serves over 25,000 water customers. The section is responsible for installing water services and meters to new customers, for checking large meters for accuracy and repairing as needed, and for maintaining critical back flow prevention valves. The distribution system uses almost 1,500 parts and supplies.

When new parts and supplies arrive, they are verified and placed in proper warehouse locations. Parts and supplies can be removed from a warehouse and transferred to a maintenance truck, or returned to the warehouse from a maintenance truck at any time. Although parts and supplies are charged on job sheets, there are no records for slippage and damage.

BCPIS Project Parameters: BCPIS will provide the Plumbing Division with a means for tracking its inventory. You will develop and write a Visual Basic program that will permit interactive maintenance of a parts and supplies database. As new parts and supplies are placed in a warehouse, corresponding data are entered into BCPIS. When any parts or supplies are moved, a written form is completed so that the database can be updated. You will use data from job sheets to update the database.

BCPIS also must produce printed reports and provide a backup system. Only certain employees are permitted access to the database.

BCPIS Inventory Database: The inventory database contains three tables in an Access database. The name of the database is BCPISdb.mdb. The master table for the parts and supplies and the master table for the location are joined by an intersection table. Referential integrity will be enforced so that no change can be made to the intersection table unless corresponding data are contained in the other two tables. The BCPIS program will require a minimum of a master form with a logo, a maintenance form for each table, and a form for generating reports.

The master parts table (MastPart) contains data about individual parts and supplies. Figure 1-10 describes the fields in the table.

Field Name	Field Type	Field Length	Description
PartID	Text	6	Primary key, required, no zero length, no duplicates
PartName	Text	30	
PartReOrdPnt	Number	Integer	Part reorder point
PartReOrdQty	Number	Integer	Part reorder quantity

Figure 1-10: MastPart table description

Figure 1-11 shows a sample MastPart table.

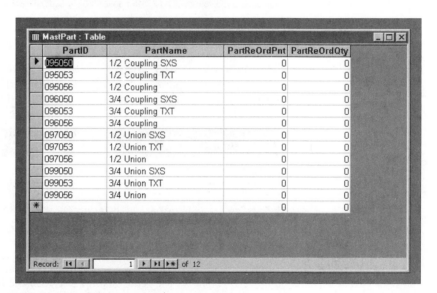

Figure 1-11: Sample MastPart table

The master location table (MastLoc) contains data about storage locations. Both warehouses and trucks are treated as locations [W*nn* = warehouse; T*nn* = truck]. Figure 1-12 describes the fields in the table.

Field Name	Field Type	Field Length	Description
LocID	Text	3	Primary key, required, no zero length, no duplicates
LocName	Text	30	

Figure 1-12: MastLoc table description

Figure 1-13 shows a sample MastLoc table.

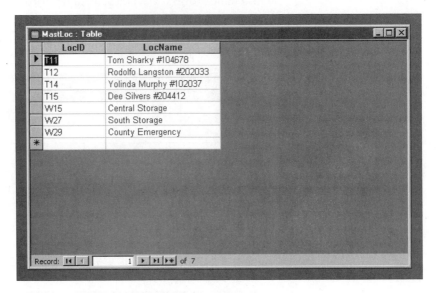

Figure 1-13: Sample MastLoc table

The master inventory table (MastInv) is an intersection table that contains data about individual parts and supplies and where they are currently stored. Figure 1-14 describes the fields in the table. The MastInv table currently contains no data.

Field Name	Field Type	Field Length	Description
LocID	Text	3	Required, must be in MastLoc
PartID	Text	6	Required, must be in MastPart
PartQty	Number	Integer	

Figure 1-14: MastInv table description

Figure 1-15 shows the relationships between the MastPart, MastLoc, MastInv tables.

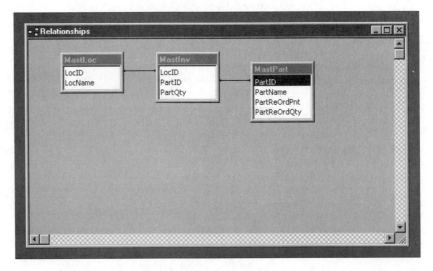

Figure 1-15: Relationships between the MastPart, MastLoc, and MastInv tables

BCPIS Password Protection: Access to the BCPIS program must be password protected with two levels of passwords. One level is for those employees who can update the PartQty field in the MastInv table and print a control break report on PartID. The second level is for all other activities. The employee identification codes and access levels will be located in a random access file. Figure 1-16 shows the record description for the BCPIS security file.

Data Description	Location in Random File
Employee ID	1 - 3 (Valid IDs = 100 to 200)
Employee Name	4 - 33
Access Level	34 (0 = all; 1 = limited)

Figure 1-16: Random access security file description

BCPIS Reports: The Plumbing Division requires three reports. Any employee with general access permission (limited) to the BCPISdb.mdb database can print a report by PartID. Any employee with full access permission (all) can print any of the three reports. Each report will contain a header showing the date the report was generated, the page number, the division's name, and a report title. Figure 1-17 shows a sample report header.

XX/XX/XX	Page
(small logo)	
Bean County Plumbing Division	
Water Division Section	
Report Title: Master Parts List for XXXXXX	

Figure 1-17: BCPIS report header

All reports also will contain a footer indicating that the report was successfully completed (End of 'report title').

The body of the first report is a master list of data about the county's storage locations. Figure 1-18 shows a sample storage location report.

Location ID	Location Name/Driver	Driver ID
W15	Central Storage	
T11	Tom Sharkey	104678
	Total Storage Locations = nn	

Figure 1-18: Body of storage location report

The body of the second report is a list of all parts sorted by part name. Figure 1-19 shows a sample parts report.

Part Name	Part ID
1/2 Coupling	0950561
XXXXXXXXXXXXXXXXXXXXXXXXXXXXXX	
	Total Number of Parts = nnnnn

Figure 1-19: Body of parts report

The body of the third report is a control break report that lists all parts, their locations, and subtotals. Figure 1-20 shows a sample body of the parts location report.

Part ID	Part Name	Location	Quantity
095050	1/2 Coupling SXS		
		W15	427
		T11	28
		Total 1/2 Coupling SXS = 455	
095053	1/2 Coupling TXT		
		W15	14
		T11	12
		Total 1/2 Coupling TXT = 26	
	Total Number of Parts = 481		

Figure 1-20: Body of parts location report

Delivering the Project: Completed projects must be delivered as proprietary executable code only. The source version, accessed by the Visual Basic application, should be unavailable to the client.

BCPIS Remote Access: The project will provide a Web page for inquiries into BCPIS. You will see the Web page design in Chapter 9.

2. Single Parents Public Service Library (SPLIB)

Project Name and Purpose: The project name is the Single Parents Public Service Library (SPLIB). The project purpose is to develop a system for managing library-related items that a single parents club makes available to its members and guests.

SPLIB Description: The single parents club has a small room at the back of a local bookstore where member volunteers store and check out library-related items (books, paperbacks, videos, CDs, etc.). The purpose of the service is to assemble items that members no longer want and that they are willing to check out in order to help each other save money.

When new items are donated to the library, data are entered on a 3" × 5" note card, and the card is filed in a small filing box. If an item is borrowed, then the name of the borrower is written on the back of the card. When the item is returned, the name is crossed out, and when the back of the card is full, a new card is made.

SPLIB Project Parameters: You will provide the library with a means of tracking its inventory. You will develop and write a Visual Basic project that will permit an interactive record of the library's inventory, a list of the members and guests who use the service, and a list of who has borrowed which item(s).

As new items are donated to the library, data about these items will be entered into a table in an Access database. Another table will be used to manage data about members and guests. When any registered member or guest wants to borrow an item, a volunteer member of the club enters the relevant data into a table in the database. A Visual Basic project will permit general management of the data in the database and will provide status reports.

SPLIB will have at least five forms: a main form with a logo, a maintenance form for each table, and a report form. The final form will be a form in which volunteers can display data upon request.

SPLIB Library Database: The library database contains two tables in an Access database. The name of the database is SPLIBdb.mdb. The primary table contains data about the items available to borrowers. A second table contains data about members and guests who can borrow library materials. A member cannot borrow an item unless both the item and the borrower's information exist in the database tables.

The master items table (MastItem) contains data about the various items available for lending. There currently are a limited number of items, which are mostly limited to books, paperbacks, CDs, and videotapes. Figure 1-21 describes the fields in the table.

Field Name	Field Type	Field Length	Description
ItemID	Text	4	Primary key, required, no zero length, no duplicates; Valid IDs = 1000 to 9999
ItemCode	Text	1	(1 = book, 2 = paperback, 3 = CD, 4 = videotape, 5 = other)
ItemTitle	Text	20	
ItemDate	Date		(if appropriate)
ItemISBN	Text	20	(if appropriate)
ItemPublisher	Text	30	(if appropriate)
opt0-5	Yes/No	Boolean	Values under $6.00
opt6-10	Yes/No	Boolean	Values $6.00 to $10.99
opt11-15	Yes/No	Boolean	Values $11.00 to $15.99
opt16-25	Yes/No	Boolean	Values $16.00 to $25.99
opt26	Yes/No	Boolean	Values $26.00 and greater
ItemNotes	Memo		
UserID	Text	3	Foreign key to MastUser table

Figure 1-21: MastItem table description

Figure 1-22 shows a sample MastItem table.

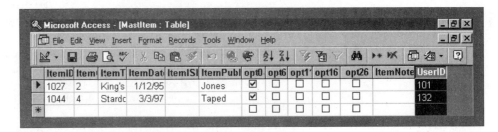

Figure 1-22: Sample MastItem table

The master users table (MastUser) contains data about those members and guests who are current users of the library's service. Figure 1-23 describes the fields in the table.

Field Name	Field Type	Field Length	Comments
UserID	Text	3	Valid IDs = 100 to 999
UserName	Text	30	
UserPhone	Text	14	(###) ###-####

Figure 1-23: MastUser table description

Figure 1-24 shows a sample MastUser table.

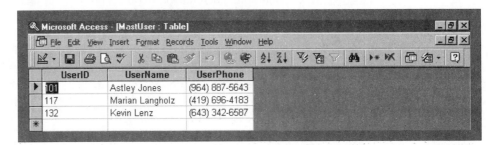

Figure 1-24: Sample MastUser table

Figure 1-25 shows the relationship between the MastItem and MastUser tables.

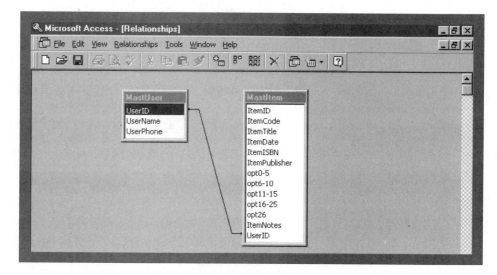

Figure 1-25: Relationship between the MastItem and MastUser tables

SPLIB Access Codes: Although security is not considered a serious threat to the data in the library system, data will be protected by general access codes that are assigned to volunteers. There are two general levels of codes: one code for volunteers who offer to help as needed and another code for volunteers who actively manage the service. The names of the volunteers and their respective codes are kept in a random file. Figure 1-26 shows the record description for the SPLIB security file.

Data Description	Location in Random File
Volunteer ID	1-2 (Valid IDs = 10 to 99)
Volunteer Name	3-32
Access Level	33 (0 = all; 1 = limited)

Figure 1-26: Random access security file description

SPLIB Reports: The library system requires three initial reports. Any volunteer with general access permission (limited) to the SPLIBdb.mdb database can print a report of borrowed items. Any employee with full access permission (all) can print any of the three reports. Each report will contain a header showing the date the report was generated, the page number, a logo, the library's name, and a report title. Figure 1-27 shows a sample report header.

XX/XX/XX	**Page**

(small logo)

Single Parents Public Service Library

Report Title: Materials Available

Figure 1-27: SPLIB report header

All reports also will contain a footer indicating that the report was completed successfully (End of 'report title').

The body of the first report is a master list of the library's users. Figure 1-28 shows a sample library user's report.

Identification	Name	Phone
101	Astley Jones	(964) 887-5643
XXX	XXXXXXXXXXXXXXXXXXXXXXXXXXXXXXX	
	Total Number of Users = nnn	

Figure 1-28: Body of library user's report

The body of the second report is a list of all borrowed items sorted by borrower by ItemID. Figure 1-29 shows a sample borrowed items report.

Borrower	Item Title
Astley Jones	Stardom (# 1044)
XXXXXXXXXXXXXXXXXXXXXXXXXXXXXX	XXXXXXXXXXXXXXXXXXXXXXXX
	Total Loaned = nnnnn

Figure 1-29: Body of borrowed items report

The body of the third report is a control break report list of all items sorted by ItemCode by ItemTitle. Figure 1-30 shows a sample body of the items listing report.

Item Code	Item Title	
1	ABC's of Child Development	
	Feeding a Family of Four	
		Total Number of Books = 2
2	King's Hill	
		Total Number of Paperbacks = 1
	Total Number of Items = 3	

Figure 1-30: Body of items listing report

Delivering the Project: Completed projects must be delivered as proprietary executable code only. The source version, accessed by the Visual Basic application, should be unavailable to the client

SPLIB Remote Access: The project will provide a Web page for inquiries into the SPLIB. You will see the Web page design in Chapter 9.

3. Short Cut Lawn Service (SCLS)

Project Name and Purpose: The project name is Short Cut Lawn Service (SCLS). The project purpose is to develop a system to manage mowing unit inventories and clients.

SCLS Description: Short Cut Lawn Service employs four to eight mowing units. Each unit consists of a van, a trailer, and the necessary mowers and implements. Units are established as needed, with the expectation of each unit cutting seven lawns, five days a week. Currently, each unit keeps track of its own materials and its customer assignments.

SCLS Project Parameters: You will provide Short Cut Lawn Service with a means for tracking its inventory and necessary data about customers assigned to each unit. You will develop and write a Visual Basic project that will permit the company's owners to match customers to mowing units and to print master lists of inventories. As new units are added, data about each unit are entered into an Access database. You must develop data maintenance routines and provide report and backup modules.

The SCLS program will require two forms. The first form will display the data about any unit, including scrollable notes. The second form will display the name of the clients assigned to that unit. The unit identification can be used to retrieve the data. Both forms will contain logos, and a Help menu will be provided for each form.

SCLS Inventory Database: The database for SCLS contains two tables. The name of the database is SCLSdb.mdb. The main inventory table contains data about the mowers and implements on each mowing unit. The current customer table provides basic data for the customers assigned to the various units. The tables are linked, with the unit ID as a foreign key in the customer table.

The unit inventory table (UnitInv) contains data about each mowing unit. The primary items are the large riding mowers that have the same manufacturer, but different models, representing size and age. Figure 1-31 describes the fields in the table.

Field Name	Field Type	Field Length	Description
UnitID	Text	3	Primary key, required, no zero length, no duplicates; Valid IDs = U01 to U99
UnitName	Text	20	
MowerA	Yes/No	Boolean	
MowerB	Yes/No	Boolean	
MowerK	Yes/No	Boolean	
MowerR	Yes/No	Boolean	
HandMower	Text	10	Type
Edger	Text	10	Type
Blower	Text	10	Type
Notes	Memo		Rakes, brooms, clippers, etc.

Figure 1-31: UnitInv table description

Figure 1-32 shows a sample UnitInv table.

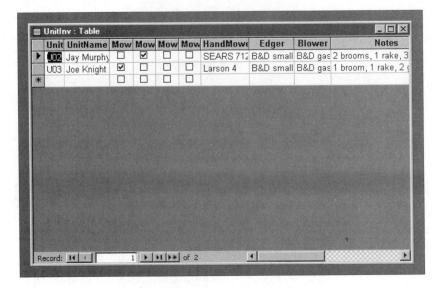

Figure 1-32: Sample UnitInv table

The data in the customer data table (CustData) contains a list of the data about customers that are needed by the various units, such as names and addresses. A unit must exist before it can be assigned a customer. Figure 1-33 describes the fields in the table.

Field Name	Field Type	Field Length	Description
CustID	Text	3	Primary key, required, no zero length, no duplicates; Valid IDs = 100 to 999
CustName	Text	30	
CustAddress	Text	30	
CustPhone	Text	8	###-####
UnitID	Text	2	Foreign key to UnitInv table

Figure 1-33: CustData table description

Figure 1-34 shows a sample CustData table.

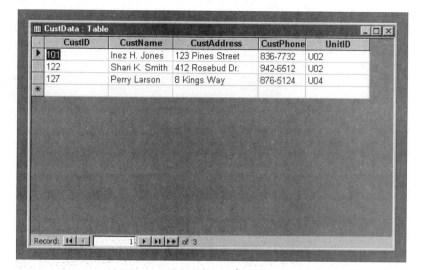

Figure 1-34: Sample CustData table

Figure 1-35 shows the relationship between the UnitInv and CustData tables.

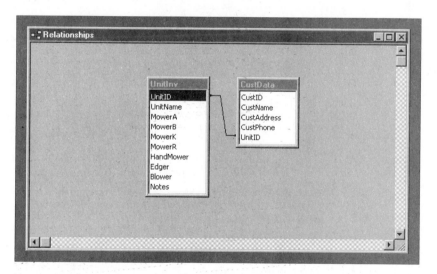

Figure 1-35: Relationship between the UnitInv and CustData tables

SCLS Password Protection: As a general precaution, access to the database must be limited to the owners and to members of a limited office staff. Members of the staff can print reports and update the unit and customer tables. Only the owner can add or delete entries in a table. The data are stored in a random file. Figure 1-36 shows the record description for the SCLS security file.

Data Description	Location in Random File
Employee ID	1 - 3 (Valid IDs = 100 to 199)
Employee Name	4 - 23
Owner	24 (1 = yes; 0 = no)

Figure 1-36: Random access security file description

SCLS Reports: Short Cut Lawn Services requires three printed reports. Any staff member can print each of the reports. Each printed report is to have a page number and a date, a small logo and the company's name, and the report title. Figure 1-37 shows a sample report header for the SCLS system.

XX/XX/XX		**Page**
	(small logo)	
	Short Cut Lawn Service	
	Report Title: XXXXXXXXXXXXX	

Figure 1-37: SCLS report header

All reports also will contain a footer indicating that the report was completed successfully (End of 'report title').

The body of the first report is a list of the units and their inventories. Figure 1-38 shows a sample inventory units report.

Unit ID	Unit Name	Large Mower	Hand Mower	Edger	Blower
U02	Murphy	A	Sears 712	B&D small	B&D gas
	Total Units = nn				

Figure 1-38: Body of inventory units report

The body of the second report is a list of any unassigned clients. Normally, all clients should be assigned. However, if this is not the case, a statement to this effect should be printed. This report is used when the possibility arises that a new unit might need to be established. Figure 1-39 shows a sample unassigned clients report.

Client ID	Client Name
101	Inez H. Jones
(There are no unassigned clients)	
	Total Unassigned Clients = nnnnn

Figure 1-39: Body of unassigned clients report

The body of the third report contains a list of all units and the clients assigned to them. Figure 1-40 shows a sample body of the clients report.

U02	Jay Murphy	
	Inez H. Jones	123 Pines St.
	Shari K. Smith	412 Rosebud Rd.
		Total Assigned to U02 = 2
U03	Joe Knight	
	Perry Larson	8 Kings Way
		Total assigned to U03 = 1
	Total Number of Customers = nnnn	

Figure 1-40: Body of clients report

Delivering the Project: Completed projects must be delivered as proprietary executable code only. The source version, accessed by the Visual Basic application, should be unavailable to the client.

Capturing Data — Creating the User Interface

Introduction ▶ You learned about the Shely Services TEMS system in Chapter 1. In Chapters 2 and 3, you will develop the first part of the project, which has two aspects. First, as Shely Services completes preliminary employment interviews, prospective temporary employees provide personal data to assist the company with job placement. Then, after the company negotiates an employee contract, the employee's personal data are entered using a Visual Basic interface and stored in a sequential file as start-up data for the new system. After the information contained on the interface is entered, the screen can be printed. This same interface also will be used to enter currently employed temporary employees into the system.

In this chapter you will design the interface (form) and add the controls for printing the screen, clearing the screen, and ending the program. You will add data editing and storage routines in Chapter 3. Figure 2-1 shows the completed Shely Services Temporary Employee Record (SSTER) interface.

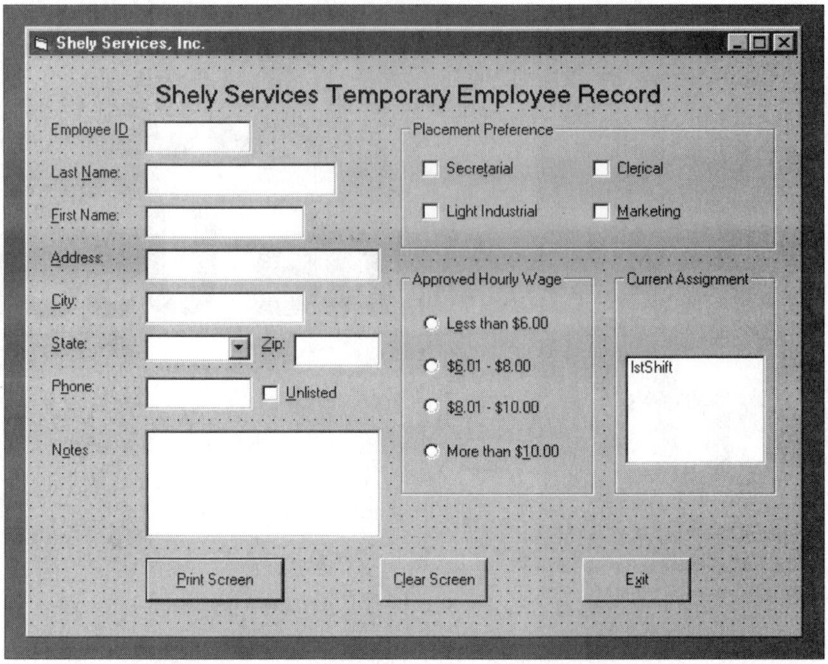

Figure 2-1: Shely Services Temporary Employee Record (SSTER) interface

Figure 2-2 shows the Task, Object, Event (TOE) chart for the SSTER application. You use a **TOE chart** to identify the tasks required of an application. Once the tasks are identified, the objects associated with the tasks are determined. The final task in creating the TOE chart is to associate the events necessary to trigger the object for processing with each object.

Task	Object	Event
Get the employee's state of residence	cboState	None—there is no code currently associated with selecting a state
Get the employee's placement preference(s)	chkClerical, chkIndustrial, chkMarketing, chkSecretary	None—there is no code currently associated with placement preference(s)
Get any unlisted phone numbers	chkUnlisted	None—there is no code currently associated with unlisted phone numbers
Clear the screen for the next employee's data	cmdClear	Click
End the application	cmdExit	Click

Figure 2-2: TOE chart for the SSTER interface

Task	Object	Event
Print the screen	cmdPrintScreen	Click
Initialize combo box states and list box shift values	frmDataEntry	Load
Get and display the preferred shift	lstShift	None—there is no code currently associated with shift selection
Get and display the preferred minimum wage	optLess6, opt6to8, opt8to10, opt10up	None—there is currently no code associated with selecting a preferred minimum wage
Highlight existing text when a control receives the focus	txtAddress, txtCity, txtEmpeID, txtFName, txtLName, txtNotes, txtPhone, txtZip	GotFocus
Get and display the employee data	txtAddress, txtCity, txtEmpeID, txtFName, txtLName, txtNotes, txtPhone, txtZip	None

Figure 2-2: TOE chart for the SSTER interface (continued)

Designing the Form

A **form** is an object that is used to contain controls that result in the user interface. **Properties** define the appearance of a form, **methods** define a form's behavior, and **events** define the form's interaction with a user. **Frames** are used to organize the form and to keep objects that belong together within the same structural unit. For example, Figure 2-1 shows a frame with the title "Placement Preference."

SSTER Form Properties

The form properties that were used to create the SSTER interface are described next. You can see a complete list of available design-time form properties in the Properties window when the form is the active object. For a detailed description of a property's function, use the Visual Basic online Help system (refer to the section entitled "Using Online Help" in Chapter 1 for directions on using online Help).

The **Name property** provides a meaningful name for keeping track of forms in event procedures. Figure 2-3 shows a recommended three-letter prefix for identifying objects and the names of controls in the TEMS system.

Object Name	ID	Related Application Examples
Check Box	chk	chkSecretary, chkClerical, chkIndustrial, chkMarketing, chkUnlisted
Combo Box	cbo	cboState
Command Button	cmd	cmdPrintScreen, cmdClear, cmdExit
Data	dat	
Directory List Box	dir	
Drive List Box	drv	
File List Box	fil	
Form	frm	frmDataEntry
Frame	fra	fraPlacement, fraShift, fraHourlyWage
Horizontal Scroll Bar	hsb	
Image	img	
Label	lbl	Only label controls whose values might change at run time
Line	lin	
List Box	lst	lstShift
OLE	ole	
Option Button	opt	optLess6, opt6to8, opt8to10, opt10up
Picture Box	pic	
Shape	shp	
Text Box	txt	txtEmpeID, txtLName, txtFName, txtAddress, txtCity, txtZip, txtPhone, txtNotes
Timer	tmr	
Vertical Scroll Bar	vsb	

Figure 2-3: Recommended naming conventions for objects

When you are writing your Visual Basic programs, subroutines, functions, and creating variable names, it is important to follow these naming conventions as closely as possible. Usually more than one person maintains a program—clearly constructed and documented programs save time and maintenance costs in the long run when conventions are described and followed.

The **Caption property** controls the text that is displayed in the form's title bar. This property is set in the property box, but it can be changed within the program. For example, to establish the caption in the title bar of the form, you could use `frmDataEntry.Caption = "Shely Services, Inc."`.

The **BorderStyle property** sets the border style for the form (the property box where BorderStyle = 3). Figure 2-4 describes some frequently used BorderStyle settings.

The **WindowState property** indicates the visual state of a form at run-time. The WindowState property settings are 0 for normal, 1 for minimized, and 2 for maximized.

The **Left property** controls the position of the left edge of the form from the left corner of the screen. The **Top property** controls the position of the top left corner of the form from the top of the screen.

BorderStyle Option	Description
0—None	No border or border-related elements
1—Fixed Single	Control-menu box, title bar, Maximize button, and Minimize button
2—Sizable (Default)	Contains all Windows standard border elements
3—Fixed Dialog	No Maximize or Minimize buttons; not resizable

Figure 2-4: BorderStyle property settings

Exercise 2.1 ▶

Start Visual Basic and create a new project. Set the following properties for the form: Caption: Shely Services, Inc.; BorderStyle: Fixed Single; WindowState: Normal; and Name: frmDataEntry. Save the form and the project as Ex2-1a in the Chapter2 folder on your Student Disk. Print the form as text. (*Hint:* Click File on the menu bar, click Print, and then select the Form as Text option.)

Exercise 2.2 ▶

Open the Ex2-2.vbp project from the Chapter2 folder on your Student Disk. Use recommended naming conventions to correct the form name. The form currently has no border or border-related elements. Change the appropriate property so the form contains all Windows standard border elements. Add an appropriate caption. Save the form and the project as Ex2-2a in the Chapter2 folder on your Student Disk. Print the form as text. (*Hint:* Click File on the menu bar, click Print, and then select the Form as Text option.)

Exercise 2.3 ▶

Create a new Visual Basic project. Experiment with the Form Properties window and define property settings of your choice for each of the following: Caption, WindowState, BorderStyle, Name, and BackColor. Save the form and project as Ex2-3a in the Chapter2 folder on your Student Disk. Print the form as text. (*Hint:* Click File on the menu bar, click Print, and then select the Form as Text option.)

The Form_Load() Event

The **Load Event procedure** is used to include initialization code that specifies default settings for controls and initializes form-level variables. The SSTER interface must be centered on the desktop. The Screen object, which is available only at run time, and associated screen properties allow the user to control the placement of the form on the screen. Example 2-1 shows how to use the Screen object to center the form vertically and horizontally.

Syntax ▶   **Screen.***propertyname*

Example 2-1 ▶   To center the form vertically, use the following code:

```
frmDataEntry.Top = (Screen.Height — frmDataEntry.Height) / 2
```

To center the form horizontally, use the following code:

```
frmDataEntry.Left = (Screen.Width — frmDataEntry.Width) / 2
```

The initial values that are required for the ComboBox and ListBox controls are specified in the Form_Load event. These values are loaded into the appropriate controls using the AddItem method.

object.AddItem *item, index*

In this syntax, *item* is a string expression specifying the item to add to the object, and *index* is an optional integer value that specifies the location of where to place the new item in the object. Figure 2-5 shows the code for the Form_Load event.

```
🖪 DataEntry_1 - frmDataEntry (Code)                              _ □ ✕
Form                                    ▼   Load                           ▼
    Private Sub Form_Load()
    'Center the form on the desktop
        frmDataEntry.Top = (Screen.Height - frmDataEntry.Height) / 2
        frmDataEntry.Left = (Screen.Width - frmDataEntry.Width) / 2
    'Add states to the combobox control
        cboState.AddItem "WV"
        cboState.AddItem "KY"
        cboState.AddItem "OH"
    'Add shift to the listbox control
        lstShift.AddItem "Flexible"
        lstShift.AddItem "7:00am - 3:00pm"
        lstShift.AddItem "3:00pm - 11:00pm"
        lstShift.AddItem "11:00pm - 7:00am"
        lstShift.AddItem "7:00am - 7:00pm"
        lstShift.AddItem "7:00pm - 7:00am"
    'Establish default values
        cboState.ListIndex = 0
        lstShift.ListIndex = 0
        optLess6.Value = True
    End Sub
```

Figure 2-5: Form_Load() event

Exercise 2.4 ▶

Open the project Ex2-4.vbp from the Chapter2 folder on your Student Disk. Open the code window for the Form_Load event. Use the Screen object and its associated Width property to complete the code necessary to center the form on the desktop. Save the form and project as Ex2-4a. Print the code.

Exercise 2.5 ▶

Open the project Ex2-5.vbp from the Chapter2 folder on your Student Disk, and then save the form and project as Ex2-5a. Run the project. Notice that the form is not centered on the desktop. Correct the code in the Form_Load event to center the form on the desktop. Save the project. Print the code.

Exercise 2.6 ▶

Open the project Ex2-3a.vbp from the Chapter2 folder on your Student Disk that you created in Exercise 2-3, or create a new project. Save the form and project as Ex2-6a. Use the Screen object and form properties to center the form on the desktop. Save the project. Print the code.

Adding Controls

Controls are objects that are contained within form objects. A control's properties, methods, and events dictate the appropriate use of the control. The controls and their associated properties that are used on the SSTER interface are described next by their function. For more information on Visual Basic controls, consult online Help.

The CommandButton Control for Event Processing

You use the **CommandButton control** to begin, interrupt, or end a process. Windows applications use command buttons to perform an immediate action when clicked. Figure 2-6 describes the CommandButton control properties.

Run-time syntax ▶	*object.property = value*
Example ▶	cmdExit.Visible = True

Property	Description
Cancel	Sets a value indicating whether a command button is the Cancel button on a form; the Cancel property values are True (the command button is the Cancel button) and False (which is the default; the command button is not the Cancel button). A user can activate the Cancel CommandButton by pressing the Esc key.
Caption	Determines the text displayed in the CommandButton control.
Default	Sets a value that determines which CommandButton control is the default command button on a form. The Default values are True (the command button is the Default button) and False (which is the default; the command button is not the Default button). Pressing the Enter key activates the default CommandButton.
TabIndex	Returns or sets the tab order of most objects within their parent form.
Visible	Sets a value indicating whether an object is visible or hidden.

Figure 2-6: CommandButton control properties

Controls for Displaying and Entering Text

You use the **Label control** to display text that a user cannot change directly. Figure 2-7 describes the Label control properties.

Run-time syntax ▶	*object.property = value*
Example ▶	lblCity.Caption = "City:"

Property	Description
Alignment	Sets a value that determines the alignment of text in the label control; the Alignment values are 0 for left justified (default), 1 for right justified, and 2 for centered.
Appearance	Sets the paint style of the label on the Form object at design time; the Appearance values are 0 for Flat and 1 for 3D (default). The 3D effect is reserved for controls that receive information from the user, thus the Appearance property should be set to 0 for label controls that only display information.

Figure 2-7: Label control properties

Property	Description
AutoSize	Sets a value that determines whether a control is resized automatically to display its entire contents. The default value is false.
BackColor	Sets the background color of the label.
BackStyle	Sets a value indicating whether a label control is transparent (0) or opaque (1, default).
BorderStyle	Sets a value indicating the control's border style; the BorderStyle values are 0 for None (default) and 1 for Fixed Single.
Caption	Determines the text displayed in the label control.
Font	Identifies a specific Font object whose properties you want to use. Font objects include font, font style, size, effects, and script. The default font is 8-point regular MS Sans Serif font.
Left	Sets the distance between the internal left edge of an object and the left edge of its container.
Name	Returns the name used in code to identify a label.
TabIndex	Returns or sets the tab order of most objects within their parent form.
Top	Sets the distance between the internal top edge of an object and the top edge of its container.
Visible	Sets a value indicating whether an object is visible or hidden.

Figure 2-7: Label control properties (continued)

A **TextBox control** displays information entered at design time, entered by the user, or assigned to the control in code at run time (an edit control). The TextBox control contains string data. Figure 2-8 describes the TextBox control properties.

Run-time syntax ▶	*object.property = value*
Example ▶	`txtFName.Text = ""`

In this example, the empty or zero-length string replaces existing text in the TextBox control. Code of this type is used in a subroutine that clears the contents of the screen.

Property	Description
Alignment	Sets a value that determines the alignment of text in the text box control; Alignment values are 0 for left justified (default), 1 for right justified, and 2 for centered.
Appearance	Sets the paint style of the text box at design time; Appearance values are 0 for Flat and 1 for 3D (default). The 3D effect is reserved for controls that receive information from the user.
BackColor	Sets the background color of the text box.
BorderStyle	Sets a value indicating the control's border style; BorderStyle values are 0 for None and 1 for Fixed Single (default).

Figure 2-8: TextBox control properties

Property	Description
Enabled	Sets a value that determines whether the text box can respond to user-generated events.
Font	Use the Font property of an object to identify a specific Font object whose properties you want to use. Font objects include font, font style, size, effects, and script. The default font is 8-point regular MS Sans Serif font.
Left	Sets the distance between the internal left edge of an object and the left edge of its container.
MultiLine	Returns or sets a value indicating whether the TextBox control can accept and display multiple lines of text; read only at run time.
Name	Returns the name used in the code to identify a text box.
ScrollBars	Returns or sets a value indicating whether the text box has horizontal or vertical scroll bars; read only at run time.
TabIndex	Returns or sets the tab order of most objects within their parent form.
Text	Sets the text contained in the edit area of the text box.
Top	Sets the distance between the internal top edge of an object and the top edge of its container.
Visible	Sets a value indicating whether an object is visible or hidden.

Figure 2-8: TextBox control properties (continued)

Controls for Presenting Choices to Users

There are many controls that you can use to give users different ways of inputting information. The following controls are used on the SSTER interface and are described next: CheckBox control, OptionButton control, ListBox control, and ComboBox control.

You use a **CheckBox control** to give the user a true/false or yes/no option. When selected, a check box appears with a check mark in the box; when the check box is cleared, the box is not selected. Use CheckBox controls in groups to display multiple choices from which the user can select one or more boxes by checking them. Figure 2-9 shows four check boxes in a check box group named "Placement Preference."

Run-time syntax ▶	*object.property = value*
Example ▶	chkIndustrial.Value = 0

CheckBox controls

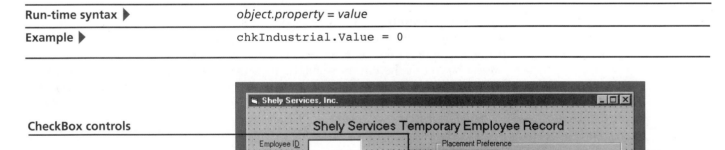

Figure 2-9: CheckBox controls on the SSTER interface

Figure 2-10 describes the CheckBox control properties.

Property	Description
Alignment	Sets a value that determines the alignment of a CheckBox control; Alignment values are 0 for left justified (the text is left-aligned and the control is right-aligned), and 1 for right justified (the text is right-aligned and the control is left-aligned). The default for the Alignment property is 0 (left justified).
Appearance	Sets the paint style of the CheckBox control at design time; Appearance values are 0 for Flat and 1 for 3D (default). The 3D effect is reserved for controls that receive information from the user.
BackColor	Sets the background color of the check box.
Caption	Determines the text displayed in the CheckBox control.
Enabled	Sets a value that determines whether the check box can respond to user-generated events.
Font	Use the Font property of an object to identify a specific Font object whose properties you want to use. Font objects include font, font style, size, effects, and script. The default font is 8-point regular MS Sans Serif font.
Left	Sets the distance between the internal left edge of an object and the left edge of its container.
Name	Returns the name used in code to identify a check box.
TabIndex	Returns or sets the tab order of most objects within their parent form.
Top	Sets the distance between the internal top edge of an object and the top edge of its container.
Value	Sets a value that determines whether the check box is unchecked (0), checked (1), or grayed (2). The default CheckBox property is unchecked (0).
Visible	Sets a value indicating whether an object is visible or hidden.

Figure 2-10: CheckBox control properties

An **OptionButton control** displays an option that can be turned on or off. OptionButton controls are used in an option group to display options from which the user can select only one. When an option button is selected, it has a mark (dot) in the button; if the button is empty, then the option button is not selected. The selection of an OptionButton control makes all other option buttons within the same group unavailable.

Run-time syntax ▶	*object.property = value*
Example ▶	`optLess6.Value = True`

Figure 2-11 shows an OptionButton control group on a form.

OptionButton controls

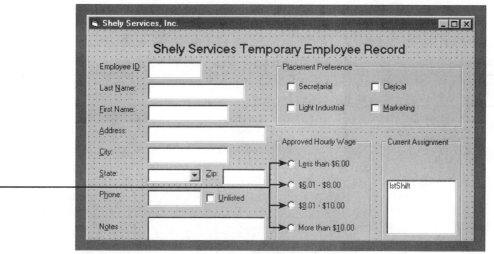

Figure 2-11: OptionButton controls on the SSTER interface

Figure 2-12 describes the OptionButton control properties.

Property	Description
Alignment	Sets a value that determines the alignment of an OptionButton control; Alignment values are 0 for left justified (text is left-aligned and the control is right-aligned), or 1 for right justified (text is right-aligned and the control is left-aligned). The default value for the Alignment property is 0 (left justified).
Appearance	Sets the paint style of the OptionButton control at design time; Appearance values are 0 for Flat or 1 for 3D (default). The 3D effect is reserved for controls that receive information from the user.
BackColor	Sets the background color of the option button.
Caption	Determines the text displayed in the OptionButton control.
Enabled	Sets a value that determines whether the option button can respond to user-generated events.
Font	Use the Font property of an object to identify a specific Font object whose properties you want to use. Font objects include font, font style, size, effects, and script. The default font is 8-point regular MS Sans Serif font.
Left	Sets the distance between the internal left edge of an object and the left edge of its container.
Name	Returns the name used in code to identify an option button.
TabIndex	Returns or sets the tab order of most objects within their parent form.
Top	Sets the distance between the internal top edge of an object and the top edge of its container.
Value	Sets the state of the control. Boolean values (true or false) indicate whether the option button is selected (true) or not selected (false).
Visible	Sets a value indicating whether an object is visible or hidden.

Figure 2-12: OptionButton control properties

A **ListBox control** displays a list of items from which the user can select one or more choices. The selected item appears highlighted in the list. If the number of items exceeds the number that can be displayed, a scroll bar is added automatically to the ListBox control (see the example for the Form_Load event in Figure 2-5).

Run-time syntax ▶	*object.property = value*
Example ▶	`lstShift.ListIndex = 0`

In this example, the ListIndex property establishes the first item in the list (a count relative to zero) as the item that will be highlighted when the program is executed. Figure 2-13 shows a list box control on the SSTER interface.

ListBox control ──────────────▶

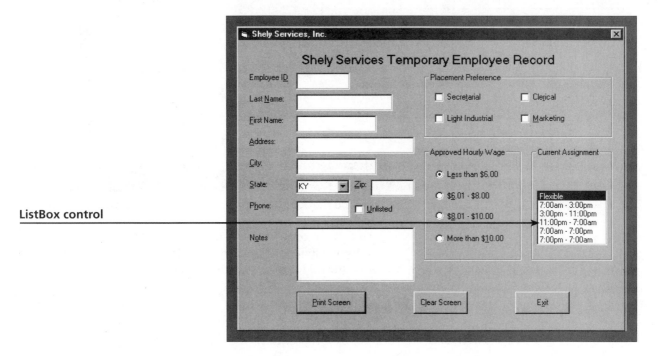

Figure 2-13: ListBox control on the SSTER interface

Figure 2-14 describes the ListBox control properties.

Property	Purpose
Appearance	Sets the paint style of the ListBox control at design time; Appearance values are 0 for Flat and 1 for 3D (default). The 3D effect is reserved for controls that receive information from the user.
Enabled	Sets a value that determines whether the list box can respond to user-generated events.
Font	Use the Font property of an object to identify a specific Font object whose properties you want to use. Font objects include font, font style, size, effects, and script. The default font is 8-point regular MS Sans Serif font.

Figure 2-14: ListBox control properties

Property	Purpose
Left	Sets the distance between the internal left edge of an object and the left edge of its container.
ListIndex	Returns or sets the index of the currently selected item in the list box; not available at design time.
Sorted	Returns a value indicating whether the elements of the ListBox control are automatically sorted alphabetically.
TabIndex	Returns or sets the tab order of most objects within their parent form.
Text	Returns the selected item in the list box; available only at run time.
Top	Sets the distance between the internal top edge of an object and the top edge of its container.
Visible	Sets a value indicating whether an object is visible or hidden.

Figure 2-14: ListBox control properties (continued)

A **ComboBox control** combines the features of a TextBox control and a ListBox control to allow users to enter information in the text box portion or select an item from the list box portion of the control. When an item is selected in a combo box, it appears selected in the list and in the text box.

Run-time syntax ▶	*object.property = value*
Example ▶	`cboState.ListIndex = 0`

In this example, the ListIndex property is set to 0, which selects (highlights) the first item in the list. Figure 2-15 shows a ComboBox control.

ComboBox control →

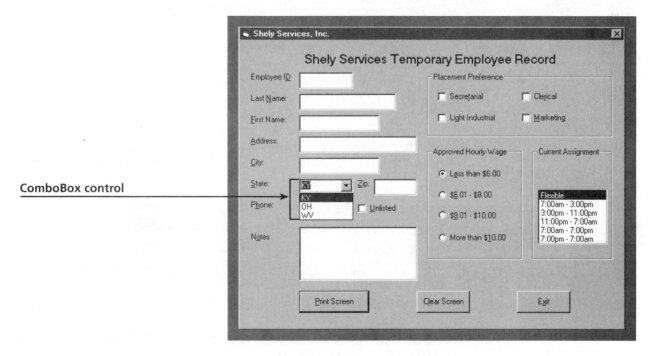

Figure 2-15: ComboBox control on the SSTER interface

Figure 2-16 describes the ComboBox control properties.

Property	Description
Appearance	Sets the paint style of the ComboBox control at design time; Appearance values are 0 for Flat and 1 for 3D (default). The 3D effect is reserved for controls that receive information from the user.
BackColor	Sets the background color of the ComboBox.
Enabled	Sets a value that determines whether the combo box can respond to user-generated events.
Font	Use the Font property of an object to identify a specific Font object whose properties you want to use. Font objects include font, font style, size, effects, and script. The default font is 8-point regular MS Sans Serif font.
Left	Sets the distance between the internal left edge of an object and the left edge of its container.
ListIndex	Returns or sets the index of the currently selected item in the combo box; not available at design time.
Sorted	Returns a value indicating whether the elements of the ComboBox control are automatically sorted alphabetically.
TabIndex	Returns or sets the tab order of most objects within their parent form.
Text	Returns the selected item in the list box; available only at run time.
Top	Sets the distance between the internal top edge of an object and the top edge of its container.
Visible	Sets a value indicating whether an object is visible or hidden.

Figure 2-16: ComboBox control properties

The Frame Control for Grouping Controls

The **Frame control** provides an identifiable grouping for controls that can be used to group other controls on a form functionally (i.e., separate groups of OptionButton controls). Figure 2-17 shows a Frame control. The Frame control serves as a container for other controls. Controls placed on a form are considered to be part of the form. Controls placed inside a frame are treated as part of the frame. Existing form controls must be detached from the form (using cut and paste) before placing them in the frame. You must use the Frame control to include more than one group of option buttons on a form.

Frame control

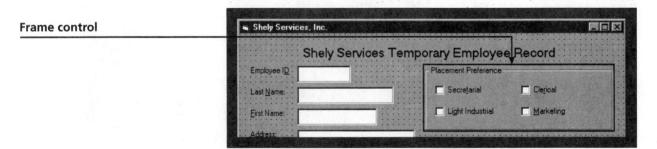

Figure 2-17: Frame control on the SSTER interface

Run-time syntax ▶	*object.property = value*
Example ▶	`fraPlacement.Visible = False`

Figure 2-18 describes the Frame control properties.

Property	Description
BorderStyle	Sets a value indicating the control's border style; BorderStyle values are 0 for None and 1 for Fixed Single (default).
Caption	Determines the text displayed in the Frame control.
TabIndex	Returns or sets the tab order of most objects within their parent form.
Visible	Sets a value indicating whether an object is visible or hidden.

Figure 2-18: Frame control properties

Exercise 2.7 ▶

Open the project Ex2-7.vbp from the Chapter2 folder on your Student Disk, and then save the form and project as Ex2-7a. Complete the form using the following specifications:

a. Add a TextBox control named txtFName for capturing the first name. Clear the Text property for the control.

b. Add a Label control below the State label adjacent to the unlabeled TextBox control. Add a caption named Phone: for the label.

c. Change the State TextBox control to a ComboBox control and name it cboState. Use the AddItem method in the Form_Load event to add "WV," "KY," and "OH" (without the quotation marks) to the combo box. The items should appear in alphabetical order when the program runs. The default item is KY.

d. Create a Frame control named fraWage with the caption "Approved Hourly Wage." Place the OptionButton controls in the frame.

e. Add four CheckBox controls to the Placement Preference frame based on the following information:

Name	Caption
chkSecretary	Secretarial:
chkClerical	Clerical:
chkIndustrial	Light Industrial:
chkMarketing	Marketing:

f. Save and run the application.

g. Print the form image, the form as text, and the code.

Exercise 2.8 ▶

Create a new Visual Basic project, and then save the form and project as Ex2-8a in the Chapter2 folder on your Student Disk. Use Figure 2-19 to create the appropriate user interface. When you are finished, print the form image, the form as text, and the code. (*Hint:* The Analysis & Design label requires the use of the ampersand (&) as a character. To create this character, use &&.)

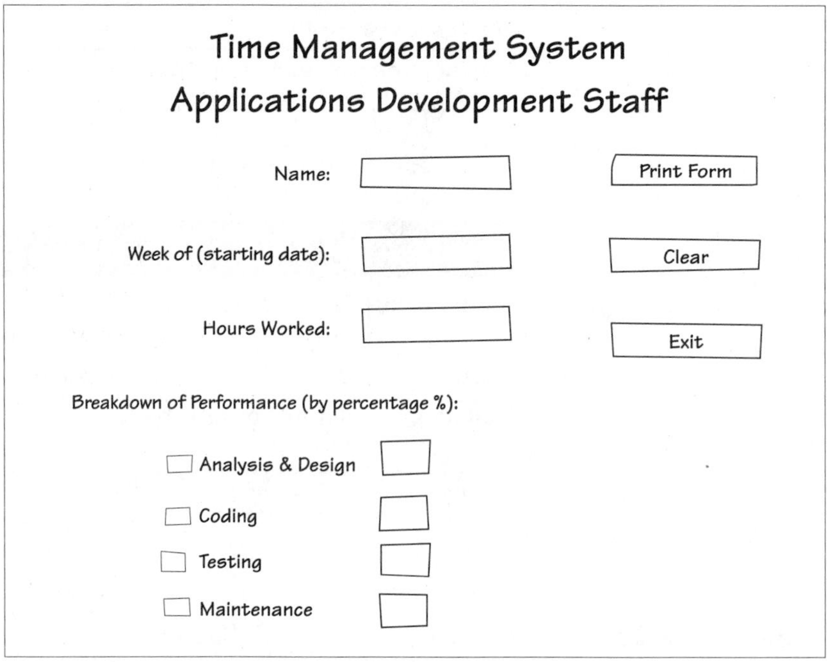

Figure 2-19: Sketch of user interface

Enhancing Data Capture

All Windows applications use standards that assist the user in making correct choices. Examples of these enhancements include setting the focus and tab order, highlighting existing text when a control receives the focus, using access keys, and setting the Default and Cancel properties.

Focus and Tab Order

Focus refers to the ability of an application to receive user input through the mouse or keyboard. In code, you use the SetFocus method to give a specific control the focus for immediate input of information. The object must be a control that can receive the focus.

Syntax ▶	*object*.SetFocus
Example ▶	`txtEmpeID.SetFocus` (used in the cmdClear_Click() event procedure)

The **TabIndex property** determines the order in which a control receives the focus when the user presses the Tab key to move through the application. Initial values of the TabIndex property represent the order in which the control was added to the form. To control the tab order, it is necessary to reset the TabIndex to reflect the desired focus order.

Highlighting Existing Text

You use Visual Basic's SelStart and SelLength properties to highlight existing text in Windows applications so that new text entered by the user automatically replaces existing text. The **SelStart property** indicates to Visual Basic where to start the text selection. The **SelLength property** tells Visual Basic how many characters to select.

Syntax ▶	*object*.**SelStart** [= *index*]
Example ▶	txtEmpeID.SelStart = 0

In this syntax, *object* is the name of the control and *index* is a number indicating the position of the insertion point. The index number uses a count relative to zero, which means that the first position in the control is position 0.

Syntax ▶	*object*.**SelLength** [= *number*]
Example ▶	txtEmpeID.SelLength = 5

In this syntax, *number* indicates the number of characters to select. To replace all existing text, the number should represent the number of existing characters. You use the **Len function** to determine the number of characters in a text box.

Syntax ▶	**Len**(*string/varname*)

In this syntax, *string* represents any valid string expression and *varname* represents any valid variable or control name. For example, Len(txtEmpeID.Text) returns the number of existing characters in the txtEmpeID TextBox control. The combined use of the SelLength property and Len function in the statement txtEmpeID.SelLength = Len(txtEmpeID.Text) has the effect of highlighting all existing code in the txtEmpeID control (see the example in Figure 2-20).

When a control receives the focus, its existing text should be highlighted. The **GotFocus event** occurs when an object receives the focus. An object can receive the focus when the user tabs to or clicks the object. The focus can be changed in code using the **SetFocus method**. Figure 2-20 shows the GotFocus event for the txtEmpeID control.

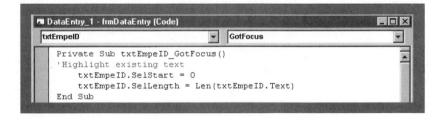

Figure 2-20: The txtEmpeID_GotFocus() event

Access Keys

Access keys allow the user to select an object by pressing the Alt key in combination with a letter. You can assign an access key to an object in the object's Caption property by typing an ampersand (&) before the desired access letter. The access key appears with an underscore on the interface—for example, the File menu is written as <u>F</u>ile, where the access key is Alt + F. When you assign access keys to labels, using the access key results in the focus being received by the next object in the tab order sequence that can receive the focus. Figure 2-21 shows the tab order sequence for the SSTER interface.

Control Name	Caption (if applicable)	TabIndex
Label2	Employee I&D:	0
txtEmpeID		1
Label3	Last &Name:	2
txtLName		3
Label4	&First Name:	4
txtFName		5
Label5	&Address:	6
txtAddress		7
Label6	&City:	8
txtCity		9
Label7	&State:	10
cboState		11
Label8	&Zip:	12
txtZip		13
Label9	P&hone:	14
txtPhone		15
chkUnlisted	&Unlisted	16
chkSecretary	Secre&tarial	17
chkClerical	Cle&rical	18
chkIndustrial	Li&ght Industrial	19
chkMarketing	&Marketing	20
fraWage	Approved Hourly Wage	21
optLess6	L&ess than $6.00	22
opt6to8	$&6.01 - $8.00	23
opt8to10	$&8.01 - $10.00	24
opt10up	More than $&10.00	25
lstShift		26
Label10	N&otes	27
txtNotes		28
cmdPrintScreen	&Print Screen	29
cmdClear	C&lear Screen	30
cmdExit	E&xit	31

Figure 2-21: TabIndex sequence for the SSTER interface

The Default and Cancel Properties

The **Default property** is used to establish which CommandButton control is the default command button on a form. The default command button immediately has the focus so that the Event procedure associated with that command button occurs when the user presses the Enter key. Only one command button on a form can be the default. The cmdPrintScreen control is the default command button for the SSTER interface.

Syntax ▶	object.**Default** [= *boolean*]

The **Cancel property** sets a value indicating whether a command button is the Cancel button on a form. This command button can be the CommandButton control or any object within an OLE container control that behaves like a command button. Use the Cancel property to give the user the option of canceling uncommitted changes and returning the form to its previous state. The cmdClear control is the Cancel button for the SSTER interface. When a CommandButton control's Cancel property setting is True and the form is the active form, the user can choose the CommandButton by clicking it, pressing the Esc key, or pressing the Enter key when the button has the focus.

Syntax ▶	object.**Cancel** [= *boolean*]

Exercise 2.9 ▶

Open the project Ex2-9.vbp from the Chapter2 folder on your Student Disk, and then save the form and project as Ex2-9a and do the following:

a. Use the following information to change the access keys:

Caption	Access Key
Employee ID	D
Last Name	N
First Name	F
Address	A
City	C
State	S
Zip	Z
Phone	h
Secretarial	t
Clerical	r
Light Industrial	g
Marketing	M
Less than $6.00	e
$6.01 - $8.00	6
$8.01 - $10.00	8
More than $10.00	1
Print Screen	P
Clear	l
Exit	x

b. Adjust the TabIndex values so the focus moves through the controls in the order presented in the table.

c. Code the GotFocus event for the Last Name text box so the existing text is highlighted. (*Hint:* Use the SelStart and SelLength properties.)

d. Make the Print button the default command button, and then change the Clear button to a Cancel button.

e. Save and run the application. Create an executable file that your instructor can use to check your work.

Exercise 2.10 ▶

Open the project Ex2-10.vbp from the Chapter2 folder on your Student Disk, and then save the form and project as Ex2-10a and do the following:

a. Run the application. Use the Tab key to check the sequence in which each control receives the focus. Make the necessary adjustments to improve the tab sequence so it is logical and functional.

b. Test the functionality of the access keys. Make the necessary adjustments to ensure that all access keys function appropriately. Ensure that de facto Windows standards, such as letter selection, are followed when defining the access keys. Remember that controls with access keys that are associated with TextBox controls must have a TabIndex of one less than that of the TabIndex of the TextBox control.

c. Save and run the application.

d. Create an executable file named Ex2-10a.exe that your instructor can use to verify the accuracy of your application.

Exercise 2.11 ▶

Open a new project and save it as Ex2-11a.vbp in the Chapter2 folder on your Student Disk. Use the sketch shown in Figure 2-22 to create the appropriate user interface. Add the access keys, and then make necessary adjustments to improve the tab sequence. Create an executable file named Ex2-11a.exe that your instructor can use to run the program to check the tab sequence.

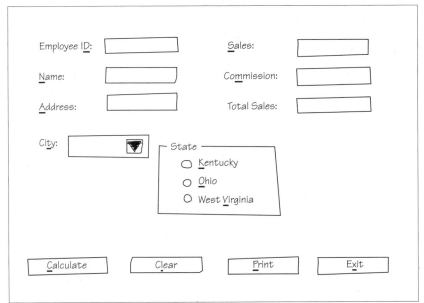

Figure 2-22: Sketch of user interface

Writing Code

Visual Basic instructions that tell the objects in the interface how to respond to events are called **code**. Code is written for each object that has an event associated with it. Code was introduced for the Form_Load event that occurs after program initialization and the GotFocus events that are associated with the TextBox controls. The Click event is associated with each of the CommandButton controls.

The cmdPrintScreen_Click() Event

When the user clicks the Print command button, the application data is printed on paper (also known as a hard copy or printout). You use the Visual Basic **PrintForm method** to print the form.

Syntax ▶ PrintForm

A printout of the form does not require the presence of the CommandButton controls. You can use the Visible property of the CommandButton controls in an assignment statement to hide the controls (set to False) prior to printing, and redisplay the controls (set to True) after the data prints. Figure 2-23 shows the cmdPrintScreen_Click() event.

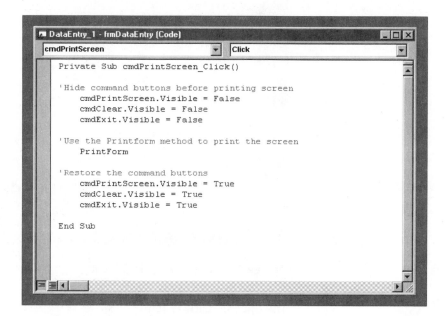

```
DataEntry_1 - frmDataEntry (Code)                           _ □ ×
cmdPrintScreen                    ▼   Click                          ▼

    Private Sub cmdPrintScreen_Click()

    'Hide command buttons before printing screen
        cmdPrintScreen.Visible = False
        cmdClear.Visible = False
        cmdExit.Visible = False

    'Use the Printform method to print the screen
        PrintForm

    'Restore the command buttons
        cmdPrintScreen.Visible = True
        cmdClear.Visible = True
        cmdExit.Visible = True

    End Sub
```

Figure 2-23: The cmdPrintScreen_Click() event

The cmdClear_Click() Event

The user clicks the Clear command button to remove previously entered data from the form and prepare the application to capture new data. Data are removed from TextBox controls by setting the value of the Text property to the **null** (or **empty** or **zero-length**) **string**, which is written as a set of empty quotation marks (" ").

You use the **Value property** to restore default values to CheckBox and OptionButton controls.

Syntax ▶ *object.***Value** = [*value*]

In this syntax, *value* specifies the state, content, or position of a control. Valid value settings for the CheckBox control are 0 for Unchecked (default), 1 for Checked, and 2 for Grayed (dimmed). The True value for the OptionButton control indicates that the button is selected; the False value (default) indicates that the button is not selected.

The **ListIndex property** of ComboBox and ListBox controls returns or sets the index of the currently selected item in the control.

Syntax ▶

*object.***ListIndex** [= *index*]

In this syntax, *index* is the value of the currently selected item. Figure 2-24 shows the cmdClear_Click() event.

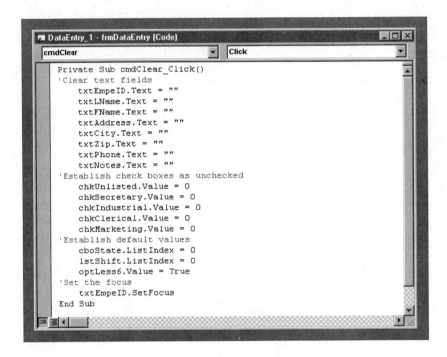

```
Private Sub cmdClear_Click()
'Clear text fields
    txtEmpeID.Text = ""
    txtLName.Text = ""
    txtFName.Text = ""
    txtAddress.Text = ""
    txtCity.Text = ""
    txtZip.Text = ""
    txtPhone.Text = ""
    txtNotes.Text = ""
'Establish check boxes as unchecked
    chkUnlisted.Value = 0
    chkSecretary.Value = 0
    chkIndustrial.Value = 0
    chkClerical.Value = 0
    chkMarketing.Value = 0
'Establish default values
    cboState.ListIndex = 0
    lstShift.ListIndex = 0
    optLess6.Value = True
'Set the focus
    txtEmpeID.SetFocus
End Sub
```

Figure 2-24: The cmdClear_Click() event

The cmdExit_Click() Event

When the user clicks the Exit command button, the application terminates. The **End statement** in Visual Basic is used to terminate the current application. Figure 2-25 shows the cmdExit_Click() event.

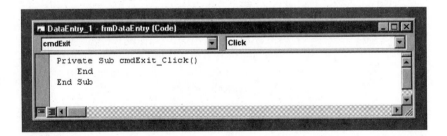

```
Private Sub cmdExit_Click()
    End
End Sub
```

Figure 2-25: The cmdExit_Click() event

Exercise 2.12 ▶

Open the project Ex2-12.vbp from the Chapter2 folder on your Student Disk, save the form and project as Ex2-12a, and then do the following:

    a. Code the cmdClear_Click() Event procedure control to clear the TextBox controls and set the focus to the Last Name TextBox control on the form.

    b. Code the cmdPrintScreen_Click() Event procedure to print the form without the command buttons showing.

    c. Save and run the application. Create an executable file named Ex2-12a.exe that your instructor can use to check your work.

Exercise 2.13 ▶

Open the project Ex2-13.vbp from the Chapter2 folder on your Student Disk, and then save the form and project as Ex2-13a. Run the application, and then do the following:

    a. Notice that the Clear Screen command button does not clear all necessary controls. Make the following changes to the cmdClear_Click() event to clear all controls:

       1. Reset the state to KY.

       2. Set the Less than $6.00 option button as the default.

       3. Set the Flexible shift as the default.

       4. Clear all check boxes.

    b. Print the form. Notice that the command buttons appear on the printed form. Make the necessary changes to the cmdPrintScreen-Click () event to hide the command button controls before printing the form. Create an executable file named Ex2-13a that your instructor can use to check your work.

Review of BASIC Fundamentals

As a descendant of the original BASIC language, it is helpful to review concepts fundamental to the entire BASIC family. In this and subsequent chapters, a review of these concepts will follow a description of the current application's code.

The primary processing mechanism used in the current form of the Shely project is **sequential processing**, which is a programming structure referred to as the sequence structure. In the **sequence structure**, the compiler processes the code instructions one at a time in the order that they were entered in the Code window.

The **assignment statement** is a BASIC instruction used to assign a value to the property of an object while the program is running. Assigning the False value to the Visible property of a CommandButton control hides the command button on the form.

Methods allow BASIC instructions to be executed to accomplish predefined procedures. Methods introduced in Chapter 2 include AddItem, SetFocus, and PrintForm.

PROGRESSIVE   PROJECTS

The projects in this chapter represent the first of two steps in an initial project to collect and prepare start-up data for the master project that begins in Chapter 4. It would be useful to review Chapter 3, without studying the details, in order to gain a better perspective for designing the screen. If some redesign does become necessary in the next step, it should be minimal.

Although this is only the first step of the projects, you might spend a great deal of time working if you fail to review the project requirements adequately. *Make sure that you enter all the data needed, and only the data needed!*

1. Bean County Plumbing Inventory System (BCPIS)

Bean County has agreed to supply start-up data in the form of printed inventory lists. It has also agreed that it will be responsible for putting the data into machine-readable format. Even though the county has accepted responsibility for its own data (as it must!), it remains in the interest of the project team to install the project as cleanly as possible.

You will develop a program to edit and enter the data into a sequential file for the table MastPart (see Figure 1-11). For general purposes of review and control, provisions will be made for printing the contents of the sequential file to hard copy. The first assignment, which you will complete in this chapter, is to design the screen carefully. Use the database table MastPart in the BCPISdb.mdb database described in Chapter 1 to determine which fields to include to capture the data. In order to make provisions for printing the form, clearing all controls of data, and ending the application, use CommandButton controls with the appropriate labels. In Chapter 3, you will add provisions for writing edit routines and adding records to the sequential file.

Make sure to review all of the project documents in Chapter 1, especially the charts with respect to necessary field and data formats. Consider, for example, that field trucks are treated as warehouses, and that inventory items have a limited number of product codes and size possibilities, which can be handled by CheckBox controls. The data in this file are to be as correct as possible at this point.

How will the county handle the problem of ensuring that the current inventory lists in the appendix will be accurate when the project is ready to be installed? You will address this question and others as you work through the projects in this book. The success of your project depends on delivering the promised project with the correct data.

Save the form and project as Ch2BCPIS in the Chapter2 folder on your Student Disk.

2. Single Parents Public Service Library (SPLIB)

While you are testing and developing the project, SPLIB plans to solicit materials through its members. Because it is a new library and there is no current catalog of its holdings, the library must develop a program so volunteers can enter data about each new item donated to the library. As items are entered, the data will be edited as reasonably as possible and entered into a sequential file. The program will have an option for printing a copy of the data so volunteers can review current materials.

The first step is to design the screen carefully. Use the database table MastItem in the SPLIBdb.mdb database described in Chapter 1 (see Figure 1-21) to determine which fields to include to capture the data. In order to make provisions for printing the form, clearing all controls of data, and ending the application, use CommandButton controls with the appropriate labels. In Chapter 3, you will add provisions for writing edit routines and adding records to the sequential file. There will not be many items at first. Nevertheless, the project description contains a data form for the master database, as well as permissible codes and data formats. For example, there are provisions for notes on the materials, as well as estimated dollar value ranges that can be entered using CheckBox controls. The editing routines that you develop for the program will need to reflect these constraints.

SPLIB volunteers also must be available to make corrections to the master database at start-up time. What is your plan for how the project team will work with SPLIB to ensure a smooth start-up? You will address this question and others as you work through the projects in this book. Save the form and project as Ch2SPLIB in the Chapter2 folder on your Student Disk.

3. Short Cut Lawn Service (SCLS)

SCLS employs anywhere from four to eight teams that cut seven lawns each, five days a week. Currently, each team keeps track of its own inventory and supplies. In preparation for the project, SCLS will need a program that collects and prepares its data for the database.

To do this, you will develop a program for the current inventory. The program also will need a form for entering its current customers. To ensure data accuracy as the data are entered, data should be edited to conform to the data layout and the descriptions of the data. The data will be stored in sequential files, with an option for a printed list.

The first step is to design the screen carefully. Use the database table UnitInv in the SCLSdb.mdb database described in Chapter 1 (see Figure 1-31) to determine which fields to include to capture the data. In order to make provisions for printing the form, clearing all controls of data, and ending the application, use CommandButton controls with the appropriate labels. In Chapter 3, you will add provisions for writing edit routines and adding records to the sequential file.

How will you train SCLS to manage the project after it is completed? Who will be available for training and for how long? What might go wrong at start-up? How will you handle such problems? You will address these questions and others as you work through the projects in this book. Save the form and project as Ch2SCLS in the Chapter2 folder on your Student Disk.

INDEPENDENT PROJECTS

1. Harold's CD-ROM Listing

Harold has CD-ROMs all over the place, and he wants to have a list of them so he can see what he has. After creating the list, he will decide how he wants to manage his CDs. Write a program that will permit Harold to enter data about each CD and print the form as he enters the data. After the data are captured to paper, clear the screen for the next entry. Design the form for Harold to have as much opportunity to enter various aspects of his data as possible. Remember to provide a control for ending the application. Save the project as Harold in the Chapter2 folder on your Student Disk.

2. Little League Roster

In this project, the term "Little League" is loosely defined as any group of young people in a volunteer organization, such as Babe Ruth League, Girl Scouts, etc. The task is to develop a roster of the organization's members. The form for entering the data should include as many of the items covered in this chapter as possible. Print the form as the data are entered. After data are captured to paper, clear the screen for the next entry. Remember to provide a control for ending the application. Save the project as LLRoster in the Chapter2 folder on your Student Disk.

3. Grandma's Recipe Box

Bring a favorite family recipe to class, and design a project to enter and edit all the recipes. Before the project is developed, careful consideration will need to be given to appropriate controls for entering data. How will users enter a "pinch" of salt? What controls are available (see Figure 2-1) for entering the data? Print each form as the data are entered. After data are captured to paper, clear the screen for the next entry. Remember to provide a control for ending the application. Save the project as Recipes in the Chapter2 folder on your Student Disk.

CHAPTER

3

Capturing Data — Editing and Storing Data

Introduction ▶ A natural extension to data entry processing is ensuring that all necessary data are captured. Usually you store your data for future reference. In this chapter, you will enhance the Shely Services Temporary Employee Record (SSTER) interface that you developed in Chapter 2 to verify data entry and store data in a sequential access file.

Prior to writing data to the file, the program uses processing instructions that use the selection programming structure to edit existing data. In this chapter, you will learn about the three programming control structures: the selection structure, the sequence structure, and the repetition structure. You also will learn about dialog boxes in the form of input and message boxes as tools for capturing additional data and informing the user of problems with processing.

You use sequential file processing to capture data when all or most of the data will be saved for future processing. Once edited, a temporary employee's data will be written as a record to a sequential access file. Records in the sequential access file will be used to load the corporate database when the system is loaded in Chapter 8. Figure 3-1 shows the enhanced SSTER interface that you will create in this chapter.

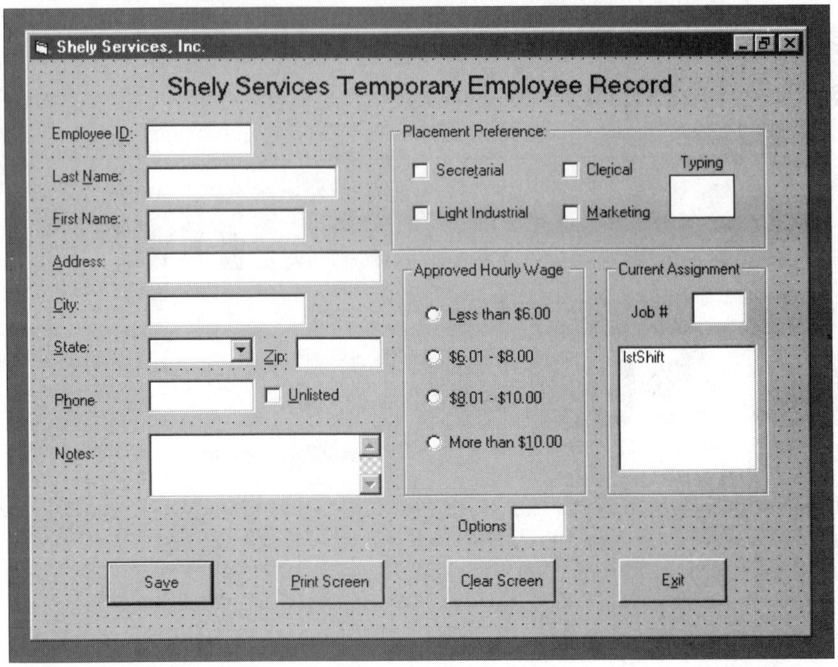

Figure 3-1: Enhanced SSTER interface

Enhancing the SSTER Interface

The SSTER interface shown in Figure 3-1 contains a label for reporting the typing speed when the typing speed is provided. The control is placed on the form and has the name lblTypingSpeed, a Flat appearance, and a BorderStyle of Fixed single. A label with the caption "Typing" is included to identify the data.

The Current Assignment frame is enhanced to include a TextBox control named txtJobID, with the label "Job #," for entering the job ID when the employee is assigned a job. The txtJobID and lstShift controls will be disabled in the Form_Load() event when the program is executed. The txtJobID.Text property is set to "000".

Finally, a TextBox control named txtOptionStorage is added to the form and given the label "Options". The text box and label controls' Visible properties should be set to False. You will see a description of how these controls are used later in this chapter.

Enhancing the SSTER interface is accompanied by more detailed processing considerations. These processing considerations will use three programming structures that determine the order in which program instructions are processed. These control structures are the sequence, selection (decision), and repetition (looping) structures.

The Sequence Structure

Until now, program instructions have been processed one after another in the order that they appear in the Code window. This control structure—the sequence structure—is common when the program must process all instructions associated with an event. The processing order depends strictly on the order in which the code is written in the procedure. In the cmdClear_Click() Event procedure, processing ensures that all values are cleared from controls and default values are restored. The order in which code in this event is accomplished is not significant, but it corresponds to the order in which the code appears in the Code window. For example, the event could restore the default values before clearing the control values. In Figure 3-2, the adjacent Code windows accomplish the same processing, but in a different order.

Example 1: cmdClear_Click()

```
Private Sub cmdClear_Click()
'Clear text fields
        txtEmpeID.Text = ""
        txtLName.Text = ""
        txtFName.Text = ""
        txtAddress.Text = ""
        txtCity.Text = ""
        txtZip.Text = ""
        txtPhone.Text = ""
        txtNotes.Text = ""
        lblTypingSpeed.Caption = ""
'Establish check boxes as unchecked
        chkUnlisted.Value = 0
        chkSecretary.Value = 0
        chkIndustrial.Value = 0
        chkMarketing.Value = 0
        chkClerical.Value = 0
'Establish default values
        cboState.ListIndex = 0
        lstShift.ListIndex = 0
        optLess6.Value = True
'Set the focus
        txtEmpeID.SetFocus
'Disable the Save button
        cmdSave.Enabled = False
End Sub
```

Example 2: cmdClear_Click()

```
Private Sub cmdClear_Click()
'Establish check boxes as unchecked
        chkUnlisted.Value = 0
        chkSecretary.Value = 0
        chkClerical.Value = 0
        chkMarketing.Value = 0
        chkIndustrial.Value = 0
'Establish default values
        cboState.ListIndex = 0
        lstShift.ListIndex = 0
        optLess6.Value = True
'Clear text fields
        txtEmpeID.Text = ""
        txtLName.Text = ""
        txtFName.Text = ""
        txtAddress.Text = ""
        txtCity.Text = ""
        txtZip.Text = ""
        txtPhone.Text = ""
        txtNotes.Text = ""
        lblTypingSpeed.Caption = ""
'Set the focus
        txtEmpeID.SetFocus
'Disable the Save button
        cmdSave.Enabled = False
End Sub
```

Figure 3-2: Comparing the processing order of two code examples

The Selection Structure

When the processing of an instruction depends on the result of a decision or comparison from a previous instruction, use the selection structure. You implement the selection structure in Visual Basic using the **If...Then...Else statement**, which is described next.

There are two forms of the If...Then...Else statement.

Syntax ▶   If *condition* **Then** [*statements*] [**Else** *elsestatements*]

In this syntax, the *condition* is the decision or comparison mechanism that might contain variables, constants, properties, functions, mathematical operators, relational operators, and logical operators. The result of the condition test might require only a single, simple action and therefore might not require the Else component of the If statement. The code in Example 3-1 shows that if the state is KY, then the state tax value is .06 and processing proceeds to the statement following the If statement.

Example 3-1 ▶   `If txtState.Text = "KY" Then lblStateTax.Caption = ".06"`

The block form syntax is generally preferred when the Else statement is necessary or more than one statement is required.

Syntax ▶
```
If condition Then
        [instructions to be executed when the condition is true]
[ElseIf condition-n Then
        [elseif instructions to be executed when the condition is false and condition-n is true] ...
[Else
        [elsestatements to be executed when both conditions are false]]
End If
```

In this syntax, the *condition* is the decision or comparison mechanism that might contain variables, constants, properties, functions, mathematical operators, relational operators, and logical operators. The result of the condition test might require alternate processing that contains one set of instructions if the condition test is true, and another set of instructions if the condition test is false. Example 3-2 shows the alternate processing that occurs if the selected state is not KY.

Example 3-2 ▶
```
If txtState.Text = "KY" Then
        lblStateTax.Caption = ".06"
Else
        lblStateTax.Caption = ".04"
End If
```

You use operators in a program to form an expression that results in a true or false value. The program conditionally executes the instructions depending on the value of an expression. Figure 3-3 describes the mathematical, relational, and logical operators that you use to create valid condition tests.

Mathematical Operators	Description
^	Exponentiation (raises a number to a power)
-	Negation
*	Multiplication
/	Division
\	Integer division (returns only the integer portion of a division operation)
Mod	Modulus arithmetic (returns only the remainder of a division operation)
+	Addition
-	Subtraction

Relational Operators	Description
=	Equal to
>	Greater than
>=	Greater than or equal to
<	Less than
<=	Less than or equal to
< >	Not equal to

Logical Operators	Description
NOT	Reverses the value of the condition
AND	All conditions connected by the AND operator must be true for the compound condition to be true
OR	Only one of the conditions connected by the OR operator must be true for the compound condition to be true

Figure 3-3: Summary of mathematical, relational, and logical operators

An instruction that is executed as a result of a true or false condition can include additional If...Then...Else statements. Such structures are called **nested selection structures**. For example, the following nested selection structure, presented using both the Else and ElseIf syntax, checks to see if an employee worked overtime hours during a single work week.

Processing Using Else Example	Processing Using ElseIf Example
| ```
If chkHourly.Value = 1 Then
  If Val(txtHoursWorked.Text) > 40 Then
   txtNote.Text = "Employee worked overtime!"
  Else
   txtNote.Text = _
    "Employee did NOT work overtime!"
  End If
End If
``` | ```
If chkHourly.Value = 0 Then
 'Employee is not an hourly
 'employee; no processing necessary
ElseIf Val(txtHoursWorked.Text) > 40 Then _
  txtNote.Text = "Employee worked overtime!"
End If
``` |

Figure 3-4: Comparison of processing using Else and ElseIf

In the first example, an End If is required for all If statements. If the ElseIf is used in the place of Else, as in the second example, only the End If associated with the initial If statement is required. In order to accomplish this, the direction of the condition test was changed from chkHourly.Value = 1 to chkHourly.Value = 0. The choice of Else or ElseIf structures is largely a matter of preference.

The Else statement is not required; you use it when alternate processing is necessary based on a condition test. For clarity, programmers usually try not to embed the If…Then…Else selection structure more than three deep.

Special Selection Structure Processing Considerations

There are four special selection structure processing considerations: the Select…Case statement, the VAL function, the Format function, and the UCase and LCase functions. You use these special selection structure processing considerations to process the selection structure when more than two alternatives exist, to examine data for numeric values, to describe numbers using non-numeric characters, and to allow for string case comparisons.

The Select…Case Statement

You use the **Select…Case statement** form of the selection structure when there are several alternate paths based on the condition test. Referred to as the **extended selection structure**, the Case statement offers a clearer alternative to the use of the If…Then…Else statement. A good rule of thumb is to use the Case statement when more than two alternatives to the condition test exist.

Syntax ▶

```
Select Case testexpression
[Case expressionlist_1
        [instructions for the first Case]]
[Case expressionlist_2
        [instructions for the second Case]]
[Case expressionlist_n
        [instructions for the nth Case]]
[Case Else
        [instructions for when the testexpression does not match any of the expressionlists]]
End Select
```

In this syntax, the *testexpression* is any valid numeric expression or string expression. The *expressionlist_n* is a delimited list of one or more of the following forms: *expression*, *expression* To *expression*, or Is *comparisonoperator expression*. The **To** keyword specifies a range of values, as in 1 to 4. If you use the To keyword, the smaller value must appear before To. Use the **Is** keyword with comparison operators to specify a range of values, as in Is > 4. If not supplied, the Is keyword is inserted automatically. Example 3-3 compares the use of the If...Then...Else and Select...Case structures.

Example 3-3 ▶

Consider the state tax structure in each of three states: Kentucky ("KY"), .06; Ohio ("OH"), .05; and West Virginia ("WV"), .0575. Figure 3-5 shows two ways to compute the state tax amount for each state.

The Select...Case Structure	The If...Then...Else Structure
| ```
Select Case cboState.Text
    Case "KY"
        txtRate.Text = ".06"
    Case "OH"
        txtRate.Text = ".05"
    Case "WV"
        txtRate.Text = ".0575"
End Select
txtTax.Text = Val(txtGross.Text) * _
  Val(txtRate.Text)
``` | ```
If cboState.Text = "KY" Then
        txtRate.Text = ".06"
Else
    If cboState.Text = "OH" Then
            txtRate.Text = ".05"
    Else
        If cboState.Text = "WV;" Then
            txtRate.Text = ".0575"
        End If
    End If
End If
txtTax.Text = Val(txtGross.Text) * _
        Val(txtRate.Text)
``` |

Figure 3-5: Computing the tax amount

After the program determines the appropriate tax rate, control flows to the statement following the End Select (or the final End If) statement where the tax amount is calculated.

The Val Function

The **Val function** tells Visual Basic to treat a character string as a numeric value. TextBox controls contain character strings. In order to calculate the tax amount in Example 3-3, the Val function was used to treat the values in the txtRate and txtGross text boxes as numeric values. If the values in the text box were in fact numeric values (including only numbers and the decimal point), the Val function would return the actual numeric value; otherwise, the Val function would return a zero.

Syntax ▶ **Val**(*string*)

In this syntax, *string* is the character string to be treated as a number. Figure 3-6 shows values returned for selected Val function examples.

Val Function Example	Value Returned	Explanation
Val("123")	123	String contains numeric values; all values returned
Val("13,500")	13	String contains a non-numeric value, the comma; numeric values are returned until the comma is encountered
Val("$25.00")	0	String contains a non-numeric value, the $, as the first character; string is converted automatically to zero
Val("xyz")	0	String contains character data

Figure 3-6: Val function examples

The Format Function

You use the **Format function** to describe numbers by using dollar signs, commas, percent signs, and date and time formats as appropriate.

Syntax ▶ **Format**(*expression, format*)

In this syntax, *expression* specifies the number, date, time, or string whose appearance is to be formatted, and *format* specifies the format to use. The specified format can be one of the predefined Visual Basic formats or a string containing special symbols that identify how you want to display the expression. Figure 3-7 describes the predefined formats in Visual Basic.

Format Name	Description	Example
Currency	Displays a number with a dollar sign and two decimal places. Uses the thousand comma separator if appropriate. Negative numbers are enclosed in parentheses.	lblTotal.Caption = Format(lblTotal.Caption,"currency") 425.5 displays as $425.50
Fixed	Displays a number with at least one digit to the left and two digits to the right of the decimal point.	lblTotal.Caption = Format(lblTotal.Caption,"fixed") .5 displays as 0.50

Figure 3-7: Predefined formats in Visual Basic

Format Name	Description	Example
Standard	Displays a number with at least one digit to the left and two digits to the right of the decimal point. Uses the thousand comma separator if appropriate.	`lblTotal.Caption = Format(lblTotal.Caption,"standard")` 1234 displays as 1,234.00
Percent	Multiplies a number by 100 and displays the number with a percent sign (%). Displays two digits to the right of the decimal point.	`lblTotal.Caption = Format(lblTotal.Caption,"percent")` .667 displays as 66.70%

Figure 3-7: Predefined formats in Visual Basic (continued)

You cannot use formatted values in selection structure condition tests when you are comparing the formatted value to a numeric value. Remember, formatted values are no longer numeric.

The UCase and LCase Functions

String comparisons in Visual Basic are case-sensitive; that is, the value "K" is different from the value "k." You cannot be sure of the case that any given user will use to enter data, so you use the UCase or LCase functions to convert inputted data into a specific format. The **UCase function** returns a string containing the specified string that has been converted to uppercase letters. The **LCase function** returns a string containing the specified string that has been converted to lowercase letters. Figure 3-8 shows examples of using the UCase and LCase functions with the selection structure.

Syntax ▶   **UCase**(*string*)
         LCase(*string*)

Condition Test	Evaluation
`If UCase(txtState.Text) = "KY" Then`	Compares the uppercase version of the string entered in the text box with the string "KY"
`If LCase(txtCity.Text) = "morehead" Then`	Compares the lowercase version of the string entered in the textbox with the string "morehead"
`If UCase(txtState.Text) = "ky" Then`	ERROR: Compares the uppercase version of the string entered in the text box with the lowercase string "ky", which will never be true

Figure 3-8: Using the UCase and LCase functions with the selection structure

Exercise 3.1 ▶

On a piece of paper, code the Select...Case selection structure to accomplish the same processing as in the following If...Then...Else statement:

```
If UCase(txtState.Text) = "KY" Then
    lblState.Caption = "Kentucky"
Else
    If UCase(txtState.Text) = "OH" Then
        lblState.Caption = "Ohio"
    Else
        If UCase(txtState.Text) = "WV" Then
            lblState.Caption = "West Virginia"
        Else
            lblState.Caption = "Out of area"
        End If
    End If
End If
```

Exercise 3.2 ▶

Hourly employees who work overtime hours (more than 40 hours during a single week) should receive time and one-half pay (hourly wage * 1.5) for all hours over 40 worked during a single week. All other employees receive straight pay. Examine the following If...Then...Else statement. On a piece of paper, write the correction to reflect the described overtime pay method.

```
If UCase(txtEmpeCode.Text) = "H" Or Val(txtHoursWked.Text) > 40 Then
    lblGross.Caption = Val(txtHoursWked.Text) * Val(lblRate.Caption)
End If
```

Exercise 3.3 ▶

Registration fees are charged based on the number of registrants per organization as follows:

Number of Registrants	Charge per Person
1 to 3	$250
4 to 9	$200
10 or more	$175

However, when the following Select Case statement executes, the result is consistently a data input error. Carefully examine the following code. On a piece of paper, write the statement to make the necessary corrections.

```
Select Case txtRegistrants.Text
    Case 1 To 3
        lblRegistrationFee.Caption = Val(txtRegistrants.Text) * 250
    Case 4 To 9
        lblRegistrationFee.Caption = Val(txtRegistrants.Text) * 200
    Case Is >= 10
        lblRegistrationFee.Caption = Val(txtRegistrants.Text) * 175
    Case Else
        lblRegistrationFee.Caption = "Data Input Error"
End Select
```

Exercise 3.4 ▶

Use the If...Then...Else selection structure to write Visual Basic code to accomplish each of the following tasks. If a condition test requires more than two alternatives, use the Select...Case form of the selection structure. Code your responses on a piece of paper.

a. Display the string "Reorder" in the lblMsg.Caption control if the txtQuantity.Text control contains a number less than 25; otherwise, display the string "Quantity Available".

b. Assume that customers in Kentucky and Ohio receive a 5% discount. Examine the txtState.Text control for the state name, and then compute the discount using the lblTotal.Caption control. Store the discount (formatted as currency) in the lblDiscount.Caption control.

c. Assume that you are offering quantity discounts on widgets to customers. The number of widgets purchased is entered in the txtNumWidgets control on the program interface. The cost per widget depends on the number of items purchased as follows:

Number of Widgets	Cost per Widget
1 to 49	$25.00
50 to 99	$22.00
100 or more	$19.00

Store the total cost of widgets (formatted as currency) in the lblTotalCost.Caption property.

The Repetition Structure

You use the **repetition structure**, also known as **looping**, to execute an instruction or a sequence of instructions repeatedly. For example, instructions necessary to create paychecks will be executed repeatedly for all employees paid based on the same criteria. The three forms of the repetition structure are For Next, Do While, and Do Until.

The For Next Loop

The **For Next loop** is an automatic counter loop that repeats a block of statements a specified number of times.

Syntax ▶

> **For** *counter* = *startvalue* **To** *endvalue* [**Step** *stepvalue*]
>   [*instructions*]
> **Next** *counter*

In this syntax, *counter* is a numeric variable that stores a number that keeps track of the number of times the loop instructions are processed. The *startvalue*, *endvalue*, and *stepvalue* are numeric items that control the number of times the loop instructions are processed. The *startvalue* identifies the beginning of the loop. The *endvalue* identifies the end of the loop. The *stepvalue* tells the loop how much to increment or decrement the *counter*. The For Next loop often is used in processing tables. Example 3-4 prints the odd integers in the range 1 to 5.

Example 3-4 ▶

```
For intCount = 1 To 5 Step 2
        Print intCount
Next intCount
```

The Do While Loop

The **Do While loop** is a pretest loop that repeats a block of instructions *while* a condition is true. The loop tests a condition *before* processing instructions within the loop. Thus, instructions within the loop might not be processed at all.

Syntax ▶

Do While *condition*
        [*loop instructions*]
Loop

In this syntax, *condition* is a condition test like the selection structure condition test that results in a true or false value that determines if the loop instructions will be processed. The code in Example 3-5 prints the numbers 1 through 5, inclusive. You should notice that the programmer is required to initialize a counter variable (`intCount`) and to ensure that the counter is incremented (`intCount = intCount + 1`). You will learn more about variables in Chapter 4.

Example 3-5 ▶

```
intCount = 1
Do While intCount <= 5
    Print intCount
    intCount = intCount + 1
Loop
```

The Do Until Loop

The **Do Until loop** is a posttest loop that repeats a block of instructions *until* a condition is true. The loop tests a condition *after* processing instructions within the loop. Thus, the Do Until loop always processes the loop instructions at least once.

Syntax ▶

Do
        [*loop instructions*]
Loop Until *condition*

For example, the code in Example 3-6 prints the numbers 1 through 5, inclusive. Again the programmer is responsible for initializing and incrementing the counter.

Example 3-6 ▶

```
intCount = 1
Do
        Print intCount
        intCount = intCount + 1
Loop Until intCount > 5
```

You will learn more about using the repetition structure when random access file processing is introduced in Chapters 4 and 8 when you load the existing applicant pool from the sequential file into the corporate database.

Dialog Boxes

You use dialog boxes in Windows applications to prompt the user for additional data necessary to the application or to display information to the user. Dialog boxes, as a specialized type of form object, can be created in three ways:

- **Predefined** dialog boxes are created from code using the MsgBox or InputBox functions.
- **Customized** dialog boxes are created using a standard form or by customizing an existing dialog box.
- **Standard** dialog boxes (such as Print and File Open) are created using the CommonDialog control.

The InputBox Function

The **InputBox function** displays a prompt, text box, OK button, and Cancel button in a dialog box. The dialog box waits for the user to input text or click a button, and then returns a string containing the contents of the text box. If no text is entered, the InputBox function returns the null (empty) string.

Syntax ▶	InputBox(*prompt*[, *title*] [, *default*] [, *xpos*] [, *ypos*] [, *helpfile, context*])

In this syntax, *prompt* is a string expression that appears as the message in the dialog box; *title* is a string expression that appears in the title bar of the dialog box; *default* is a string expression that appears in the text box as the default response if no other input is provided; *xpos* and *ypos* are used to specify the horizontal and vertical distance of the upper-left corner of the dialog box from the top-left corner of the screen; *helpfile* is a string expression that identifies the Help file used to provide context-sensitive Help for the dialog box; and *context* is used with helpfile as the numeric expression that is the Help context number assigned to the appropriate Help topic by the Help author.

In the code shown in Example 3-7, an InputBox allows the user to enter a typing speed. The typing speed entered is converted to a numeric value and stored in the intWordsPerMinute variable.

| **Example 3-7 ▶** | ```
intWordsPerMinute =
  Val(InputBox("Enter your typing speed (in words per minute):", _
  "Temporary Employee Record"))
``` |

The InputBox function is used in the SSTER application to capture typing speed, as shown in Figure 3-9. The value entered in the InputBox text box (or the null string if nothing is entered) is stored as a numeric value in the variable named intWordsPerMinute. You will learn more about using variables in Chapter 4.
```

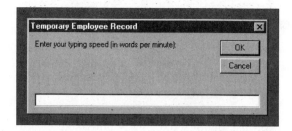

Figure 3-9: InputBox function to capture typing speed

Exercise 3.5 ▶

Data captured by the input area of the InputBox function is string data. Make the necessary correction to the following code to ensure that the typing speed stored in intSpeed is a numeric value. Write your response on a piece of paper.

```
intSpeed = _
    InputBox("Enter typing speed (in words per minute):", _
    "Typing Speed")
```

Exercise 3.6 ▶

On a piece of paper, write the Visual Basic statements to create the InputBox shown in Figure 3-10. Store the salary captured in the InputBox input area in the lblSalary.Caption. Format the label control as currency.

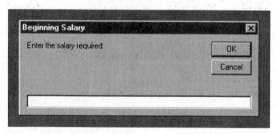

Figure 3-10: InputBox function to capture salary

The MsgBox Function

The **MsgBox function** displays a message in a dialog box along with one or more command buttons and an optional icon. After the dialog box opens, the MsgBox function waits for the user to click a button and then it returns an integer value that indicates which button the user clicked.

Syntax ▶   **MsgBox**(*prompt*[, *buttons*] [, *title*] [, *helpfile, context*])

In this syntax, *prompt* is a required string expression that appears as the message in the dialog box; *buttons* is a numeric expression that is the sum of values specifying the number and type of buttons to display, the icon style to use, the identity of the default button, and the modality of the message box; *title* is a string expression that appears in the title bar of the dialog box; *helpfile* is a string expression that identifies the Help file used to provide context-sensitive Help for the dialog box; and *context* is used with helpfile as the numeric expression that is the Help context number assigned to the appropriate Help topic by the Help author. You can use Visual Basic online Help for a detailed list of constants representing buttons, argument settings, and return values.

The code shown in Example 3-8 displays the Data Entry Error dialog box, shown in Figure 3-11, when the user does not enter a last name in the text box on the interface. The dialog box will contain an OK button and an information icon.

Example 3-8 ▶

```
intUserResponse = MsgBox("Missing employee last name", _
        vbOKOnly + vbInformation + vbDefaultButton1 + _
        vbApplicationModal, "Data Entry Error")
```

Figure 3-11: Data Entry Error dialog box

The SSTER interface uses the MsgBox function as an aid for editing data before writing information to a sequential file. For any data entry field whose contents are empty, a MsgBox function will be sent reminding the user to capture that data. In addition, a MsgBox function is used to verify that the user wants to exit the application when the Form_Unload(Cancel As Integer) event is executed, as shown in Figure 3-12.

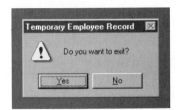

Figure 3-12: MsgBox function to exit

Exercise 3.7 ▶

On a piece of paper, write the MsgBox function statement to create the MsgBox shown in Figure 3-13. Store the response in a variable named intResponse. Use Example 3-8 and Figure 3-12 as a guide, and then code the Select...Case statement to store the response in the lblResponse control as follows:

Case	Response
Yes	"Overwrite the file"
No	"Do NOT overwrite the file"
Cancel	"Cancel the save operation"

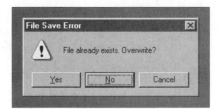

Figure 3-13: MsgBox function for Exercise 3.7

Use Visual Basic online Help to ascertain the return value constants necessary to code the selection structure.

Customized Dialog Boxes

You create customized dialog boxes using a standard form. You use standard forms to create more professional-looking dialog boxes that can request additional input. When a project requires a customized dialog box, special processing is required that considers the multiform project. You will learn more about customized dialog boxes in Chapter 6.

Standard Dialog Boxes

The CommonDialog control provides a standard set of dialog boxes for operations such as opening and saving files, setting print options for printing files, and selecting colors and fonts. You will learn more about the CommonDialog control and its associated methods in Chapter 7.

Sequential Processing

The information captured on the SSTER interface must be saved for future reference in a **sequential access data file**. Information in these data files is stored as a collection of related records. Each **record** might contain multiple single items, or **fields**, of information about an entity or a record might contain only a single field. Fields in sequential access files usually vary in length, and thus records in sequential access files often are referred to as **variable-length records**. Visual Basic automatically appends a carriage control and a line feed to the end of each record in a sequential access file.

You use sequential access files to store and retrieve data records in consecutive order using the **FIFO (First-In, First-Out) method**. No matter how the system handles the data, the records are considered by the program to be contiguous. The first record stored in the file is followed by the second record, and then the third record, and then the fourth record, and so on until the last record. In the same manner, records retrieved from a sequential file will be retrieved in the order in which they were created—first, second, third, etc. New records are appended to the end of the file.

Sequential access file processing requires the use of the Open, Write # or Print #, Input #, and Close statements.

The Open Statement

The **Open statement** enables input/output (I/O) to a file.

Syntax ▶   **Open** *pathname* **For** *mode* [**Access** *access*] [*lock*] **As** [#]*filenumber* [**Len**=*reclength*]

In this syntax, *pathname* is a required string expression that specifies a file-name; *mode* is a keyword specifying the file mode (Append, Binary, Input, Output, or Random); *access* allows for optional specification of the operations permitted on the open file (Read, Write, or Read Write); *lock* specifies the operations permitted on the open file by other processes (Shared, Lock Read, Lock Write, and Lock Read Write); *filenumber* is a valid file number in the range 1 to 511, inclusive; and *reclength* is used for random access files to specify the record length. You also can use a variable name for the file. You must be careful to use filenames that fit standard conventions for most computers. Remember that rules for DOS and Windows filenames are quite different.

A file must be opened before any I/O operation can be performed on it. The Open statement allocates a buffer for I/O to the file and determines the mode of access to use with the buffer. If the file specified by *pathname* doesn't exist, it is created when a file is opened for Append, Binary, Output, or Random modes. If the file is currently open by another process, then the Open operation fails and an error occurs. The data file is opened in this project for Append so the Shely staff members can add data to the file until you are ready to copy the data into the personnel database. If the data file is opened in Output mode, any previous data is erased. Example 3-9 shows an Open statement.

Example 3-9 ▶   `Open "A:EAP.dat" For Append As #1`

The Write # Statement

The **Write # statement** writes data to a sequential file.

Syntax ▶   **Write #**filenumber, [outputlist]

In this syntax, *outputlist* is one or more comma-delimited numeric expressions or string expressions to write to a file. The Write # statement inserts commas between items and quotation marks around strings as they are written to the file. When you use Write # to write data to a file, data other than string data might be interpreted as follows:

- Numeric data always are written using the period as the decimal separator.
- For Boolean data, either #TRUE# or #FALSE# is printed.
- Date data are written to the file using the universal date format (#yyyy-mm-dd hh:mm:ss#). When either the date or the time component is missing or is zero, only the part provided is written to the file.
- Nothing is written to the file if *outputlist* data is empty; however, for null data, #NULL# is written.

For example, the code in Example 3-10 writes the data captured on the SSTER interface to a sequential file opened as #1.

Example 3-10 ▶

```
'Data written to the EAP.dat file
  Write #1, frmDataEntry!txtEmpeID, _
    frmDataEntry!txtLName, _
    frmDataEntry!txtFName, _
    frmDataEntry!txtAddress, _
    frmDataEntry!txtCity, _
    frmDataEntry!cboState.Text, _
    frmDataEntry!txtZip, _
    frmDataEntry!txtPhone, _
    frmDataEntry!chkUnlisted, _
    frmDataEntry!chkSecretary.Value, _
    frmDataEntry!lblTypingSpeed, _
    frmDataEntry!chkClerical.Value, _
    frmDataEntry!chkMarketing.Value, _
    frmDataEntry!chkIndustrial.Value, _
    frmDataEntry!txtJobID.Text, _
    frmDataEntry!lstShift.Text, _
    frmDataEntry!txtOptions.Text, _
    frmDataEntry!txtNotes.Text
```

Notice the use of the underscore (_) character in the code. You use the underscore to continue a Visual Basic statement to the next line. Remember that Visual Basic associates the Enter key with the end of a statement. Using the underscore makes it possible to subdivide lengthy statements across lines. Additionally, notice that the name of the form is given and separated from the control name by an exclamation point (!). The form name is not required when only one form exists in the application. As the Shely Services system grows, multiple form processing will become necessary.

Example 3-11 shows a record written to the sequential file created in this project.

Example 3-11 ▶

```
"343","Jones","Loretta","3526 Maple Ave.","Green
City","KY","22987","(543) 555-8866","0",1,"55",0,0,0,"000",
"7:00am - 3:00pm","3","Can work on special weekend assignments."
```

The Print # Statement

The **Print #** statement writes display-formatted data to a sequential file.

Syntax ▶

Print #*filenumber*, [*outputlist*]

In this syntax, *filenumber* is any valid file number and *outputlist* is an expression or list of expressions to print. The Print # statement presents a second option for writing data to a sequential file. The Print # statement accepts formatted data as generated. The data often take up less space but must be parsed within the program itself when retrieved.

The Input # Statement

The **Input # statement** reads data from an open sequential file and assigns the data to variables.

Syntax ▶ | **Input #***filenumber, varlist*

In this syntax, *filenumber* is the integer assigned to the file in the Open statement, and *varlist* is a comma-delimited list of variables that are read from the file. You use this statement only with files opened in Input or Binary mode. (You can use LINE INPUT to read a complete record.) For example, the code in Example 3-12 reads the employee ID, last name, and first name from a sequential access file into the variable names strID, strLastName, and strFirstName—the compiler assumes that the ID, last name, and first name appear in the record in the order specified.

Example 3-12 ▶ | `Input #1, strID, strLastName, strFirstName`

The Close Statement

The **Close statement** concludes input/output (I/O) to a file that was opened using the Open statement.

Syntax ▶ | **Close** [*filenumberlist*]

In this syntax, *filenumberlist* can be one or more valid file numbers. If included, the filenumber should be preceded by the # (pound) sign. If you omit the *filenumberlist*, all active files opened by the Open statement are closed. The following code closes the file opened as file number one: `Close #1`.

End of File Detection

You use **end of file (EOF) detection** to detect the end of the file to prevent errors that result from attempting to read past the end of the file.

Syntax ▶ | `EOF(n)`

In this syntax, *n* is the filenumber assigned in the Open statement. The code in Example 3-13 reads the ID, last name, and first name from a sequential file for each record in the file. When the strID variable contains the value 100, the data are assigned to the appropriate controls on the interface.

Example 3-13 ▶
```
Do While Not EOF(1)
        Input #1, strID, strLastName, strFirstName
        If strID = "100" Then
                txtID.Text = strID
                txtLastName.Text = strLastName
                txtFirstName.Text = strFirstName
        End If
Loop
```

Exercise 3.8 ▶

You work for a professor who wants you to write a Visual Basic application that captures each student's name, major, current grade point, and grade expected in her Visual Basic programming course. The data should be written to a sequential access file named Ch3Ex3-8.dat that is stored in the Chapter3 folder on your Student Disk. Create the interface shown in Figure 3-14. Code the cmdSave_Click() Event procedure to write the data to the file. Code the cmdClear_Click() Event procedure to clear the screen for the next data entry. Code the cmdExit_Click() Event procedure to end the application. Save the form and project as Ex3-8a in the Chapter3 folder on your Student Disk.

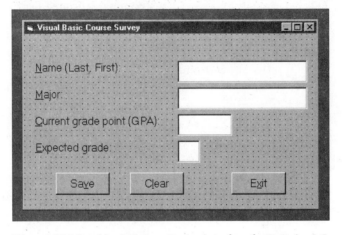

Figure 3-14: Visual Basic Course Survey interface for Exercise 3-8

Writing Code for Approved Hourly Wage Processing

The approved hourly wage options are mutually exclusive—selecting an option deselects any previously selected option. The sequential file needs to store only the value of the selected option. The program uses the txtOptionStorage.Text text box, which is invisible to the user, to store values as follows:

- optLess6.Value = True, txtOptionStorage.Text = "1"
- opt6to8.Value = True, txtOptionStorage.Text = "2"
- opt8to10.Value = True, txtOptionStorage.Text = "3"
- opt10up.Value = True, txtOptionStorage.Text = "4"

Example 3-14 shows how these values are stored by the option buttons Click() Event procedure.

Example 3-14 ▶

```
Private Sub optLess6_Click()
    txtOptionStorage.Text = "1"
End Sub
```

Code for the chkSecretary_Click() Event Procedure

Selecting or deselecting a check box control executes the control's Click() event. In the case of the check box, it is necessary to know whether clicking the check box adds or removes a check mark. The Value property contains a Boolean value that equals 1 when the check box contains a check mark. For example, when the Secretary Placement Preference check box is checked, the program opens an input box to capture the applicant's typing speed. Figure 3-15 shows the code for the chkSecretary_Click() event.

```
DataEntry_2 - frmDataEntry [Code]                                    _ □ ×
chkSecretary                              ▼   Click                          ▼
Private Sub chkSecretary_Click()
'Prompt the user for the typing speed if the
'Secretary preference is checked
    If chkSecretary.Value = 1 Then
        intWordsPerMinute = _
        Val(InputBox("Enter your typing speed (in words per minute):", _
        "Temporary Employee Record"))
        lblTypingSpeed.Caption = intWordsPerMinute
    Else
        lblTypingSpeed.Caption = ""
        intWordsPerMinute = 0
    End If
End Sub
```

Figure 3-15: The chkSecretary_Click() event

Using Code Modules

As its name suggests, a **code module** is a separate file that contains only code. You can add code modules to any number of applications. When sections of code are used in different places in a program or might be referenced from different forms or programs, it is appropriate to use the code module. Code organized effectively in code modules is easier to find in large programs. You create and add modules to the project by selecting the Add Module command on the Project menu. To change a module's name, click the module name and then activate the Properties window. Figure 3-16 shows the Project Explorer window for the current application.

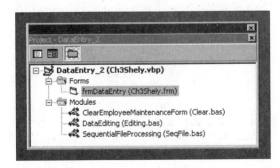

Figure 3-16: Project Explorer window

Code for the cmdSave_Click() Event Procedure

The cmdSave_Click() event performs two functions. First, it verifies that the user actually wants to write the data to the sequential file, and then it either exits the subroutine or calls the Basic code module that contains the routine to check the data.

The process of examining each data entry field for data is a routine that might be required by different forms in the Shely Services system. The **Call statement** transfers control to a Sub procedure (subroutine), Function procedure, or dynamic-link library (DLL) procedure. In this case, the Call CheckData statement transfers control to the CheckData subroutine in the DataEditing code module. After all code has been executed, control is transferred to the statement following the Call statement. You will learn more about the Call statement in Chapter 5. Figure 3-17 shows the code for the cmdSave_Click() event.

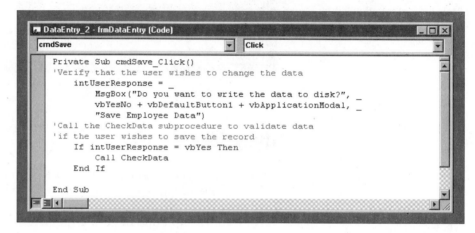

```
DataEntry_2 - frmDataEntry (Code)                              _ □ ×
cmdSave                          ▼     Click                          ▼

    Private Sub cmdSave_Click()
    'Verify that the user wishes to change the data
        intUserResponse = _
            MsgBox("Do you want to write the data to disk?", _
            vbYesNo + vbDefaultButton1 + vbApplicationModal, _
            "Save Employee Data")
    'Call the CheckData subprocedure to validate data
    'if the user wishes to save the record
        If intUserResponse = vbYes Then
            Call CheckData
        End If

    End Sub
```

Figure 3-17: The cmdSave_Click() event

Code for the CheckData() Subroutine

The employee ID, last name, first name, address, city, zip, and phone fields are checked for data by a simple If statement. A condition test checks the control for null strings that indicate that no data were input. When the condition identifies a null string, a message box containing an appropriate message opens, and the control that is missing the data receives the focus. Then the subroutine exits with no further processing.

The Value property of the four check box controls is examined using the compound condition form of the If statement with the AND logical operator. If all four placement preference check boxes are empty (value = 0), then the user is prompted to indicate a placement preference. The chkSecretary control receives the focus, and the subroutine is exited.

If all of the data entry edits are satisfactory, then the subroutine performs Calls to additional subroutines to write the data to the sequential file and subsequently clear all data entry fields for further processing.

After the WriteToSequentialFile and ClearEmployeeMaintenanceFields subroutines have executed, control returns to the cmdSave_Click() event, and this Event procedure is exited. The user can begin processing again. The code in Example 3-15 shows the CheckData() subroutine for editing data on the SSTER interface.

Example 3-15 ▶

```
Sub CheckData()
'Check each required data field for data
  If frmDataEntry!txtEmpeID.Text = "" Then
     intUserResponse = MsgBox("Missing Employee ID", _
        vbOKOnly + vbInformation, "Data Entry Error")
     frmDataEntry!txtEmpeID.SetFocus
  End If

  If Val(frmDataEntry!txtEmpeID.Text) < 100 Or _
     Val(frmDataEntry!txtEmpeID.Text) > 499 Then
     intUserResponse = MsgBox("Incorrect employee ID" + _
        vbNewLine + "ID should be between 100 and 499", _
        vbOKOnly + vbInformation, "Data Entry Error")
     frmDataEntry!txtEmpeID.SetFocus
     Exit Sub
  End If

  If frmDataEntry!txtLName.Text = "" Then
     intUserResponse = MsgBox("Missing employee last name", _
        vbOKOnly + vbInformation, "Data Entry Error")
     frmDataEntry!txtLName.SetFocus
     Exit Sub
  End If

  If frmDataEntry!txtFName.Text = "" Then
     intUserResponse = MsgBox("Missing employee first name", _
        vbOKOnly + vbInformation, "Data Entry Error")
     frmDataEntry!txtFName.SetFocus
     Exit Sub
  End If

  If frmDataEntry!txtAddress.Text = "" Then
     intUserResponse = MsgBox("Missing address", _
        vbOKOnly + vbInformation, "Data Entry Error")
     frmDataEntry!txtAddress.SetFocus
     Exit Sub
  End If

  If frmDataEntry!txtCity.Text = "" Then
     intUserResponse = MsgBox("Missing city", _
        vbOKOnly + vbInformation, "Data Entry Error")
     frmDataEntry!txtCity.SetFocus
     Exit Sub
  End If

  If frmDataEntry!cboState.Text <> "WV" And _
     frmDataEntry!cboState.Text <> "OH" And _
     frmDataEntry!cboState.Text <> "KY" Then
        intUserResponse = MsgBox("State must be WV, OH, or KY", _
           vbOKOnly + vbInformation, "Data Entry Error")
        frmDataEntry!cboState.SetFocus
     Exit Sub
  End If
```

```
        If frmDataEntry!txtZip.Text = "" Then
            intUserResponse = MsgBox("Missing zip code", _
                vbOKOnly + vbInformation, "Data Entry Error")
            frmDataEntry!txtZip.SetFocus
            Exit Sub
        End If

        If frmDataEntry!txtPhone.Text = "" Then
            intUserResponse = MsgBox("Missing phone number" _
                vbOKOnly + vbInformation, "Data Entry Error")
            frmDataEntry!txtPhone.SetFocus
            Exit Sub
        End If

        If frmDataEntry!chkSecretary.Value = 0 And _
            frmDataEntry!chkClerical.Value = 0 And _
            frmDataEntry!chkMarketing.Value = 0 And _
            frmDataEntry!chkIndustrial.Value = 0 Then
            intUserResponse = _
                MsgBox("Please indicate placement preference", _
                    vbOKOnly + vbInformation, "Data Entry Error")
            frmDataEntry!chkSecretary.SetFocus
            Exit Sub
        End If

        Call WriteToSequentialFile
        Call ClearEmployeeMaintenanceFields

End Sub
```

If all data are edited successfully, the data from the interface is written as a record to the sequential file opened in the OpenSequentialAppend subroutine, which is called by the Form_Load() Event procedure. The sequential file found on the disk in drive A was opened for Append in the Form_Load() event. In this way, the program adds subsequent records to the end of the file until the file is copied to the corporate database. While developing and testing applications, it often is desirable to open the sequential file for Output in order to erase previously added records that might contain errors.

Code for the Form_Unload(Cancel As Integer) Event

The **Unload event** occurs when a form is about to be removed from the screen. The user triggers the event by clicking the Close button. The Unload statement in code also triggers the Unload event. To verify that the user wants to exit the application, the appropriate code is placed in the form's Unload event. Setting the **Cancel argument** to any non-zero value stops Visual Basic from removing the form as is the case when the user clicks the No button in the "Do you want to exit?" message box. Figure 3-18 shows the code for the Unload event.

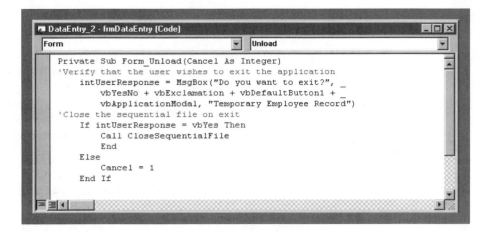

Figure 3-18: The Form_Unload() event

Exercise 3.9 ▶

Open the project Ex3-9.vbp from the Chapter3 folder on your Student Disk. Code the Form_Unload() Event procedure to ask the user if he or she wants to exit. To capture the user's response, use the variable intUserResponse, as shown in Figure 3-18. Code the Unload statement in the cmdExit_Click() Event procedure. Save the form and project as Ex3-9a.

Review of BASIC Fundamentals

Chapter 3 introduced the programming control structures (sequence, selection, and repetition) by syntax and example. The enhanced SSTER application uses the sequence and selection structures as processing mechanisms. The selection structure, implemented as If...Then...Else in this application, provides for alternate processing based on a condition test. Remember that Visual Basic provides extensive help files that need to be consulted as often as necessary. Sometimes by selecting and copying the examples, you can paste excellent routines into the program. It is often easier to work from an example than to read general discussions of program structures.

Functions are used extensively in this chapter. Functions, like methods, allow BASIC instructions to be executed to accomplish predefined alternatives. Unlike methods, functions result in a value. Functions introduced in Chapter 3 include InputBox, MsgBox, Val, Format, UCase, and LCase.

File processing statements allow BASIC instructions to communicate file processing requirements to the operating system. This chapter employs the use of sequential file processing statements including the Open, Input #, Write #, and Close statements.

Constants are items of data whose values do not change while the program is running. **Intrinsic constants**—for example, True, vbCancel, and vbYes—are built into Visual Basic and are used to contain values that can be checked. Intrinsic constants are easier to read and understand than the values they represent. For example, the code in Example 3-16 checks to see if the user clicked the Yes button in a dialog box.

Example 3-16 ▶   `If intUserResponse = vbYes Then …`

PROGRESSIVE PROJECTS

The progressive projects in this chapter build on the initial project that was assigned in Chapter 2 to collect and prepare start-up data. You might need to make some room across the bottom of the screen so you can add the command controls. Do this now, so you can use the screen in the next chapters.

Warning: Check and recheck the data to be sure they are stored properly. It might be messy to have to return to this step later in the project. *Again, be sure all the data needed, and only the data needed, are entered!*

1. Bean County Plumbing Inventory System (BCPIS)

You are writing a program to edit and enter the data into a sequential file. Use the form developed in the last chapter to add events for writing the data to a sequential file. Make sure to review all of the project documents. Save the form and project as Ch3BCPIS in the Chapter3 folder on your Student Disk. Use Ch3BCPIS.dat as the sequential filename. After executing the program, examine the Ch3BCPIS.dat file by opening it in WordPad.

2. Single Parents Public Service Library (SPLIB)

SPLIB needs a program to enter data that is edited as reasonably as possible. You completed the first step in preparing the program in Chapter 2. Now you add provisions for writing the data to a sequential file. Note from the program developed throughout the chapter that there is an area for command controls across the bottom of the screen. Save the form and project as Ch3SPLIB in the Chapter3 folder on your Student Disk. Use Ch3SPLIB.dat as the sequential filename. After executing the program, examine the Ch3SPLIB.dat file by opening it in WordPad.

3. Short Cut Lawn Service (SCLS)

You are writing a program for SCLS to collect and prepare its data for the project database. To do this, you started a program in Chapter 2 for entering and editing data. The data now must be stored in sequential files. Work from the sample program in the chapter to complete this program. Make sure to examine all data carefully for accuracy. Save the form and project as Ch3SCLS in the Chapter3 folder on your Student Disk. Use Ch3SCLS.dat as the sequential filename. After executing the program, examine the Ch3SCLS.dat file by opening it in WordPad.

INDEPENDENT PROJECTS

1. The Book Collection Listing

Harold has a set a books that are part of a larger collection—something like the *Hardy Boys*—and he wants to list them so he can see what he has. After he has the list, he can decide which books he still needs to purchase. Write a program for Harold so he can enter data about each book. Design editing procedures so that there will be some consistency in the data. Append the data from each form to a sequential file as Harold enters his books. Create code modules for the data edits and sequential processing routines as was done in the Shely Services program. Save the form and project as Ch3IP1 in the Chapter3 folder on your Student Disk. Use Ch3IP1.dat as the sequential filename. After executing the program, examine the Ch3IP1.dat file by opening it in WordPad.

2. The University Classroom Listing

The university needs a master list of classrooms with data about each room, such as number of seats, computers, labs, etc. You need to develop a list of the university's rooms that takes into consideration necessary editing and storage routines. The form for entering the data should include as many of the items covered in this chapter as possible, such as dialog boxes created using the MsgBox function, program control of the editing process, and validation of data. You must store the data in a sequential file. Save the form and project as Ch3IP2 in the Chapter3 folder on your Student Disk. Use Ch3IP2.dat as the sequential filename. After executing the program, examine the Ch3IP2.dat file by opening it in WordPad.

3. A Master Disk File

Prepare a list of your disks and the data needed about each type, such as production, master, backup, etc. Then develop a program to enter, edit, and store data about each disk in a sequential file. Include provisions for editing the data, using the MsgBox function to inform the user of invalid data, and the use of code modules. Remember that you can view the data using WordPad after writing it to the file. Save the form and project as Ch3IP3 in the Chapter3 folder on your Student Disk. Use Ch3IP3.dat as the sequential filename.

Managing Data — Database Access

Introduction ▶ In Chapter 3, you developed the Shely Services Temporary Employee Record (SSTER) interface to capture all data needed to place temporary employees in the appropriate employment positions. While the Shely Services application is being developed in this and the following chapters, Shely staff members can enter data about temporary employees into the sequential file named EAP.dat. You will use this data in Chapter 8 to load the corporate database. In this chapter, you will work on a way to view the captured data using a test database.

Although the interface resembles the SSTER interface, in this chapter you will create a transition that incorporates access to the data collected via the corporate database. Protection of corporate data is paramount—applications in production normally require password access, and so will the new SSTER interface (frmEmpeMaint). You will create routines to enter and store staff passwords.

During the development process, a programmer tests applications against test datasets. Even though the actual process will run against corporate data, you need to test sample data that is representative of actual data. No one wants to destroy a corporate dataset with untested code. The Shely Services project needs three test datasets: a random file containing the passwords and a test corporate database containing the TemporaryEmployees table and the CurrentJobs table.

The most frequently used data access mechanism is the corporate database. After reviewing the use of variables, constants, variable arrays, and control arrays for managing data in applications, you will review the fundamentals of database processing. You will explore the Data Manager as a way to generate Microsoft Access database tables from within the Visual Basic environment. You will use the Data control to connect the SSTER interface to an Access database. Figure 4-1 shows the enhanced SSTER interface created in this chapter.

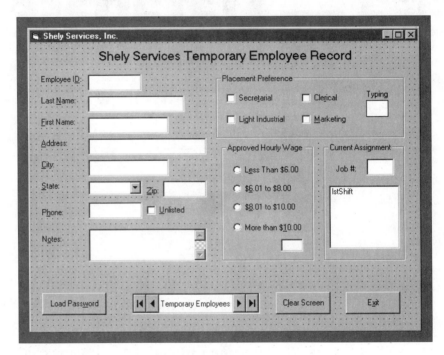

Figure 4-1: Enhanced SSTER interface

Using Variables and Constants

You use variables and constants to temporarily store data needed by an application in memory locations inside the computer. **Variables** are memory locations whose contents *can* change as the program executes. Constants are memory locations whose contents *cannot* change as the program executes.

Working with Variables

In Chapter 3, the Shely Services application required the use of variables with the InputBox and MsgBox functions. These functions returned values for typing speed (intWordsPerMinute) and keys pressed (intResponse), but there were no associated controls on the interface for these values. In addition to the need for variables in situations where necessary data are not found on the form, there are two advantages for using variables. First, using variables allows the programmer to assign properties of controls to variables in order to control the preciseness of numbers used in calculations. Second, storing data in variables makes code more efficient because data stored in a variable are processed faster than data stored in the property of an object.

Good programming practice requires good variable names. Although good variable names are not required by Visual Basic, they are a must when writing programs. It is preferable when using variables to declare the variable by indicating the name and, for efficiency, the data type. To require the use of declared variables in a program, use the **Option Explicit statement** in the form's General Declarations section. Without the Option Explicit statement, Visual Basic automatically creates a variable of the Variant data type for all undeclared variables. Figure 4-2 shows the General Declarations code window for the Shely Services program.

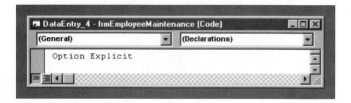

Figure 4-2: General Declarations code window

Use the **Dim statement** or the **Public statement** to create a variable. A section of the computer's internal memory (RAM) is reserved for each variable created. The syntax for the Dim and Public statements is:

Syntax ▶

Dim *variablename* [**As** *datatype*]
Public *variablename* [**As** *datatype*]

In this syntax, *variablename* is a descriptive name for the variable that indicates the data type and purpose of the variable, and *datatype* is the most efficient data type for the variable's purpose. The rules for naming variables are:

- Variable names must begin with a letter.
- Variable names can contain only letters, numbers, and the underscore character.
- A variable name cannot exceed 255 characters in length.
- A variable name cannot be a **reserved word**, which is a word with special meaning in Visual Basic, such as Open, Write, and Close.

Figure 4-3 shows some suggested data type prefixes that you can use when naming variables. An example of a string data type with the str prefix might be strFirstName.

Data Type	Data Type Prefix
Byte	byt
Boolean	bln
Currency	cur
Date (Time)	dtm
Double	dbl
Integer	int
Long	lng
Object	obj
Single	sng
String	str
Variant	vnt

Figure 4-3: Suggested data type prefixes

Figure 4-4 describes the type of values each data type can store, the maximum size of that data, and the range of valid data allowed for that data type.

Data Type	Allowable Data	Maximum Size	Valid Data Range
Byte	Binary numbers	1 byte	0 to 255
Boolean	Logical values	2 bytes	True or False
Currency	Up to 15 digits to the left of the decimal point and up to 4 digits to the right of the decimal point	8 bytes	+/- 9E14
Date (Time)	Date and time information	8 bytes	January 1, 100 to December 31, 9999
Double	Floating-point numbers	8 bytes	+/- 5E-324 to 1.8E308
Integer	Integers	2 bytes	-32,768 to 32,767
Long	Integers	4 bytes	+/- 2 billion
Object	Any object reference	4 bytes	
Single	Floating-point numbers	4 bytes	+/- 1E-45 to 3E38
String	Text information	Fixed-length (1 byte per character): 1 to 65,400 bytes	Variable-length (11 bytes per character): 0 to 2 billion bytes
Variant	Any of the other data types	Memory varies by data type	

Figure 4-4: Data type specifications

Example 4-1 shows some variable declarations.

Example 4-1 ▶

```
Dim intWordsPerMinute as Integer
Public intUserResponse as Integer
Dim curSales as Currency
Dim lngPopulation as Long
```

Scope of Variables

The location where you declare a variable in a program determines which procedures in the application can use the variable. You can declare variables in one of three locations:

1. In an object's Event procedure (local variables)
2. In a form's General Declarations section (form-level variables)
3. In a code module's General Declarations section (global variables)

You use the Dim statement to declare local and form-level variables. **Local variables** are known only to the procedure in which they are declared. **Form-level variables** are known to all procedures of the form and to the form's associated control procedures.

You use the Public statement to declare global variables. **Global variables** are known to all procedures in every form and control included in the application.

Storing Data in a Variable

You use the assignment statement to store data in a variable. The format for storing a value in a variable is *variablename = value*. A variable can store only one item of data at a time. When multiple assignment statements use the same *variablename*, the last item of data assigned is stored in the variable location. The use of variables in code typically follows a three-step process:

1. Declare variables
2. Assign values to variables
3. Manipulate variables

Exercise 4.1 ▶

Your application needs to store an employee ID, accepted pay rate, number of hours worked, and whether or not the employee is an hourly employee. (*Hint:* The indication for an hourly employee is True for an hourly employee and False for a salaried employee.)

a. On a piece of paper, write the appropriate Dim statements to create the necessary variables.
b. The employee ID and hourly employee check variables are required in multiple Event procedures on the form. Where will you declare these variables?
c. The accepted pay rate and number of hours worked variables are found only in the cmdCalculate_Click() Event procedure. Where will you declare these variables?

Variable Arrays

A **variable array** is a group of related variables that has the same name and data type. For example, variables in an array might contain valid state codes (a **one-dimensional array**, or a **list**), or state codes and their associated state names (a **two-dimensional array**, or a **multidimensional array**). Sometimes variable arrays are referred to as **subscripted variables** because one variable name is combined with a number in parentheses to reference a single variable in a logically organized set of variables. Figure 4-5 shows examples of a one-dimensional and a two-dimensional array.

One-dimensional array: `Dim strStateCode(1 to 5) As String`				
strStateCode(1) AL	strStateCode(2) AK	strStateCode(3) AR	strStateCode(4) OH	strStateCode(5) WY
To change AR to WV, the code would be `strStateCode(3)` **=** `"WV"` **with the result:**				
strStateCode(1) AL	strStateCode(2) AK	strStateCode(3) WV	strStateCode(4) OH	strStateCode(5) WY

Two-dimensional array: `Dim strStates(1 to 5, 1 to 2)`			
strStates(1,1)	AL	strStates(1,2)	Alabama
strStates(2,1)	AK	strStates(2,2)	Alaska
strStates(3,1)	AR	strStates(3,2)	Arkansas
strStates(4,1)	OH	strStates(4,2)	Ohio
strStates(5,1)	WY	strStates(5,2)	Wyoming

To change AR to WV in this table requires the code:
`strStates(3,1) = "WV"`
`strStates(3,2) = "West Virginia"`			

strStates(1,1)	AL	strStates(1,2)	Alabama
strStates(2,1)	AK	strStates(2,2)	Alaska
strStates(3,1)	WV	strStates(3,2)	West Virginia
strStates(4,1)	OH	strStates(4,2)	Ohio
strStates(5,1)	WY	strStates(5,2)	Wyoming

Figure 4-5: Sample one- and two-dimensional arrays

Syntax ▶

Dim *arrayname([lower subscript1* **To***] upper subscript1[,[lower subscript2* **To***] upper subscript2[...,[lower subscriptn* **To***] upper subscriptn]])*

In this syntax, *arrayname* is the name of the variable array; *lower subscript1...lower subscriptn* represents the lowest subscript in the respective dimension of the array; and *upper subscript1...upper subscriptn* represents the highest subscript in the respective dimension of the array. If the lower bound value is not explicitly stated, the Option Base statement controls the lower bound value of an array. If no Option Base statement is present, the lower bound value is zero.

The **subscript** is the unique number required to reference a particular variable in the variable array. Refer to the variable by the array name, and specify the variable's subscript(s) in parentheses immediately following the name. Use a comma to separate each subscript. For example, the following statement creates a two-dimensional array named strArray. The array is global, which is indicated by the use of Public. The first dimension varies from 1 to 50 while the second dimension varies from 1 to 4. The following array declaration prepares room for 200 string locations in memory (50 sets of 4):

```
Public strArray(1 To 50, 1 To 4) As String
```

The associated code that follows stores the employee ID in the location (intArrayCounter, 1), where intArrayCounter is an integer variable written as:

```
strArray(intArrayCounter, 1) = txtEmpeID.Text
```

The **Option Base statement** is used at module level to declare the default lower bound for array subscripts. The statement is not required, but when used it must appear in the module before any subprocedures.

Syntax ▶	Option Base {0 | 1}
Example 4-2 ▶	Option Base 1 Dim strStateCode(50) As String

In Example 4-2, the Option Base statement initializes the lower bound for the subscript to 1. Most business applications use the value 1 as the lowest subscript number in each dimension and limit the number of array dimensions to no more than three. Visual Basic provides for up to 60 dimensions in a variable array. Even though it is easy to create many physical dimensions, using too many dimensions can cause logic problems, especially when someone else must work with the program.

One of the advantages of using subscripted variables is that referencing data in the array is simplified. In Example 4-3, each of the variables in the state codes array is set to the null string (" ") using the For...Next loop.

Example 4-3 ▶	For intX = 1 to 5 strStateCode(intX) = "" Next intX

When you declare an array, space is reserved in memory to contain array data. Storing data in variable arrays in memory increases application efficiency because data in memory can be read and written faster than data stored in files on disk. In addition, data can be stored once at the beginning of the application and referenced as often as necessary.

The Shely Services application will use a two-dimensional array to store the employee ID, last name, access code, and password from a corporate random access file. These data will be used to provide data access via an accepted password and access privilege (browse, update, delete, and backup) via the access code. The If statement used to reference the access level from the array is:

```
If strArray(intArrayPosition, 4) = strPassword Then
        strAccessLevel = strArray(intArrayPosition, 3)
End If
```

When the program finds a valid password in the password field, the program stores the corresponding access code.

Exercise 4.2 ▶

On a piece of paper, complete the following:
  a. Use Visual Basic to write the appropriate Dim statement to declare a variable array named strMonthCodes. Each variable will store a string. Write the assignment statements that will store the three-character month codes (JAN, FEB, etc. as uppercase letters) in the array.
  b. Draw the array. Include each variable's name and its contents in the drawing.

Exercise 4.3 ▶

This exercise requires that you complete Exercise 4-2 first. On a piece of paper, complete the following:

    a. You decide to print the spelled out month on reports rather than using the three-character month codes. Use strMonths as the variable name. Modify the code created in Exercise 4-2 to create a two-dimensional array that contains month codes and month names.

    b. Assume that the array contains the month data. Code the cmdConvertMonths_Click() Event procedure that will convert the month code entered in txtMonth to the month name.

    c. Draw the array on paper. Include each variable's name and its contents in the drawing.

Control Arrays

A **control array** is a group of controls of the same type that share the same set of Event procedures, and, like the variable array, have the same name. The unique number assigned to each of the controls in a control array is an **index**. Just as the subscript reflects the variable's position in a variable array, the index reflects the control's position in a control array. The **Index property** returns or sets the number that uniquely identifies a control in a control array and is available only if the control is part of a control array.

Syntax ▶   *object*[(*number*)].**Index**

In this syntax, *object* is the name of the control, and *number* is a numeric expression that evaluates to an integer that identifies an individual control within a control array. If the number does not exist, the control is not a member of a control array. A control array can contain up to 32,767 controls. The first control in a control array is referenced with the number 0. Visual Basic automatically assigns the next integer available within the control array. You must use the Index property in code to specify a particular control in the array. An index must appear as an integer (or a numeric expression evaluating to an integer) in parentheses next to the control array name—for example, `optPlacement(0)`.

If the controls to be included in the array are *not* already on the form, you can use the copy and paste commands to create the control array. If the controls to be included in the array *are* already on the form, rename each of the controls using the same name. In either case, respond Yes to the dialog box question shown in Figure 4-6.

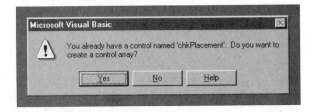

Figure 4-6: Control array dialog box

When a control in the array recognizes that an event has occurred, Visual Basic calls the control array's Event procedure and passes the applicable Index setting as an additional argument. You can override this assigned value as well as skip integers in the Properties window. In this chapter, the Shely Services application is revised to create a control array of placement preferences named chkPlacement.

Open the Ch4Shely.vbp program and examine the indexes of each of the controls in the placement preferences array.

Exercise 4.4 ▶

You recently learned about control arrays and decide to modify an existing application to optimize performance by using control arrays.

    a. Open the file Ex4-4 in the Chapter4 folder on your Student Disk, and then save the form and project as Ex4-4a.

    b. Create a control array of placement preferences using the chkSecretary, chkClerical, chkIndustrial, and chkMarketing controls. Name the control array chkPlacement.

    c. Examine the program code and replace all occurrences of chkSecretary, chkClerical, chkIndustrial, and chkMarketing with the appropriate chkPlacement(Index) value.

    d. Create a control array of hourly wages required using the optLess6, opt6to8, opt8to10, and opt10up controls. Name the control array optHourlyWage.

    e. Examine the program code and replace all occurrences of optLess6, opt6to8, opt8to10, and opt10up with the appropriate optHourlyWage(Index) value.

    f. Save the project. Create an executable file named Ex4-4a.exe.

Using Constants

There are two types of constants in Visual Basic: intrinsic constants and user-defined constants. Intrinsic constants are defined by Visual Basic. The programmer uses a Visual Basic statement to create **user-defined constants**.

Intrinsic Constants

You use Visual Basic's intrinsic constants to make a program more readable. The Object Browser dialog box is available only at design time and provides information about the objects available to your application. When you use intrinsic constants, you can use meaningful words in place of values that are less clear. For example, in the statement `frmEmpeMaint.BackColor = vbWhite`, it is clear that the background color of the form is being changed to white.

User-Defined Constants

You create user-defined constants using the **Const statement**.

Syntax ▶   **[Public | Private] Const** *constantname* **[As** *type***]** = *expression*

    In this syntax, *constantname* is the name of the symbolic constant following the naming convention of using a three-letter prefix (*con*) followed by a descriptive name; *type* is a valid Visual Basic data type; and *expression* represents a Visual Basic expression that becomes the value of the constant. For example, the following code creates a user-defined constant named conButtons that contains constant values necessary to provide Yes (the default) and No command buttons, an exclamation icon, and an application modal processing environment:

```
Const conButtons = vbYesNo + vbDefaultButton1 + _
  vbExclamation + vbApplicationModal
```

Using user-defined constants makes a program more readable and easier to maintain. When the value of a constant changes, you need to change the value only at the location of the constant declaration.

Random Access File Processing

The project description for the Shely Services application calls for password-protected access to data as well as access privileges that control an employee's level of access to data (browse only or update access). Shely staff employee passwords and access codes are stored in a random access file that is maintained by another corporate application.

A **random access file** contains records that can be stored and retrieved in any order. Random access records are similar to one-dimensional arrays stored in a file, and are stored and retrieved by their physical locations. The first record in the file is record number 1, the second record in the file is record number 2, and so on. When you use this method, the record number represents the relative position of the record in the file. The length of the fields in a random access file is identical from record to record. Thus direct access to records is possible because random access file records are **fixed-length records**. The fixed record length allows for quick computation of any record's location. Unlike sequential access files, random access file records do not contain a carriage control and line feed and are normally not created using a word processor. You create and write records to a random access file. Prior to writing records to a random access file, the file is initialized. **Initializing** a random access file involves estimating the maximum size of the file (number of records * individual record length) and writing spaces to the string fields and zero to the numeric fields of all records. Initializing ensures that there are no residual data from a previous application residing in the area reserved for the random access file.

The Type Statement

To create a random access file, you must define the file's record structure. The **record structure** describes the names, data types, and lengths of the fields in the record that results in the description of the fixed-length record definition for the random access file. You use the **Type statement** to create a user-defined data type that contains the names of the fields and their data types. After creating the user-defined data type, you can declare a variable of that data type using the udt prefix.

Syntax ▶

Type *structurename*
    fieldname1 **As** *datatype*
    [*fieldname2* **As** *datatype*]
    [*fieldnamen* **As** *datatype*]
End Type

For example, the Type statement shown in Example 4-4 creates a record structure that contains six fields. Data relevant to this application are the employee ID, last name, access code, and password. Lengths for the string fields (strEmployeeID, strEmployeeLastName, strPassword, strOtherData1, and strOtherData2) are indicated using String * *n*, where *n* is the number of characters contained in the string. The Dim statement creates a user-defined data type, udtSecurityDataRec, of the type SecurityDataStruc.

Example 4-4 ▶

```
Type SecurityDataStruc
        strOtherData1 As String * 1
        strEmployeeID As String * 3
        strEmployeeLastName As String * 30
        strOtherData2 As String * 214
        intAccessCode As Integer
        strPassword As String * 6
End Type
'Variable declaration
        Dim udtSecurityDataRec As SecurityDataStruc
```

A sample udtSecurityDataRec record will contain the following fields:

strOtherData1	strEmployeeID	strEmployeeLastName	strOtherData2	intAccessCode	strPassword

To reference the complete record, refer to udtSecurityDataRec. For example, you can print the complete record using the command `Printer.Printudt SecurityDataRec`. To refer to a field contained in the record, enter the record name (udtSecurityDataRec) and the field name, separated by a period. For example, to print the employee last name (strEmployeeLastName), use the command `Printer.Print udtSecurityDataRec.strEmployeeLastName`.

Creating and Writing to Random Access Files

Random access file processing requires the use of the Open, Put, Get, and Close statements, which are described next.

The **Open statement** enables input/output (I/O) to a file.

Syntax ▶

Open *pathname* **For** *mode* [**Access** *access*] [*lock*] **As** [#]*filenumber* **Len**=*reclength*

In this syntax, *pathname* is a required string expression that specifies a filename; *mode* is a keyword specifying the file mode (here, Random); *access* allows for optional specification of the operations permitted on the open file (Read, Write, or Read Write); *lock* specifies the operations permitted on the open file by other processes (Shared, Lock Read, Lock Write, and Lock Read Write); *filenumber* is a valid file number in the range from 1 to 511; and *reclength* is required for random access files to specify the record length. You also can use a variable name for the file.

Random access files are opened as Random. If the file specified by *pathname* does not exist, it is created. If the file already was opened by another process, the Open operation fails and an error occurs. In Example 4-5, the SSicher.txt file found in the root directory of drive A is opened. The length of the records in the file, which is required, is obtained using the Len function as the length of the user-defined data type, udtSecurityDataRec.

| **Example 4-5** ▶ | ```
Dim strFileName As String
Dim intRecordLength As Integer
strFileName = "A:\SSicher.txt"
intRecordLength = Len(udtSecurityDataRec)
Open strFileName For Random As #1 Len = intRecordLength
``` |

The **Put statement** writes data to a random access file.

Syntax ▶	**Put** [#]*filenumber*, [*recordnumber*], *variablename1*[, *variablename2, ... variablenamen*]

In this syntax, *filenumber* is the number used in the Open statement; *record-number* is the record number where writing begins; and *variablename* is the name of the variable containing data to be written to disk. For example, the following statement writes a record of the udtSecurityDataRec type to the record location stored in the intRecordNumber variable.

```
Put #1, intRecordNumber, udtSecurityDataRec
```

The appropriate data must be stored in each of the fields in the udtSecurityDataRec record structure before the program executes the Put statement. In Example 4-6, data captured from text box controls on the screen are stored in each required data field.

| **Example 4-6** ▶ | ```
udtSecurityDataRec.strEmployeeID = txtEmployeeID.Text
udtSecurityDataRec.strEmployeeLastName = txtLName.Text
udtSecurityDataRec.intAccessCode = CInt(txtAccessCode.Text)
udtSecurityDataRec.strPassword = txtPassword.Text
``` |

The **Get statement** reads a record from a random access file.

Syntax ▶	**Get** [#]*filenumber*, [*recordnumber*], *variablename1*[, *variablename2, ... variablenamen*]

In this syntax, *filenumber* is the number used in the Open statement; *record-number* is the record number where writing begins; and *variablename* is the name of the variable containing data to be written to disk. Data read with the Get state-ment usually are written to the file with the Put statement. For example, in the fol-lowing statement, data in the intRecordNumber location are read into the udtSecurityDataRec record structure:

```
Get #1, intRecordNumber, udtSecurityDataRec
```

The **Close statement** concludes input/output (I/O) to a file opened using the Open statement.

Syntax ▶	**Close** [*filenumberlist*]

In this syntax, *filenumberlist* can be one or more valid file numbers. If the *filenumberlist* is included, you precede the file number by the # (pound) sign. If the *filenumberlist* is omitted, all active files opened by the Open statement are closed. For example, the following statement closes the file opened as file number 1: `Close #1`.

Exercise 4.5 ▶

In Exercise 4-3, you created a two-dimensional array that contained month codes and month names. The data were hard-coded into the array. Assume a file named MonthCodes.txt exists in the root directory of drive A and contains the valid month codes and month names based on the following record structure:

```
Type MonthCodeStruc
  strMonCode As String * 3
  strMonName As String * 12
End Type
```

Complete the following exercises on a piece of paper.
  a. Code the Dim statement to declare a user-defined variable of the MonthCodeStruc type.
  b. Code the cmdLoadMonthsArray_Click() event to load the data from the file into the state codes array.

Exercise 4.6 ▶

On a piece of paper, create a record structure that contains the faculty ID (the Social Security number), faculty name, faculty department (a three- or four-letter code), and faculty status (1 = Assistant Professor; 2 = Associate Professor; 3 = Full Professor), and then complete the following exercises:
  a. Write a Dim statement that declares a variable of the user-defined record structure.
  b. Write an Open statement that opens a random access file named A:\FacStat.dat.

The Build Random Access File Program

Password protection and data access for Section IV, Temporary Employee Management, at Shely Services are controlled via maintenance of a random access file. The file contains, among other data, the staff employee ID, password, and an access code used to determine each employee's access privileges (2 = browse; 4 = browse, add, update; 8 = full access, which includes browse, add, update, delete, and backup). The Shely Services data access program requires access to the random access file for the purpose of creating a two-dimensional variable array of security data used to password-protect the company database. Staff IDs are numbers in the range 101 to 150. The array, strArray, is defined as 50 by 4, `strArray(1 to 50, 1 to 4)`, and holds the variables strEmployeeID, strEmployeeLastName, intAccessCode, and strPassword. The BldRand.vbp program in the Chapter4 folder on your Student Disk is used to create the random access file required by the Shely Services application.

Because it can damage data, developing and testing a program against a master file is not recommended. Programs under construction typically are tested using sample data. Unlike sequential access files, simply typing the data in a word processor is not the best way to create random access files. You must create and write records to the file using random access file statements. This section describes the program used to build a test random access file from which the data access program can build the required array. Figure 4-7 shows the user interface used to capture the random access file data. The array is built here as a function of program component development and testing. As programs become large and contain many areas of processing, it is often desirable to code and test incrementally.

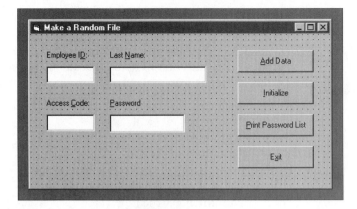

Figure 4-7: BldRand.vbp interface

Using Variables, Constants, and Arrays

Figure 4-8 shows the General Declarations code window for the RandomFileProcessing code module. You use the General Declarations section to create the record structure using the Type statement and to declare global variables that will be referenced throughout the code (the user-defined record structure, two-dimensional array, and a counter variable).

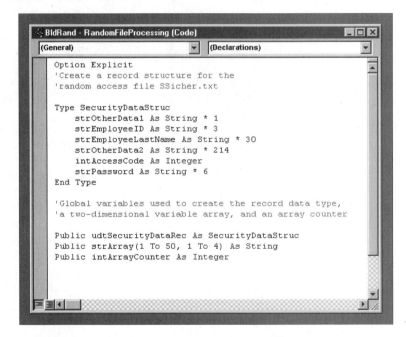

Figure 4-8: The General Declarations code window for the RandomFileProcessing code module

The cmdInitialize_Click() Event Procedure

The cmdInitialize_Click() Event procedure performs the task of clearing any existing records from the random access file. In addition, the initialize code is used to set aside space on the disk that has been cleared of any existing data prior to its first use. Figure 4-9 shows the code to initialize a random access file named SSicher.txt to contain 50 records.

```
Private Sub cmdInitialize_Click()
'This routine initializes a file of fifty records to be used
'as the security file (SSicher.txt) for the Shely application

    Dim strFileName As String
    Dim intRecordLength As Integer
    Dim intResponse As Integer
    Dim intRecordNumber As Integer
    Const conBtns As Integer = vbYesNo + vbExclamation _
        + vbDefaultButton2 + vbApplicationModal

'Store the file name
    strFileName = "A:\SSicher.txt"
'Store the record length
    intRecordLength = Len(udtSecurityDataRec)

'Open the file for processing
    Open strFileName For Random As #1 Len = intRecordLength

'Verify that the user wants to rebuild the file with blank records
    intResponse = MsgBox("Do you want to initialize the file?", _
            conBtns, "Clear File Check")
    If intResponse = vbYes Then
    'Initialize the fields in the security record
    'Spaces for strings, 0 for the integer
        With udtSecurityDataRec
          .strOtherData1 = Space(1)
          .strEmployeeID = Space(3)
          .strEmployeeLastName = Space(30)
          .strOtherData2 = Space(214)
          .intAccessCode = 0
          .strPassword = Space(6)
        End With
    'For each of 50 records, write a blank record to the file
        For intRecordNumber = 1 To 50
            udtSecurityDataRec.strEmployeeID = _
            Str(intRecordNumber)
```

Figure 4-9: The cmdInitialize_Click() event

```
          Put #1, intRecordNumber, udtSecurityDataRec

      Next intRecordNumber

   End If

   Close #1

   txtEmployeeID.SetFocus
```

Figure 4-9: The cmdInitialize_Click() event (continued)

Variables declared within the Initialize Event procedure are local variables. These variables are declared, initialized, and manipulated (as necessary) strictly within this Sub procedure. Any future reference to the same variable names will have no effect on values received here. In addition, the symbolic constant conBtns is declared and initialized here to contain the necessary constant values used to construct the MsgBox.

You use the With...End With statement (which is described in the Review of BASIC fundamentals section at the end of this chapter) to initialize string variables in the record to spaces, and integer variables to zero. Then the repetition structure is used to initialize a 50-record area.

The cmdAddData_Click() Event Procedure

You use the cmdAddData_Click() event to build the random access file. This Click event examines the employee ID text box for a valid value in the range 101 to 150. If the value is valid, data from the screen are assigned to a variable in the record structure, and the file is opened, written to, and closed. Then all screen controls are cleared for future processing, as shown in Figure 4-10.

```
Private Sub cmdAddData_Click()

  Dim strFileName As String

  Dim intRecordLength As Integer

  Dim intRecordNumber As Integer


'Store the filename

  strFileName = "A:\SSicher.txt"

'Determine the record length

  intRecordLength = Len(udtSecurityDataRec)


'Verify that the employee ID is in the range 101 to 150

  If Val(txtEmployeeID.Text) < 101 Or _

    Val(txtEmployeeID.Text) > 150 Then

    MsgBox "Staff ID must be in the range 101 to 150", _

     vbOKOnly, "Incorrect Staff ID"

    txtEmployeeID.SetFocus
```

Figure 4-10: The cmdAddData_Click() event

```
        Close #1

        Exit Sub

   End If


 'Store the interface data in the appropriate field
    With udtSecurityDataRec

       .strOtherData1 = Space(1)

       .strEmployeeID = txtEmployeeID.Text

       .strEmployeeLastName = txtLastName.Text

       .strOtherData2 = Space(214)

       .intAccessCode = CInt(txtAccessCode.Text)

       .strPassword = txtPassword.Text

    End With


 'Compute the record location
    intRecordNumber = CInt(txtEmployeeID.Text) - 100
 'Open the file, write a record, close the file
    Open strFileName For Random As #1 Len = intRecordLength

    Put #1, intRecordNumber, udtSecurityDataRec

    Close #1


 'Clear the user interface, frmMakeRandom
    txtEmployeeID.Text = ""

    txtLastName.Text = ""

    txtAccessCode.Text = "0"

    txtAccessCode.SelLength = 1

    txtPassword.Text = ""

    txtEmployeeID.SetFocus
 End Sub
```

Figure 4-10: The cmdAddData_Click() event (continued)

The cmdPrint_Click() Event Procedure

Figure 4-11 shows the cmdPrint_Click() event, which uses the printer object and its associated print method to provide a printout of the employee ID, last name, access code, and password for existing records in the file.

```
Private Sub cmdPrint_Click()

  Dim intCount As Integer

  Dim strFileName As String

  Dim intRecordLength As Integer

'Store the filename

  strFileName = "A:\SSicher.txt"

'Determine the record length

  intRecordLength = Len(udtSecurityDataRec)

'Open the security file

  Open strFileName For Random As #1 Len = intRecordLength


'For each of the records in the security file with an access

'code other than zero, print the record data

  For intCount = 1 To 50

    Get #1, intCount, udtSecurityDataRec

    If udtSecurityDataRec.intAccessCode <> 0 Then

      With udtSecurityDataRec

        Printer.Print .strEmployeeID; " ";

        Printer.Print .strEmployeeLastName; " ";

        Printer.Print CStr(.intAccessCode); " ";

        Printer.Print .strPassword

      End With

    End If

Next intCount


'Send the output to the printer

  Printer.EndDoc

  Close #1

End Sub
```

Figure 4-11: The cmdPrint_Click() event

The cmdExit_Click() Event Procedure

In addition to its standard function of ending the application, the cmdExit_Click() Event procedure provides the opportunity for the programmer to build and print the array required for future processing. Based on a MsgBox response of yes, the SetUpArray and PrintArray code modules are called to create and print the array.

The SetUpArray routine uses the random access file to access records with existing access codes and to build a two-dimensional array of relevant system access data. Levels of access are obtained using the Mod operator (`intAccessCode Mod 16`). For purposes of flow control, the line label and GoTo statements are employed to branch around code within the same module.

If the calculated access code is 2, 4, or 8, and the computed base code Mod 16 result is 0, then data are written to the next row location in the array. Figure 4-12 shows the variable names and contents of the sample data used to test the application. (Note: In Figure 4-12, the Roman numeral IV followed by the numbers 2, 4, or 8 represents section numbers and access codes available for use in testing and debugging.) After the SetUpArray code terminates, the PrintArray routine is called to print the contents of the array using the Printer object.

Employee ID	Employee Last Name	Access Code	Password
strArray(1,1) 101	strArray(1,2) Maitland IV/2	strArray(1,3) 2	strArray(1,4) pass01
strArray(2,1) 103	strArray(2,2) Carruthers IV/4	strArray(2,3) 4	strArray(2,4) pass03
strArray(3,1) 105	strArray(3,2) James IV/8	strArray(3,3) 8	strArray(3,4) pass05
strArray(4,1) 130	strArray(4,2) Masterly IV/2	strArray(4,3) 2	strArray(4,4) pass09
strArray(5,1) 140	strArray(5,2) Porterfield IV/4	strArray(5,3) 4	strArray(5,4) pass12
strArray(6,1) 146	strArray(6,2) Lamar IV/8	strArray(6,3) 8	strArray(6,4) pass13
strArray(7,1) 147	strArray(7,2) Lowell IV/2	strArray(7,3) 2	strArray(7,4) pass14

Figure 4-12: Variable names and contents of the sample data

Exercise 4.7

Ex4-7.vbp contains a partially completed program to create a random access file and build an array containing valid security data. Open the program Ex4-7.vbp in the Chapter4 folder on your Student Disk, and then save the form, module, and project as Ex4-7a. Examine the existing code to ascertain the random file record layout. Then complete the following steps to complete the partially developed code.

a. Valid employee IDs are positive integers less than 50. These IDs are entered as strings containing leading zeros in the txtEmployeeID.Text property (i.e., 01). In the cmdAddData_Click() Event procedure, records are automatically written to the random file. Modify the code to verify that the employee ID is in the range 01 to 50 prior to writing a record. Send an appropriate error message for invalid employee IDs.

b. Valid access codes for this application are "A", "D", "U", and "All". In the SetUpArray Sub procedure, validate the access code prior to writing the record to the array. Bypass all records with invalid access codes.

c. Save and run the application, and then test the application using the following data:

d. Print the data stored in the Ex4-7Sec.txt file.

e. Create an executable file named Ex4-7a.exe.

Employee ID	Last Name	Access Code	Password
01	Appleby	A	123456
03	Cassidy	D	987654
04	Eggleston	U	135790
05	Jones	All	999999
99	ErrinID	A	102938
50	ErrinAccess	Xyz	135642

Database Access

A **database** is an organized collection of related information stored electronically (in a file on a disk). A **relational database** stores information in tables that are composed of rows and columns. Each column (or **field**) in a relational database represents a single item of information (or **property**) about a person, place, or thing. Each row (or **record**) in a relational database contains all of the necessary information (or **instance**) about a person, place, or thing. A group of related records pertaining to the same topic (or **entity**) makes up a database **table**. A relational database can contain one or more tables.

Visual Basic lets you access the data stored in a relational database, or you can use Visual Basic to create a Microsoft Access relational database.

Using the Visual Data Manager

You can use the Visual Data Manager to create a Microsoft Access database that includes indexes and validation rules from within the Visual Basic environment. After creating the database, you can use the Data Manager to browse the database, or to add, delete, or update records. You start the Visual Data Manager from the Add-Ins menu. The Visual Data Manager is automatically installed when you install a typical installation of Visual Basic 5.0 or 6.0. If you are using the Control Creation Edition of Visual Basic, the Visual Data Manager and the Data control are not available. From within the Data Manager, you use the File menu to access an existing database and to create a new database. Figure 4-13 shows the VisData window that contains the Database Window and the SQL Statement window for navigating databases. You will learn more about Structured Query Language (SQL) commands in Chapter 6.

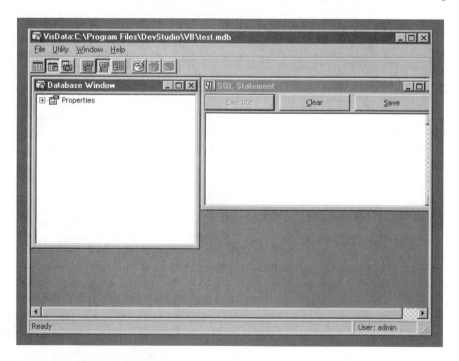

Figure 4-13: VisData window

Creating a Table Using the Visual Data Manager

Creating a relational database and its associated tables requires a thorough design based on the user's information requirements. The basic design steps include:

■ Organizing the data requirements into tables

- Describing the required fields for each table
- Establishing relationships between tables, if more than one table exists
- Creating indexes, if necessary
- Defining any required validation rules

You open the Table Structure dialog box shown in Figure 4-14 by right-clicking the Database window and then clicking New Table. You use the Table Structure dialog box to name a table and to define the characteristics of each field in the table, including the field name, data type, and size. You also can create indexes and validation rules using this dialog box. You use the Build the Table button to save the table information.

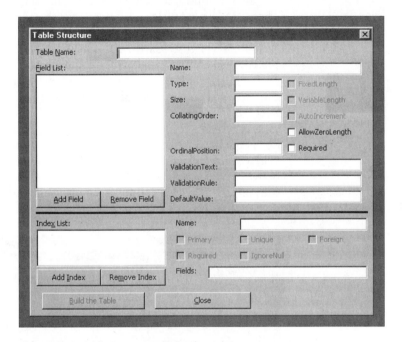

Figure 4-14: Table Structure dialog box

Figure 4-15 shows the CurrentJobs and TemporaryEmployees tables in the Shely Services database.

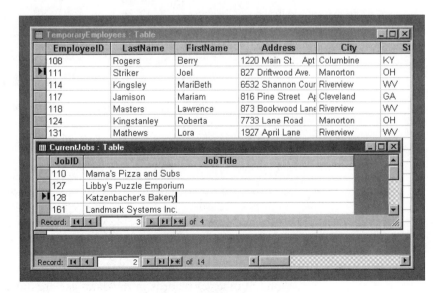

Figure 4-15: CurrentJobs and TemporaryEmployees tables

An **index** is a special table that is created and maintained by Visual Basic to arrange database records in a specific order. The index and pointer fields of the index table store, respectively, the values contained in the indexed field and the record number of the corresponding record in the table being indexed. A table can have one or more indexes.

A **data validation rule** places restrictions on the data entered in a field. You use data validation rules to ensure that the data in the database are accurate. You can use mathematical, relational, and logical operators with numbers and strings to create validation rules.

ShelyTemps.mdb consists of two tables: CurrentJobs and TemporaryEmployees. The .mdb file extension indicates that the file is a Microsoft Access database. The CurrentJobs table is maintained by another application in the Shely Services Human Resources (HR) Department. The CurrentJobs table stores the JobID and the JobTitle fields. The CurrentJobs table eventually will contain additional data added by the HR Department. The CurrentJobs table is **read only**, which means that you cannot write data to the table. Figure 4-16 shows the relationship diagram for the ShelyTemps.mdb database, where the JobID primary key in the CurrentJobs table is established as a foreign key (JobID) in the TemporaryEmployees table. The **primary key** is the field(s) whose value(s) uniquely identify each record in a table. When the primary key from one table is used as a field in a second table to form a relationship between the two tables, it is called a **foreign key** in the second table. This relationship implies that you cannot assign a JobID to an employee unless the JobID exists in the CurrentJobs table.

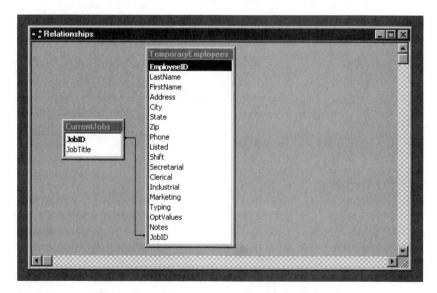

Figure 4-16: Relationships window for the ShelyTemps database

Accessing a Database Using the Visual Data Manager

You can use the Visual Data Manager to open an existing database and browse through existing records. In addition, you can add and delete records and search for specific records.

You open the Open table window shown in Figure 4-17 by clicking the Open DataBase command on the File menu on the VisData menu bar and then clicking the appropriate database software, selecting the database and clicking the Open button, and then double-clicking the table to open it. The record pointer location and number of records in the database are indicated to the right of the scroll bar at the bottom of the screen. You use the scroll bar to browse through existing records in the TemporaryEmployees table.

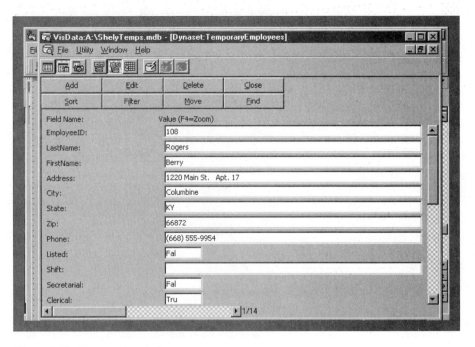

Figure 4-17: Open table window

Exercise 4.8 ▶

Use the Visual Data Manager to create an Access database named StuRecords.mdb that contains one table named Student that consists of the following fields:

- Student ID (a text field containing the Social Security number, 11 characters in length)
- Student Last Name (a text field 30 characters in length)
- Student First Name (a text field 15 characters in length)
- Student Phone Number (a text field 12 characters in length)
- Major (a text field 20 characters in length)
- Classification (a text field 2 characters in length; valid entries are Fr, So, Jr, Sr)
- Current Grade Point Average (a single field)

Using the Data Control

You cannot customize the user interface that is provided with the Visual Data Manager. However, you can create a Visual Basic application to customize an interface that you can use to access stored database records. Visual Basic's **Data control** allows the application to become data-aware. **Data-aware applications** can access and manipulate stored database data.

Figure 4-18 shows the Data control in the SSTER interface. The Data control establishes a link between the database and other controls in the interface, in a process called **binding**. Bound controls automatically display database field contents when the Data control is present. Required property settings for the Data control include the **DatabaseName property**, which specifies the complete path to the database, and the **RecordSource property**, which indicates the table to use from the database. To allow the user to add records to the database, use the **EOFAction property**, which indicates the action to take when the user tries to move past the last record in a table: 0 for Move Last, 1 for EOF (end of file, default), or 2 for Add New. Figure 4-19 shows the Properties window for the datTempEmpe control.

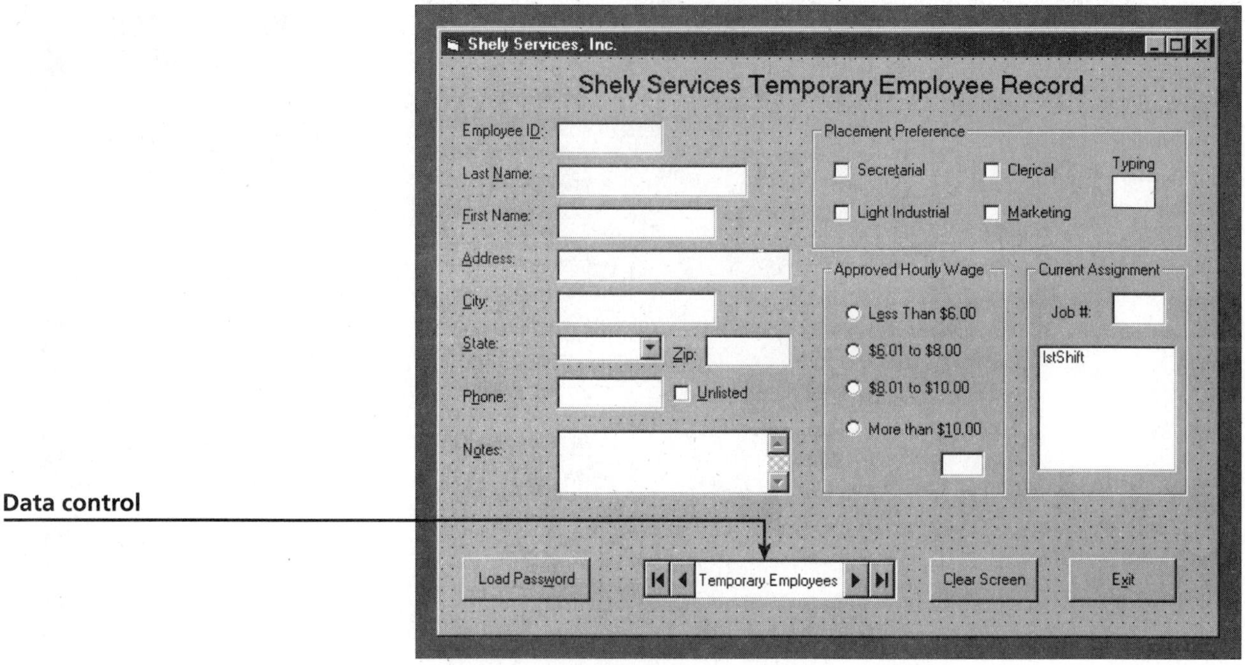

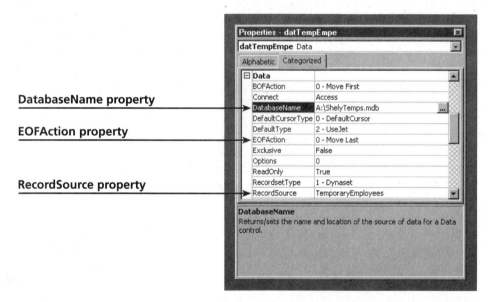

Figure 4-18: SSTER interface Data control

Figure 4-19: Properties window for the datTempEmpe control

To create **bound (data-aware) controls,** set the **DataSource property** (the name of the Data control to which the desired control is bound) and the **DataField property** (the name of the table field to which the desired control is bound). Figure 4-20 shows the DataSource and DataField property settings for the txtEmpeID control. The DataSource and DataField properties should be set for all form controls that access database data.

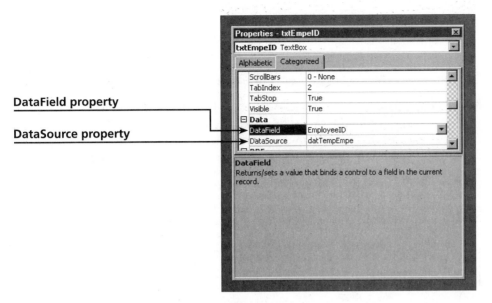

DataField property

DataSource property

Figure 4-20: Properties window for the txtEmpeID control

Writing Code

The Ch4Shely.vbp project uses a random access file of security data (A:\SSicher.txt) to build a variable array of passwords and access codes. Once security access has been obtained, the Data control is used to bind the SSTER interface controls to the Access database.

The first of three data management programs, Ch4Shely.vbp, was created from the Ch3Shely.vbp project and is saved in the Chapter4 folder on your Student Disk. The Chapter 3 form and its associated code modules were saved as the new Ch4Shely.vpb project. The SSTER interface (Ch4Shely.frm) was changed to include the Load Password command button and the Data control. The form name, frmDataEntry, used in Chapter 3, was changed to frmEmpeMaint in Chapter 4 to reflect the introduction of the maintenance function in the TEMS system. The Save and Print Screen command buttons were removed because they are no longer necessary.

Once included in the interface, the Data control DatabaseName property is set to reflect the test database (A:\ShelyTemps.mdb), and the RecordSource property is set to reflect the database table (TemporaryEmployees). Then the interface controls related to database fields are bound to each other using the DataSource and DataField properties.

Project Variables

Variables created in the Ch4Shely.vbp project are local and global variables. Global variables are required for the record structure, variable array, and array counter variable declarations. Remember that global variables are required when all forms, controls, and subroutines within the project will require access to the data. All other variables are declared and initialized locally.

The Form_Load() Event Procedure

Updating the Form_Load() event to reflect changes in Chapter 4 involves removing references to the cmdSave_Click() event and any statements that disable controls. The references to the sequential file subroutine code also need to be removed.

The SetUpArray subroutine is called to read the random access file and load the variable array used in password processing.

The cmdLoadPassword_Click() Event Procedure

The cmdLoadPassword_Click() event uses the InputBox function to capture the user password. The string ****** indicates to the user how many characters are contained in the password. After an assignment statement initializes the strAccessLevel variable to zero, a For...Next loop iterates through the array looking for a matching password. If a match exists, the security access level is stored in the strAccessLevel variable and the Data control is made visible allowing the user to browse the test database (see Figure 4-21). You will use the access level code in Chapters 5 and 6 to allow the user update and backup access to the database.

```
Private Sub cmdLoadPassword_Click()
'Declare variables
  Dim strAccessLevel As String * 1
  Dim strPassword As String
  Dim intArrayPosition As Integer
'Accept the user password
  strPassword = _
     InputBox("Enter Password", "Check Password", "******")
'If Cancel is clicked, bypass further checks
  If strPassword = "" Then
'If a  password was entered, check the password
  ElseIf strPassword <> "******" Then
'Initialize the access level
     strAccessLevel = "0"
'Examine the array for the password entered
'If the password is found, store the access level
     For intArrayPosition = 1 To intArrayCounter
        If strArray(intArrayPosition, 4) = strPassword Then
           strAccessLevel = strArray(intArrayPosition, 3)
        End If
     Next intArrayPosition
'If the password exists in the array,
'display the Data control, otherwise
'send an error message
     If strAccessLevel <> "0" Then
        datTempEmpe.Visible = True
     Else
        MsgBox "Invalid Password, try again!", , "PassWord"
     End If
```

Figure 4-21: The cmdLoadPassword_Click() event

```
    Else

      MsgBox "You must enter a password, try again!" _

        , , "Password"

    End If
```

Figure 4-21: The cmdLoadPassword_Click() event (continued)

The txtOptionStorage_Change() Event Procedure

The selected hourly wage option is stored in the database with the values 1, 2, 3, or 4, based on the values of less than $6.00, $6.01 to $8.00, $8.01 to $10.00, or more than $10.00 per hour, respectively. In order to set the appropriate option button value correctly as records are displayed on the interface, an assignment statement stores the numeric wage option value in an invisible text box (txtOptionStorage). As the user scrolls through the database records, or **browses** the database, the txtOptionStorage_Change() event shown in Figure 4-22 uses a Case statement to select the appropriate option button.

```
Private Sub txtOptionStorage_Change()

'Examine the txtOptionStorage button

'Set the appropriate option button value

'based on the stored value

      Select Case txtOptionStorage.Text

              Case 1

                      optLess6.Value = True

              Case 2

                      opt6to8.Value = True

              Case 3

                      opt8to10.Value = True

              Case 4

                      opt10up.Value = True

      End Select
```

Figure 4-22: The txtOptionStorage_Change() event

Review of BASIC Fundamentals

In this chapter as you define record structures and variable arrays, you will need to use variables as temporary storage locations. Records are read from files into a record structure location in memory in order to access the data. In this application, record access is so prevalent that you must declare the record structure (SecurityDataStruc) at the global level.

Data from multiple records are stored in a variable array location in memory, which makes access to the password data more efficient. The array data also are referenced from many locations, so the array declaration also is global. All other variables used in processing are declared within Event procedures or code modules as local variables.

BASIC code statements that extend across multiple lines often are difficult to understand. In some cases, the use of symbolic constants can shorten a code statement, in addition to isolating constant values. In the Shely Services data management application, a symbolic constant is used to describe the buttons value as follows:

```
Const conBtns As Integer = vbYesNo + vbExclamation + _
    vbDefaultButton1 + vbApplicationModal
intResponse =
MsgBox("Do you want to print the array?", conBtns,
  "Print Array")
```

The **With statement** allows you to perform a series of statements on a specified object without requalifying the name of the object. In the BldRand.vbp project described earlier, for example, the fields in the record structure are initialized to spaces and zero. Placing the assignment statements within the With control structure allows a single reference to the record name as follows:

```
With udtSecurityDataRec
  .strOtherData1 = Space(1)
  .strEmployeeID = Space(3)
  .strEmployeeLastName = Space(30)
  .strOtherData2 = Space(214)
  .intAccessCode = 0
  .strPassword = Space(6)
End With
```

The With statement also is used in the ClearEmployeeMaintenanceFields() and SetUpArray() Sub procedures.

You use the **Space function** for clearing data from fixed-length strings and for formatting output.

Syntax ▶	Space(*number*)

In this syntax, *number* is a specified number of spaces.

The CInt conversion function is used in the cmdAddData_Click() Event procedure of the BldRand.vbp program to convert the access code entered on the interface to an integer prior to writing a record to the random access file. You use **conversion functions**, such as CInt and CStr, to convert an expression to a specific data type.

Syntax ▶	CInt(*expression*)

In this syntax, the *expression* argument is any string expression or numeric expression, and the function name—CInt in this example—determines the return data type.

Data-type conversion functions are self-documenting because they show that the result of some operation should be expressed as a particular data type rather than as the default data type. For example, you use CInt to force integer conversion.

Finally, Chapter 4 uses the Mod operator, which is a mathematical operator that returns *only* the remainder portion of a division operation. For example, 34 Mod 16 returns the value 2. The Mod operator is used in the SetUpArray() Sub procedure to validate the access code.

P R O G R E S S I V E   P R O J E C T S

As with any continuing project, it is a good idea to make a backup copy of your work so you can recover from any programming errors or program problems. You can create a backup copy of your Student Disk on another disk, or copy the files from the chapter folder on your Student Disk into a "Backup" folder on the same disk. Make sure that you are consistent with whatever method you choose.

It is also time to stop and look around. The next four chapters gradually add database routines to the project. Once the project is reduced to a new starting point, the rest will follow step by step. It is often helpful to have an idea what future processing will occur in planning for current project development. You might benefit from reviewing the project descriptions described at the end of Chapter 1 at this point. In addition, you might benefit from quickly scanning the material in the next four chapters to see what will be happening. It is not necessary to do anything more than gain some idea of what to expect.

In this chapter, you will build test datasets and examine them for accuracy. Depending upon the project, these test datasets consist of random access files and an Access database. You will add the Data control to the project and bind the various controls that display data to the database to permit the user to browse back and forth through the inventory. In Chapter 5, you will add a routine for retrieving individual items from the database. Later you will add routines for adding, updating, and deleting items in the database. Finally you will use collections of data for report writing.

When you set up the primary key for the Access database, keep the following thoughts in mind:

- The primary field should consist of characters, and not integers.
- The size of the primary key and the size of the field in the database should be exactly the same.

For example, if the size of the field is three characters, then the only valid primary keys are characters—and not integers—in the range from 000 to 999. Were the primary key value to be the value 1, for example, then the primary key would be edited to be two spaces and the integer 1 so the primary key contains three characters total ("#1"). When the primary key is edited to include space characters, the structure of the primary keys might have to be edited as follows:

```
Select Case primary_key
      Case Len(primary_key) = 1
            primary_key = "  " + primary_key
      Case Len(primary_key) = 2
            primary_key = " " + primary_key
      Case Len(primary_key) > 4 Then
            MsgBox =  [error]
End Select
```

It is far better in the beginning to set the size of the valid primary keys and the size of the corresponding fields in the Access database to match. The following steps apply to Progressive Projects 1, 2, and 3:

1. Build and test the random file and the array routines. As in the chapter, go one step at a time. Code and test a single routine before going to the next one. For example, whenever data are written to the random file, use a word processor, such as WordPad, to print it. Do not just look at the data—count the characters.

You can code any noncharacter fields, but you cannot read them. If you add data, print the contents of the array, and make sure that everything is where it is supposed to be—just because Visual Basic compiles and runs without errors doesn't mean that the data are in the correct location.

2. Review the material in the chapter, and then go through the project as it now stands and mark all statements, routines, and so on that are not needed any longer with the dimension single quotation mark ('). This includes the file writing and printing routines. Also disable all (calls to) editing routines. Do not delete anything until this chapter is complete! Then run the program to make sure that it compiles without errors. If you need to use a statement that you commented, just deleting the single quotation mark can activate it.

3. Set up the Access data table to match the data layout in the project description. As noted above, be especially careful when establishing the field to hold the primary keys. Do not let Access check for duplicate keys or create an index.

4. As described in the chapter, add the data object to the form, and then bind the DatabaseName property to the Access database (use the select icon on the right, and browse until you find the database). Then bind the RecordSource property to the appropriate table. If you complete these steps correctly, the table name will appear when the RecordSource property's select icon (to the right of the field) is selected. If you have problems with this step, ask your instructor or technical support person for help. Finally, set the ReadOnly property to "True."

5. As a check, bind one of the text objects on the form to its corresponding field in the Access database by selecting the object's DataSource property and then selecting the name of the data object created in Step 4. If the text object does not appear, recheck your work in Steps 1 through 4, and then bind the DataField property by selecting the appropriate Access field name. It is best to run the program at this point to make sure that everything functions correctly. If the program runs correctly, bind the rest of the objects that reference the database. If you have option buttons, make sure to add the text box and the necessary TextBox_Change() routine as described in the chapter.

6. Run the program, and then browse back and forth to make sure that every object displays the correct data.

7. Save and backup your work.

1. Bean County Plumbing Inventory System (BCPIS)

The Bean County project needs one random file to hold the IDs and passwords of those employees who have access to the inventory database. The data is to be loaded into an array each time the project starts. Make sure you extract the relative record location carefully. Create the random access file as BCPISSicher.txt. The project requires three tables, but you will build only the MasterPart table at this time. You will add the other two tables when multiple screens are discussed. It is only necessary to have a few entries for testing, but you will need to add enough data to generate meaningful reports. Save the form and project as Ch4BCPIS in the Chapter4 folder on your Student Disk. Locate the database BCPISdb.mdb and the random access file BCPISSicher.txt in the root directory of your Student Disk with the Chapter4 folder.

2. Single Parents Public Library Service (SPLIB)

The random file contains data for between 75 and 99 volunteers who have access privileges. Note that the last two digits of the ID number give the relative record position. You will load only the user's ID, the volunteer's name, and the access level into the array, and these data items will be used either to validate a member as an occasional guest, or as an active/manager, or in a report. Create the random access file as SPLIBSicher.txt. The project description provides the database table layout for the materials table. Note that the user ID in both tables must match. Save the form and project as Ch4SPLIB in the Chapter4 folder on your Student Disk. Locate the database SPLIBdb.mdb and the random access file SPLIBSicher.txt in the root directory of your Student Disk that contains the Chapter4 folder.

3. Short Cut Lawn Service (SCLS)

You need to create and check the small random file that contains the password for the owner of the lawn service. You will enter only the employee's ID, password, and access level into an array for future checking. Create the random access file as SCLSSicher.txt. There are two tables in the SCLS database—you will build only the unit inventory table now. You will add the current customers table in Chapter 5. Note that the unit ID field in the CustData table must match the unit ID field in the UnitInv table. Save the form and project as Ch4SCLS in the Chapter4 folder on your Student Disk. Locate the database SCLSdb.mdb and the random access file SCLSSicher.txt in the root directory of your Student Disk that contains the Chapter4 folder.

INDEPENDENT PROJECTS

1. Current Construction Projects

Design a random file that holds fields for data related to a list of current construction projects for Austin Construction. Fields might include the job number, job title, location, beginning date, ending data, supervisor name, and perhaps check boxes to indicate that a project has been assigned, bid, accepted, etc. The user needs to browse, add, delete, and update data.

Design a form and write a program that will retrieve data from the random file and display it on the form. Use as many different objects as possible. Save the form and project as Ch4IP1 in the Chapter4 folder on your Student Disk.

2. The Program Library

Michelle has a lot of diskettes and no way to find out what is on them. Create a program that lets her use a random file to store data about her disks and to find data about a disk and display it on a form. Use as many objects as possible, such as option buttons for system, original, and backup (with check boxes corresponding to backups for program, data, etc.). (*Hint:* How about data read into an invisible box that then is used to set the option buttons and which corresponds to the data in the check boxes? Or add a memo field and enter enough data to enable the use of a scroll bar on the form. Or try both approaches.) Make sure that Michelle can maintain the data in her file and store information about 50 diskettes. Save the form and project as Ch4IP2 in the Chapter4 folder on your Student Disk.

3. Information Systems (IS) Department Computer Inventory

The university's IS Department has computers in each faculty office. No one knows for sure the ages, sizes, peripherals, etc., for each machine. Design a program that allows the department secretary to manage a random file that will display the computer data and configuration in each office. Design check boxes for drives, printers, and other peripherals attached to the computers, and frames and option buttons to indicate each computer's CPU, RAM, and other features. You can include a note box with scroll bar for comments, and perhaps something special—find a digital camera and display an image of the system. (*Hint:* Use the ComputerID field to load the image stored in a flat file using a Case statement.) Save the form and project as Ch4IP3 in the Chapter4 folder on your Student Disk.

Managing Data — Searching the Database

Introduction ▶ In Chapter 4, you created a transition for the SSTER interface to incorporate database access to data collected via the corporate database. The Data Manager generated Microsoft Access tables from within the Visual Basic environment. Once in place, the Data control provided a means for browsing the test database created using the Data Manager. In this chapter, you will enhance the Shely Services project to provide direct access to specific records.

As a part of everyday processing, Shely staff members frequently need to refer to specific records in a database. In the ShelyTemps.mdb database for example, the employee ID in the first and last records gives an indication of the range of employee ID numbers that currently are assigned. A staff member can use these records to find the next or previous employee ID record that is available for assignment. Perhaps more important is the ability to access a specific record by employee ID to ascertain data relevant to employee placement. These capabilities are provided in this chapter through the use of the Recordset object and its associated methods. The **Recordset object** provides an alternative view of the data as it is stored in the database.

As applications become more comprehensive, users expect to find an interface that provides alternative means for processing data. The use of menus, toolbars, and shortcut keys provide familiar alternatives. In this chapter, you will add menus and shortcut keys as a processing alternative. In Chapter 8, you will add toolbars.

The menu bar is an integral part of any Windows application. You will add menu items to let users browse the Shely database to find specific records. Menu items are associated with Recordset methods to let the application browse the database for the first, last, next, previous, and selected records.

More comprehensive applications necessitate alternative processing methods for programmers as well. Code that is appropriately organized by function and procedure is easier to maintain. This chapter introduces the use of user-defined Sub and Function procedures to organize its processing. Figure 5-1 shows the revised SSTER interface. The txtOptionStorage control has been relocated as part of the Approved Hourly Wage frame and the label has been removed.

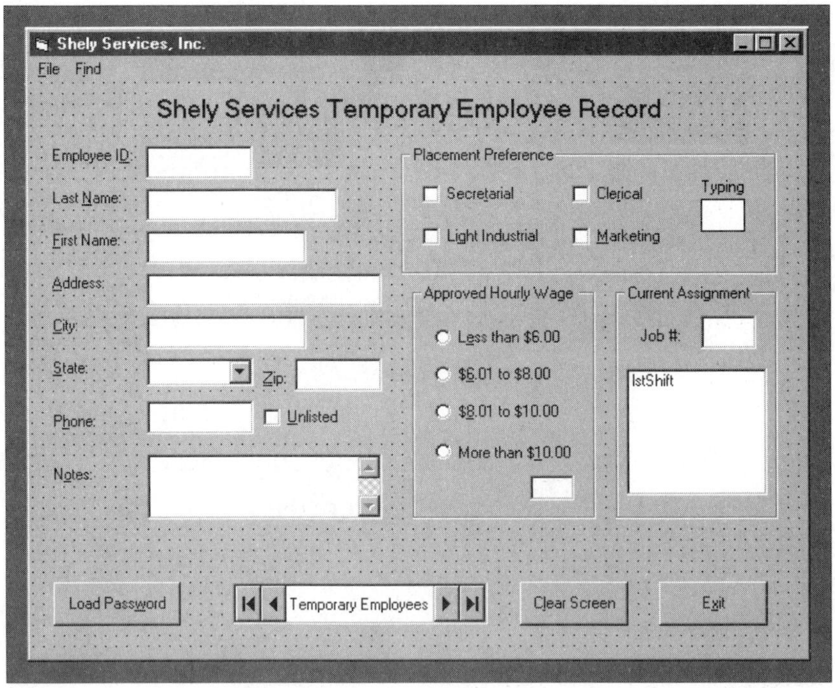

Figure 5-1: Revised SSTER interface

Creating Menus

Menus provide users with an alternative to using a command button to complete a task. You use the **Menu Editor** to create menu controls, such as menu titles, menu items, submenu titles, and submenu items. To start the Menu Editor, click Tools on the menu bar, and then click Menu Editor. You can create up to four levels of sub-menus in an application. Make sure that you follow standard conventions for other Windows applications when creating menu items. Menu design guidelines include the following:

- Menu titles should consist of one capitalized word with a unique access key.
- Menu items should consist of one to three words using book title capitalization, a unique access key, and shortcut keys for frequently used menu items.
- Menu items that require additional information from the user should contain an ellipsis (...) as part of the menu's caption.
- Placement of menu titles and items in locations should be similar to other Windows standard applications; that is, the File menu is the first in a series of menu titles.
- Disable all menu items not applicable to the initial state of the application. These menu items will be enabled by the appropriate application procedure.

Using the Menu Editor

Figure 5-2 shows the Menu Editor. The top half of the Menu Editor contains the properties associated with menu controls. Each menu item must have a caption and a name property. The Checked, Enabled, and Visible properties control whether a submenu title or item contains a check mark, appears dimmed, or whether the item is visible at run time. Assigning **shortcut keys**, which appear to the right of the menu command, allows a user to select a menu command without opening the menu.

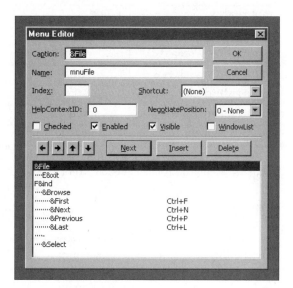

Figure 5-2: Menu Editor

The Menu Editor arrow buttons and the Next, Insert, and Delete command buttons provide navigation aids that you can use to edit menu elements as you create them. Figure 5-3 describes the purpose of each button.

Button	Purpose
← or →	Changes the indentation level of a menu control
↑ or ↓	Relocates a menu control to another location
Next	Moves the highlight to the next menu control in the list; creates a new control if the highlight is currently at the end of the list
Insert	Inserts a new control above the highlighted menu control
Delete	Deletes the highlighted menu control

Figure 5-3: Menu Editor commands

A list box at the bottom of the Menu Editor shows the menu controls as you create them. Each entry in the list is considered a separate menu control. Figure 5-4 shows the control names and the current SSTER interface menu items. The dot leaders that appear in Figure 5-4 are the result of using the right arrow to create subordinate menu controls.

Menu Control Name	SSTER Interface Menu Items	Shortcut Keys
mnuFile	&File	
mnuExit	....E&xit	
mnuFind	F&ind	
mnuFindBrowse	....&Browse	
mnuFindBrowseFirst	........&First	Ctrl + F
mnuFindBrowseNext	........&Next	Ctrl + N
mnuFindBrowsePrevious	........&Previous	Ctrl + P
mnuFindBrowseLast	........&Last	Ctrl + L
mnuFindSelect	....&Select	

Figure 5-4: Menu control names and current SSTER interface menu items

Coding Menu Items

The Click event is the only event associated with menu items. You normally code only the lowest set of items. For example, the First, Next, Last, and Previous items represent the lowest items in the Find menu title and the Exit menu item represents the lowest menu item in the File menu title. The Exit menu item functions in the same manner as the Exit command button. In these events, the Unload statement triggers the Form Unload() event, as shown in Example 5-1.

Example 5-1 ▶

```
Private Sub mnuExit_Click()
        Unload frmEmpeMaint
End Sub
```

Exercise 5.1 ▶

Open the file named Ex5-1.vbp from the Chapter5 folder on your Student Disk, and then save the form, module, and project as Ex5-1a.vbp. You will modify the interface to contain the following menu items:

File Menu	Edit Menu
Initialize	Add Data
Print Password List	
Exit	

a. Use the Menu Editor to create the menu titles and menu items. Assign access keys and use shortcut keys where appropriate.

b. Copy the code from each command button click event to the appropriate menu item click event.

c. Save and run the application. Test each menu item.

d. When you are sure that the menu items function properly, remove the code from the click events and the command button controls from the interface. Resize the form to satisfy Windows standard design guidelines.

e. Save the application, and create an executable file named Ex5-1a.exe.

Exercise 5.2 ▶

Reminder
• • • • • • • • • • • • • • • •

▶ You will need to move the .mdb file for this exercise from the Chapter5 folder to the root directory of your Student Disk. See the "Read This Before You Begin" page before Chapter 1 for more details.

Coffee Haus Wholesalers sells coffee to customers in Indiana, Kentucky, Ohio, and West Virginia. The customer database, CHCust.mdb, contains the Customers table used in the interface found in Ex5-2.vbp. Staff members use this program to contact customers when special pricing is available on their preferred coffee.

a. Open the file named Ex5-2.vbp from the Chapter5 folder on your Student Disk, and then save the form, module, and project as Ex5-2a.vbp.

b. The menu controls used in this program do not follow Windows standards. Use the Menu Editor to change the menu control structure based on the following standards:

■ Menu titles should follow Windows applications order with the File menu first.

■ Browse and Exit should be menu items within the Find and File menu titles.

■ Shortcut keys should be assigned for the First, Last, Next, and Previous menu items.

■ Access keys should exist for all menu controls.

■ Menu naming conventions require the use of the mnu prefix and names that detail the location of the menu item, for example, mnuFileExit.

c. Save the project with the new menu structure.

d. Create an executable file named Ex5-2a.exe.

Navigating the Database Using the Recordset Object

Visual Basic treats the collection of records from a table in the database as a Recordset object. The syntax for the Recordset object is:

Syntax ▶   *datacontrol*.**Recordset**

In this syntax, *datacontrol* is the name of the Data control in the interface. The Recordset object has its own methods, which you can use to navigate and manipulate records in the database. Figure 5-5 lists each method and its description.

Method	Description
AddNew	Clears the buffer for creating a new record in a table
Delete	Deletes the current record
Edit	Opens the current record for editing
Update	Saves the contents of the buffer to the table
FindFirst	Locates and makes current the first record that satisfies specified criteria
FindLast	Locates and makes current the last record that satisfies specified criteria
FindNext	Locates and makes current the next record that satisfies specified criteria
FindPrevious	Locates and makes current the previous record that satisfies specified criteria
MoveFirst	Moves to the first record in the Recordset, and makes the record current
MoveLast	Moves to the last record in the Recordset, and makes the record current
MoveNext	Moves to the next record in the Recordset, and makes the record current
MovePrevious	Moves to the previous record in the Recordset, and makes the record current

Figure 5-5: Recordset methods

When you open a database table, the Recordset becomes available. You can set the Recordset default to include all of the records in the table, or the program can request a subset of the records in the table. In either case, the program recognizes the Recordset as a group of records that a user can navigate.

For the menu items associated with the Browse method, the code works the same as the browse buttons on the Data control (datTempEmpe). The database keeps track of the currently available record in the Recordset. Conceptually, a pointer exists for the database that points to the current record. When the pointer moves forward, the next record becomes the current record. When the pointer moves backward, the previous record becomes current. In some databases, such as Access, the database permits the pointer to go one logical record beyond the beginning or the end of the Recordset so the program can check for the beginning of the file (BOF) and the end of the file (EOF) without error.

In this chapter, the program accesses a complete Recordset of the TemporaryEmployees table. The Recordset is established automatically when the program is loaded and the data object, with its various properties, is activated. In Chapter 6, you will generate and process subsets of the database table. Figure 5-6 shows the menu item code modules associated with database processing.

```
Private Sub mnuFindBrowseFirst_Click()
'Move to the first record in the Recordset
    datTempEmpe.Recordset.MoveFirst
End Sub

Private Sub mnuFindBrowseLast_Click()
'Move to the last record in the Recordset
    datTempEmpe.Recordset.MoveLast
End Sub

Private Sub mnuFindBrowseNext_Click()
'Move to the next record in the Recordset
    datTempEmpe.Recordset.MoveNext
'If the EOF condition is raised,
'move to the first record in the Recordset
    If datTempEmpe.Recordset.EOF Then
        datTempEmpe.Recordset.MoveFirst
    End If
End Sub

Private Sub mnuFindBrowsePrevious_Click()
'Move to the previous record in the Recordset
    datTempEmpe.Recordset.MovePrevious
'If the BOF condition is raised,
'move to the last record in the Recordset
    If datTempEmpe.Recordset.BOF Then
        datTempEmpe.Recordset.MoveLast
    End If
End Sub

Private Sub mnuFindSelect_Click()
'Branch to the SelectEmployee Sub procedure
    Call SelectEmployee
End Sub
```

Figure 5-6: Menu item control modules

The Recordset designation is necessary to tell the program which set of data to navigate. The actual navigation commands are MoveFirst, MoveLast, MoveNext, and MovePrevious. The MoveNext and MovePrevious commands require code that tests to see if the pointer moves beyond the first or the last record in the Recordset (BOF or EOF). For this application, when the EOF condition is raised, the first record in the database is displayed. The BOF condition causes the last record in the database to be displayed.

Exercise 5.3 ▶

Open the file named Ex5-3.vbp from the Chapter5 folder on your Student Disk, and then save the form, module, and project as Ex5-3a.vbp. Use the Recordset methods and the Shely example to code the following subroutines:

    a. mnuFileExit

    b. mnuFindBrowseFirst

Reminder

• • • • • • • • • • • • • •

▶ You will need to move the .mdb file for this exercise from the Chapter5 folder to the root directory of your Student Disk. See the "Read This Before You Begin" page before Chapter 1 for more details.

c. mnuFindBrowseLast
d. mnuFindBrowseNext
e. mnuFindBrowsePrevious

Save and run the application. Test the Exit, First, Last, Next, and Previous menu items to ensure that they function properly, and then create an executable file named Ex5-3a.exe.

General Procedures

The mnuFindSelect_Click() Event procedure uses two types of general procedures: user-defined Sub procedures (also called subroutines) and Function procedures. These procedures do not respond to an event. Thus, you must call these procedures explicitly. Using general procedures, like the Sub and Function procedures, programmers divide tasks into logical components that can be re-used within the same program or in different programs.

User-Defined Sub Procedures

A **user-defined Sub procedure** is a collection of code that you can invoke from more than one place in a program. These standard modules usually exist as separate .bas files that you can add to an application.

Code that is associated with an event on the form is bound to the form. In order to edit the code, the form must be open. If you delete the form, then the code is lost. Therefore, placing the majority of procedure code in standard modules makes sense. For example, if you change the event associated with a user-defined Sub procedure from a command button click event to a menu-item click event, the change is facilitated quickly by simply relocating the call to the Sub procedure code.

You use the Add Procedure command on the Tools menu to create user-defined Sub procedures, as shown in Figure 5-7. The rules for naming a user-defined Sub procedure are the same as for naming variables and constants.

Figure 5-7: Add Procedure dialog box

The Type section of the Add Procedure dialog box indicates the procedure as a Sub, Function, Property, or Event procedure. The Scope section indicates whether the procedure is Public or Private.

Syntax ▶

```
[Private | Public] Sub name [(arglist)]
    [statements]
End Sub
```

In this syntax, **Public** indicates that the Sub procedure is accessible to all other procedures in all modules, **Private** indicates that the Sub procedure is accessible only to other procedures in the module where it is declared, *name* is the name used to call the Sub procedure, *arglist* is a list of variables that represent arguments passed to the Sub procedure when it is called, and *statements* are the instructions that are executed when the procedure is called.

Function Procedures

One difference between Function and user-defined Sub procedures lies in how they communicate processing results to the procedure from which they were called. Function procedures return a value of a specific data type. Sub procedures pass and receive values as part of an argument list if one exists.

Syntax ▶

```
[Public | Private] Function functionname (arguments) [As datatype]
    [statements]
    [name = expression]
End Function
```

In this syntax, **Public** indicates that the Function procedure is accessible to all other procedures in all modules, **Private** indicates that the Function procedure is accessible only to other procedures in the module where it is declared, *functionname* is the name of the function used to call the procedure, *arguments* is a list of variables representing arguments that are passed to the Function procedure when it is called, *datatype* is the data type of the value returned by the Function procedure, *statements* are the instructions to be executed within the Function procedure, and *expression* is the return value of the function. The function shown in Example 5-2 is called as follows:

```
strSearchID = GetEmployeeID(strSearchID)
```

Example 5-2 ▶

```
Public Function GetEmployeeID(ByVal strSearchID)
    Dim strID As String
    strID = InputBox("Enter employee ID", "Employee ID")
    GetEmployeeID = strID
End Function
```

Note that the value of the variable strID is assigned to the Function name (GetEmployeeID) and that the value is then returned to strSearchID.

Calling a Procedure

To **call** a procedure means to have program control transfer to the code in the general procedure where the code is executed. Simply placing the procedure name in code will cause the program to execute the Function or Sub procedure code. You can use the Call statement to call the procedure to make procedure calls easier to identify. The syntax for the Call statement is:

Syntax ▶ | [**Call**] *name* [(*argumentlist*)]

In this syntax, **Call** is an optional keyword signifying transfer of program control to another procedure, *name* is the name of the procedure to pass control to, and *argumentlist* represents the variables or expressions to pass to the called procedure. The *argumentlist* is optional and might include the keywords ByVal or ByRef to describe how the arguments are treated by the called procedure. When you pass a variable **ByVal**, Visual Basic creates a copy of the variable in memory and the copy is passed to the receiving procedure. The contents of the original variable remain unchanged. If you pass a variable **ByRef**, which is the default, Visual Basic passes the variable's actual address in memory and the contents of the variable are changed permanently by the receiving procedure.

Passing arguments to the procedure creates general procedures that are more flexible. In Example 5-3, the DisplayID Sub procedure is called and the value in the variable strUserID is passed to the Sub procedure. This value is stored in the variable strUserID within the Sub procedure. In this fairly simple example, the variable is used to create a string, "The user ID is xxx!", where xxx is the value in the variable. This string is displayed in a label control on the interface. The Sub procedure shown in Example 5-3 is called as follows:

```
Call DisplayID(strUserID)
```

Example 5-3 ▶

```
Private Sub DisplayID(strUserID As String)
        Dim strMsg As String
        strMsg = "The user ID is " & strUserID & "!"
        lblMsg.Caption = strMsg
End Sub
```

Exercise 5.4 ▶

DEVELOP

Reminder
. . . .
▶ You will need to move the .mdb file for this exercise from the Chapter5 folder to the root directory of your Student Disk. See the "Read This Before You Begin" page before Chapter 1 for more details.

Melanie's Mall needs a customized Visual Basic interface to access the Stores table. Use the Visual Data Manager to open the Stores table in the Ex5-4.mdb database from the Chapter5 folder on your Student Disk. Design a customized Visual Basic interface to access the database table. You will create the following menu items:

File Menu	Find Menu
Exit	First
	Next
	Last
	Previous

a. Bind each of the controls in your interface to the Data control. Remember to assign values to the following properties: Data control—DatabaseName and RecordSource properties; other controls—DataSource and DataField properties.

b. Use the necessary Recordset objects to code the First, Next, Last, and Previous menu items.

c. If the BOF condition is raised, redisplay the first record, and then send a message indicating that this is the first record in the file.

d. If the EOF condition is raised, redisplay the last record, and then send a message indicating that this is the last record in the file.

e. Code the Exit menu item to end the application.

f. Save the form and project as Ex5-4a.vbp in the Chapter5 folder on your Student Disk.

g. Create an executable file named Ex5-4a.exe.

Writing Code for the GetEmployeeID Function Procedure

The ID search string is obtained by a function call to the user-defined function GetEmployeeID. The variable strSearchID is passed to the function by value (ByVal strSearchID). The Function subroutine uses an InputBox Function to obtain the employee ID. The function then verifies that the ID received is within the valid range and returns an ID value (or "000" for invalid ID values). Figure 5-8 shows the GetEmployeeID Function procedure.

```
Public Function GetEmployeeID(ByVal strSearchID)
'Declare variables
  Dim strID As String
  Dim strMsg1 As String
  Dim strMsg2 As String

'Declare symbolic constants
  Const conMsg1 As String = "Enter an Employee ID"
  Const conMsg2 As String = "IDs are between 100 and 499"
  Const conMsg3 As String = "Enter Correct Employee ID"
  Const conMsg4 As String = "Employee ID does not exist"
  Const conMsg5 As String = "Incorrect Employee ID"
  strMsg1 = conMsg1 & vbNewLine & vbNewLine & conMsg2

'Accept the employee ID from the user
  strID = InputBox(strMsg1, conMsg3, "000")

'Verify that the employee ID was entered and is a number
'in the range 100 to 499
  Select Case strID
      Case ""
        strID = "000"
      Case Is < "100"
        strResponse = MsgBox(conMsg4, vbOKOnly, conMsg5)
        strID = "000"
      Case Is > "499"
        strResponse = MsgBox(conMsg4, vbOKOnly, conMsg5)
        strID = "000"
  End Select

'Return the validated employee ID
  GetEmployeeID = strID
End Function
```

Figure 5-8: GetEmployeeID Function procedure

Exercise 5.5 ▶

Coffee Haus needs the ability to search the CHCust.mdb database by state in order to inform its customers of specials in their area. Open the file named Ex5-5.vbp from the Chapter5 folder on your Student Disk, and then save the form, module, and project as Ex5-5a.vbp. Create a Function procedure to allow Coffee Haus staff to enter the required two-digit state code.

a. Click Add Procedure on the Tools menu. The procedure name is GetState, the procedure type is Function, and the procedure scope is Public.

b. In the code window for the Function procedure, complete the following processing:

1. Declare variables and symbolic constants as needed.
2. Use the InputBox function to accept the state code from the user.
3. Use a Do While loop to accept the state code until a user enters a correct code as follows:
   - Declare a variable strValid as string and assign the value "N".
   - If the code is valid, set strValid to "Y".
   - If the code is the null string, send the message "Action cancelled, you must enter a state code." and set strValid to "Y".
   - If the code is not valid, send the message "Invalid state," and then use the InputBox Function to accept the state code from the user.
4. Return the validated state code.

c. Test the Function procedure by placing a function call in the mnuFindSelect code window. Use the Printer.Print method to print the returned state code. When you are sure that the Function procedure performs accurately, save the application.

d Create an executable file named Ex5-5a.exe.

Exercise 5.6 ▶

Employees at Melanie's Mall need to search the mall database for specific stores based on the store name in order to give customers the location of the store in the mall. Open the project Ex5-6.vbp from the Chapter5 folder on your Student Disk, and then save the form and project as Ex5-6a.vbp.

a. Add the Select menu item to the Find menu.
b. Click Add Procedure on the Tools menu. The procedure name is GetStore, the procedure type is Function, and the procedure scope is Public.
c. Use a MsgBox statement to print the returned state code on the form. You will complete the search procedure processing in Exercise 5-7.
   1. Declare variables and symbolic constants as needed.
   2. Use the InputBox Function to accept the store name from the user.
   3. Use a Do While loop to accept the store name until a user enters a correct store name as follows:
      - Declare a variable strValid as string and assign the value "N".
      - If the code is valid, set strValid to "Y".
      - If the code is the null string, send the message "Action cancelled, you must enter a store name." and set strValid to "Y".
      - If the code is not valid, send the message "Invalid store name," and then use the InputBox Function to accept the store name from the user.
   4. Return the validated store name.
d. Test the Function procedure by placing a function call in the mnuFindSelect code window. Use a MsgBox statement to print the returned store name on the form. When you are sure that the Function procedure performs accurately, save the application. You will complete the search procedure processing in Exercise 5-8.
e. Create an executable file named Ex5-6a.exe.

Writing Code for the SelectEmployee() Procedure

When a user searches for an individual record, the record might not exist in the database. There are three steps for finding an individual record:

1. Set up the Search command to be passed to the database.
2. Send the command.
3. Check to see if the record was found and returned.

The Search command is a string with the format `EmployeeID = '117'`. This string is used with the Recordset object's FindFirst method to search the table connected by the RecordSource property of the data object for the field name `EmployeeID` and to find the value 117.

This Search command is hard coded. To make the program function interactively (like the Find command in many Windows applications) the application needs to obtain an employee ID from the user and use it to format a command to send to the database. For example, in the following code, 'strSearchID' is the string containing the employee ID, which is obtained via a function call, and 'strSearchString' is the command that will be sent:

```
strSearchString = "EmployeeID = '" + strSearchID + "'"
```

Notice the inclusion of single quotation marks within the double quotation marks, which represents a string within a string. This format is required—the database will not process a command without correct usage of quotation marks and the error returned will not point to this statement, but rather, to the statement actually passing the call to the database.

The strSearchString variable used with the FindFirst method results in a search of the database for the first occurrence (which in the ShelyTemps.mdb should be the only occurrence) of the specified string. You use the Recordset object's NoMatch property to determine if a match is found, as shown in Example 5-4.

Example 5-4 ▶   `If frmEmpeMaint!datTempEmpe.Recordset.NoMatch`

In this example, the NoMatch property will contain the Boolean value True if the desired record was *not* found. A message will indicate that the employee does not exist and the interface control fields will be cleared. Figure 5-9 shows the user-defined Sub procedure named SelectEmployee().

```
EmpeMaint_2 - DataBaseProcessing (Code)                    _ □ ×
(General)                              SelectEmployee

    Public Sub SelectEmployee()
    'Declare variables
        Dim strSearchID As String * 3
        Dim strSearchString As String
        Dim strResponse As String
    'Call the GetEmployeeID function to validate the employee ID
        strSearchID = GetEmployeeID(strSearchID)
    'If the returned employee ID is equal to 000,
    'exit the subroutine
        If strSearchID <> "000" Then
    'Build the search string
            strSearchString = "EmployeeID = '" + strSearchID + "'"
    'Search the database for the requested record
            frmEmpeMaint!datTempEmpe.Recordset.FindFirst _
                strSearchString

            If frmEmpeMaint!datTempEmpe.Recordset.NoMatch Then
                strResponse = MsgBox("Employee does not exist", _
                    vbOKOnly, "No Current Employee")
                Call ClearEmployeeMaintenanceFields
            End If
        End If
    End Sub
```

Figure 5-9: SelectEmployee() Sub procedure

When the match is made successfully and the record pointer is moved to the desired record, the content of the record is retrieved and displayed as appropriate in the form. This occurs (as it did in Chapter 4) because each of the form's controls is bound to a field in the TemporaryEmployees table. Examine the comments in the code for an explanation of the code's processing.

Exercise 5.7 ▶

Reminder
• • • • • • • • • • • • • •

▶ You will need to move the .mdb file for this exercise from the Chapter5 folder to the root directory of your Student Disk. See the "Read This Before You Begin" page before Chapter 1 for more details.

Open the file Ex5-7.vbp from the Chapter5 folder on your Student Disk. Save the form, module, and project as Ex5-7a.vbp, and then do the following:

a. Modify the Find menu as follows. You create the separator bar by placing a hyphen in the caption. Remember that all menu items must contain a caption and name.

Find
   First
   Last
   Next
   Previous
   ——————————— (separator bar)
   Search
     Find
     Find next

b. Use the Add Procedure menu item to create a user-defined Sub procedure named SearchStates.
c. Code the SearchStates subroutine to search the Customer table for the state code and return the state data or an appropriate message.
d. Code the Find – Search – Find menu item to contain a call to the SearchStates Sub procedure.
e. There might be more than one record in the Customer table for each state. Code the Find – Search – Find Next menu item to continue the search and find the next matching state.
f. Save and run the application. Test the application for each of the valid states (IN, KY, OH, and WV) and for invalid state codes as well.
g. Save your changes and then create an executable file named Ex5-7a.exe.

Exercise 5.8 ▶

Reminder
• • • • • • • • • • • • • •

▶ You will need to move the .mdb file for this exercise from the Chapter5 folder to the root directory of your Student Disk. See the "Read This Before You Begin" page before Chapter 1 for more details.

Open the file Ex5-8.vbp from the Chapter5 folder on your Student Disk. Save the form and project as Ex5-8a.vbp, and then do the following:

a. Use the Add Procedure menu item to create a user-defined Sub procedure named SearchStores.
b. Code the SearchStores subroutine to search the Stores table for the store name and return the store data or an appropriate message. The subroutine should use the GetStore Function.
c. Add a Call to the SearchStores Sub procedure in the mnuFindSelect_Click() event. You might need to remove existing code in the mnuFindSelect_Click() event to the SearchStores Sub procedure.
d. Save and run the application. Test the application for each of the valid states' store names and for invalid store names as well.
e. Save your changes and then create an executable file named Ex5-8a.exe.

Review of BASIC Fundamentals

The GetEmployeeID Function procedure uses the concatenation operator, symbolic constants, and a Visual Basic intrinsic constant to create the InputBox prompt and title. **Concatenation** is the operation of connecting strings. The Visual Basic concatenation operators are the ampersand (&) and the plus sign (+). Using the + operator can be confusing because the operator is used for both addition and string concatenation. The & operator eliminates ambiguity and provides self-documenting code.

For example, in Example 5-5, conMsg1 and conMsg2 contain character strings and vbNewLine is an intrinsic constant.

Example 5-5 ▶

```
strMsg1 = conMsg1 & vbNewLine & vbNewLine & conMsg2
```

Figure 5-10 shows the InputBox created using the code shown in Example 5-6.

Example 5-6 ▶

```
Const conMsg1 = "Enter an Employee ID"
Const conMsg2 = "IDs are between 100 and 499"
Const conMsg3 = "Enter Correct Employee ID"
strMsg1 = conMsg1 & vbNewLine & vbNewLine & conMsg2
strID = InputBox(strMsg1, conMsg3, "000")
```

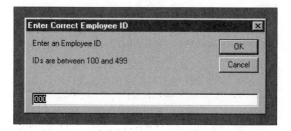

Figure 5-10: InputBox example

You learned about using symbolic constants in Chapter 4. In Chapter 5, you used symbolic constants to create character strings used with the InputBox function to streamline the InputBox function.

Intrinsic constants are built-in Visual Basic constants. An intrinsic constant can represent frequently used character codes while providing internal documentation to the code. The GetEmployeeID function uses the vbNewLine intrinsic constant that stores the character codes chr(13) and chr(10), which represent the carriage return and line feed controls, respectively. Access to available intrinsic constants is found in the Object Browser.

PROGRESSIVE PROJECTS

Now you will add menus and browsing techniques using the Recordset object and database query capabilities to your project. In Chapter 6, you will add new Function and Sub procedures for maintaining the database to the projects, so you need to make sure that everything works as expected at this point.

Add two sets of menus to each project. The first menu is the File menu, which includes the Exit menu item. The second menu is the Find menu, which includes the Browse and Select menu items. The Browse menu control contains the First, Last, Next, and Previous menu items. Establish levels for browsing and for selecting individual records. Test the Exit and the Browse menus.

Establish a new module and create a function to request a primary key from a user. The function should make sure that the primary key it returns is valid (within ranges and properly formatted). The call to the subroutine can simply be from the corresponding menu selection. Also, use a message box to ensure that the primary key is returned correctly.

After establishing that a valid primary key is returned, use the search procedure created in the chapter as an example and carefully enter and test a subroutine to make the call to the database. Everything must be perfect or the call will not return data. If the subroutine does not work as expected, disable the call to the function and reduce the code in the subroutine to a minimum. Hard code the primary key into the `'strSearch ='` segment of the call, and then test it. Use as little code as possible until everything works. If necessary, add a button to the form for now, and put the code behind it. If your code does not work correctly, ask your instructor or technical support person for help.

1. Bean County Plumbing Inventory System (BCPIS)

Use the BCPISdb.mdb database and Ch4BCPIS.vbp project you created in Chapter 4 to accomplish the previously described required processing. Be sure that all methods used to access the database function properly.

You will develop additional tables later, so it is important to enter all code as neatly and as organized as possible. Then you can copy and modify the code for each table. Save the form and project as Ch5BCPIS.

2. Single Parents Service Library (SPLIB)

Use the SPLIBdb.mdb database and Ch4SPLIB.vbp project you created in Chapter 4 to accomplish the previously described required processing. Make sure that the call to the database functions properly. In Chapter 6, you will add more routines, so you must be certain that the connections to the database function correctly. Save the form and project as Ch5SPLIB.

3. Short Cut Lawn Service (SCLS)

Use the SCLSdb.mdb database and Ch4SCLS.vbp project you created in Chapter 4 to accomplish the previously described required processing. Add the menus and then carefully construct the call to the database. In Chapter 6, you will add more forms and tables, so make sure the code on this form works properly. Also, write your code neatly and carefully so you can copy and modify the code later to save time. Save the form and project as Ch5SCLS.

INDEPENDENT PROJECTS

1. Donald's Cross Listing

Donald needs batteries for his hobby projects. The batteries are small and come in various sizes, similar to hearing-aid batteries. Because Donald buys his batteries through the Internet, he needs to know the corresponding battery number for each company that sells the batteries he needs. Establish a database with a table that holds Donald's primary battery number in the first column, and the corresponding battery numbers for each company in the following columns of the same row. Save the database as Batteries.mdb. Do not use integers for the battery numbers—use characters (where 0 and 1 are processed as characters rather than as numbers, for example, "OC7"). Make all of the primary battery numbers the same length. Then create a form and menus so Donald can browse the database or request the data for a particular battery. Save the form and project as Ch5IP1 in the Chapter5 folder on your Student Disk.

2. Maddy's Boat Dock

Maddy rents slips to boaters. She needs a better way to keep track of each slip, its size and, if leased, data about the boat that is in the slip. There are 25 slips. Slips 1 through 15 are for boats with a length (LOA) of less than 12 feet and a beam (width) of no more than five feet. Slips 16 through 20 are for boats with less than 24 feet LOA and a beam of no more than seven feet. Slips 21 through 25 are for boats up to 35 feet LOA and beams of up to nine feet. The slips are numbered 1 to 25.

Construct a database with a table to hold data about Maddy's boat slips. The primary keys for the slips in the database are 01 to 25 and should be in the first field. You might need to convert the format of the key before a call to the database. Data about the slip (LOA, beam, and depth) are in the next fields and data about the boat in a leased slip are in the succeeding fields. If the slip is not leased, then some of the columns are empty.

Write a program that will enable Maddy to navigate through the slips or request data about a particular slip. Make the form as attractive as possible. Save the form and project as Ch5IP2 in the Chapter5 folder on your Student Disk.

3. Linda's Itinerary

Linda has a vacation scheduled for two weeks in Europe, from May 11 to May 26. She is taking her laptop computer with her and wants to have her itinerary readily available. Construct a database table with a field for the day (primary key, 01 to 31), the city, the country, and other interesting data, such as currency conversions and a customs memo. Create one row in the table for each vacation day, for example: day 11: leave; day 12: Frankfurt, Germany, DM 1.80, "tip by rounding to the next unit." The form should contain menus that permit browsing the database and selecting a certain day. A creative project will increase the project to include morning, afternoon, evening schedules. Save the form and project as Ch5IP3 in the Chapter5 folder on your Student Disk.

Managing Data — Database Maintenance

Introduction▶ The Shely Services Temporary Employee Record (SSTER) interface is almost complete. In Chapter 5, you added the menu bar, which is an integral part of all Windows applications, and menu items to provide a mechanism for browsing the database. You used the Recordset object and its associated methods to access the first, last, next, and previous records in the corporate database.

In this chapter, you will explore programming concerns related to data integrity. You will use previously generated access codes to ensure data accuracy. The database maintenance function includes the ability to add, delete, and update data. Each function must be restricted to employees with the appropriate security clearances.

You will alter the SSTER interface to include database maintenance functions accessible by both menu items and command buttons. The project includes a master form (frmMaster) that an employee uses to enter the system. The master form controls initial access to data management, corporate reports, and database backup procedures. The master form and its associated SSTER interface combine to form the functional components of Shely's Temporary Employee Management System, the TEMS system. Figure 6-1 shows the frmMaster form.

Figure 6-1: The frmMaster form

Figure 6-2 shows the frmEmpeMaint form that is the enhanced SSTER interface.

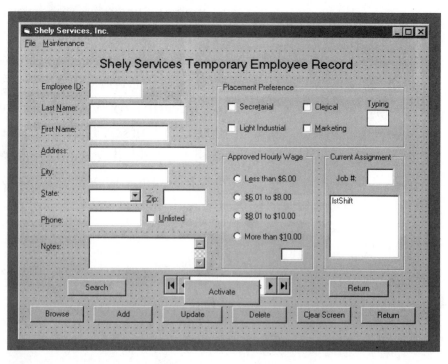

Figure 6-2: Enhanced SSTER interface

Managing Projects with Multiple Forms

A project can require more than one form. For example, most applications begin by displaying a splash screen that identifies the program's name, purpose, and copyright information. The splash screen holds the user's attention while the complete application is being loaded into memory. Windows standards impose the use of a splash screen for each application. You will add a splash screen to the Shely application in Chapter 9.

You can create the splash screen or any other required form as part of the project, or you can add it from a subset of existing forms. In either case, the form is added to the project using the Add Form command on the Project menu.

When a project contains more than one form, you must tell Visual Basic which form to display when the application runs. The **startup object** is the initial form or general procedure that is executed first when the program runs. You specify the startup object using the <*Project Name*> Properties command on the Project menu. Figure 6-3 shows a startup object for the Shely application. To select the startup object, click the General tab in the Project Properties dialog box, and then click the Startup Object list arrow to display all available forms and Sub Main.

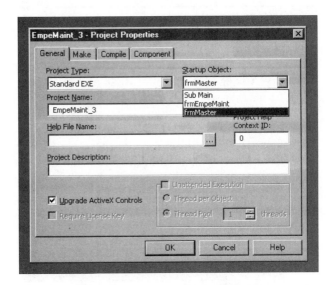

Figure 6-3: Startup object for the Shely application

Managing the Display of Forms

Two statements and two methods control the display and removal of forms from the screen while the program is running. To display a form on the screen, use the form's **Show method** or the **Load statement**.

Syntax ▶   *object*.**Show** [*style*]

In this syntax, *object* is any Form object, and *style* is an optional intrinsic constant that determines the modality of the form: 0 = modeless (the default) and 1 = modal. A **modal form** requires that the user take some action before another form or dialog box can be displayed. The Show method will load the form into memory if the form has not already been loaded and then display the form on the screen.

Syntax ▶	Load *formname*

In this syntax, *formname* is any Form object. The Load statement places the form in the computer's memory, but it does not display it on the screen. To display the form, you must call the Show or SetFocus method after the Load statement executes. When a project contains multiple forms that are alternately displayed, you can optimize the process for displaying the forms by loading all of the forms while the splash screen appears.

To remove a form from the screen, use the form's **Hide method** or the **Unload statement**. To leave the form in memory, use the Hide method.

Syntax ▶	*object*.**Hide**

When a form is hidden, the objects contained on the form still are available to the project, and you can reference them in code.

Syntax ▶	Unload *formname*

The Unload statement removes the form and its associated controls from memory. You cannot reference these objects in code. You use the Unload statement with forms that will not be used by the program any longer to improve the performance of all forms currently in use by the program.

The TEMS system uses the Hide and Show methods to manage the display of forms. When the user clicks the Data Management command button or chooses Data Management from the File menu on the frmMaster form, the frmEmpeMaint form appears on the screen and the master form is hidden. The Return command button or the Return item on the File menu on the temporary employees form hides the frmEmpeMaint form and redisplays the master form. Figure 6-4 shows the code window for the cmdDataManagement_Click() Event procedure.

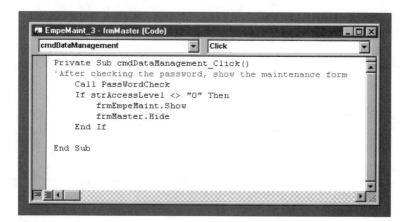

```
EmpeMaint_3 - frmMaster (Code)
cmdDataManagement                    Click

Private Sub cmdDataManagement_Click()
'After checking the password, show the maintenance form
    Call PassWordCheck
    If strAccessLevel <> "0" Then
        frmEmpeMaint.Show
        frmMaster.Hide
    End If

End Sub
```

Figure 6-4: The cmdDataManagement_Click() event

Exercise 6.1 ▶

MODIFY

In this exercise you will add a copyright form to the existing Bicycle Orders application.

    a. Open the project Ex6-1.vbp from the Chapter6 folder on your Student Disk, and then save the project as Ex6-1a.vbp. Save any forms and modules as part of the new project.

b. Add the form Ex6Copy1a.frm to the project, and use the Project –
Ch6_Ex1 Properties dialog box to make frmCopyright the startup object.

c. Code the cmdOK_Click() event on the frmCopyright form to show the
frmOrders form and to remove the frmCopyright form from the screen and
from memory.

d. Save and run the application, and then create an executable file named
Ex6-1a.exe.

Exercise 6.2

In this exercise you will add a copyright form to the existing Coffee Haus
Wholesale Distributors application.

a. Open the project Ex6-2.vbp from the Chapter6 folder on your Student
Disk, and then save the project as Ex6-2a.vbp. Save any forms and modules
as part of the new project.

b. Add the form Ex6Copy2a.frm to the project, and use the Project –
Ch6_Ex2 Properties dialog box to make frmCopyright the startup object.

c. Code the cmdExit_Click() event on the frmCopyright form to show the
frmCustData form and to remove the frmCopyright form from the screen
and from memory.

d. Save and run the application, and then create an executable file named
Ex6-2a.exe.

Exercise 6.3 ▶

DEBUG ▽

In this exercise you will debug the Melanie's Mall application to ensure that the
copyright form appears as the first form in the application.

a. Open the project Ex6-3.vbp from the Chapter6 folder on your Student Disk,
and then save the project as Ex6-3a.vbp. Save any forms and modules as part
of the new project.

b. Run the application.

c. Make the necessary adjustment to the application to ensure that
frmCopyright appears as the first form in the application.

d. Add the necessary code to the cmdExit_Click() event to remove the
frmCopyright form from the screen and from memory and to show the
frmMall form necessary for processing.

e. Save and run the application, and then create an executable file named
Ex6-3a.exe.

Maintaining the Database

So far, the data in the database have been protected so you only are allowed to
navigate the database through the records in a Recordset object. The Data object
property is set to ReadOnly (the default) and the flow of data is only one way. When
Add, Update, and Delete routines are included in a project, these defaults change, and
the data in the database become vulnerable. Therefore, you must take extra precautions to protect the data from unexpected activity. For example, in Chapter 5, the
txtEmpeID control was disabled in the Properties window because this control is the
link to the primary key in the database. Now that two forms exist in the project, you
should disable the txtEmpeID control in the Form_Load() Event procedure. Users
should not be allowed to alter the primary key.

Two subroutines in the DataBaseProcessing module control the type of access
to the data. BeSureReadOnly sets the ReadOnly property for the Data control to
True. The BeSureReadOnly subroutine is called when the user has browse access to
the database. The OpendatTempEmpe subroutine sets the ReadOnly property for
the Data control to False and is called when the user has add, delete, or update
access to the database. The Refresh method is used in both subroutines.

Syntax ▶   *[form.]Data control object.***Refresh**

The **Refresh method** causes the Data control to use the DatabaseName and RecordSource properties to create a new Recordset object that contains a copy of the object's new property settings. This process is explicit and necessary, or the changes will not take place. Figure 6-5 shows the code for the BeSureReadOnly and OpendatTempEmpe subroutines.

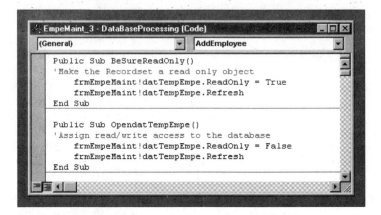

Figure 6-5: BeSureReadOnly and OpendatTempEmpe subroutines

After you finish this chapter, users must be able to browse and, when permitted, perform maintenance on the data. Although it is possible for users to enter incorrect data, *the program must maintain the integrity of the data*—even if a data value itself is incorrect. The program must ensure that what happens is *intended* to happen and that no hidden events corrupt the data. The general logic for add, update, and delete includes:

- Establishing necessary database access using the ReadOnly property
- Adding or changing the data on the form for add or update
- Verifying the requested action and processing the database to complete the action

Adding New Records

The Recordset object method that allows you to add records to a database is the **AddNew method.**

Syntax ▶   *object.***AddNew**

In this syntax, *object* must be a valid instance of a Recordset. The AddNew method acts on the current Recordset object and creates an empty database record for editing. The RecordsetType property of the datTempEmpe control is set to 1–Dynaset (the Dynaset type is a Recordset object that you can use to manipulate data in an underlying database). All new records will be added to the end of the Recordset object.

After adding the information for the new record, you need to use the **Update method** to store the new record in the database.

Syntax ▶	*object.***Update**

The Update method acts on the current Recordset object and writes the changes of a record created by the AddNew method to the database.

The code shown in Example 6-1 is simple. The data are written to the database regardless of content. You will see the add routine for the Shely application that considers both data integrity and security later in this chapter.

Example 6-1 ▶

```
frmEmpeMaint!datTempEmpe.Recordset.AddNew
frmEmpeMaint!datTempEmpe.Recordset.Update
```

Exercise 6.4 ▶

Use the AddNew and Update Recordset methods to code a procedure to allow the user to add records to the Bicycle Orders database. Before beginning this exercise, you might find it helpful to review the material in this chapter and to examine the Ch6Shely.vbp project code.

   a. Open the file Ex6-4.vbp from the Chapter6 folder on your Student Disk, and then save the project as Ex6-4a.vbp. Save any forms and modules as part of the new project.

   b. Code the cmdAdd_Click() Event procedure using the following pseudocode guidelines:

     1. Initialize the database for read-only access and refresh the database. Disable the Data control.

     2. Disable all other maintenance functions.

     3. Prompt the user for an order ID.

     4. Verify that an ID was entered and is a valid number between 101 and 399. Remember to restore all maintenance functions if the ID is invalid, send an appropriate message, and then exit the subroutine.

     5. Verify that the record is *not* in the database. If the ID currently exists, restore all maintenance functions, send an appropriate message, and then exit the subroutine.

     6. Clear fields and set focus to Customer ID.

     7. Make the database updatable.

     8. Place the ID on the screen, and disable the text box.

     9. Display the "Click to ADD" caption in the cmdActivate command button.

    10. If the user clicks the Click to ADD command button, add the record without editing. Remember to change the database so it is not updatable.

    11. Restore the command buttons to their initial values.

   c. Save and run the program, and then add a record.

   d. Create an executable file named Ex6-4a.exe.

Exercise 6.5 ▶

In this exercise you will modify the Coffee Haus application to let the user add records to the database using the AddNew and Update Recordset methods. The Add menu item will be used to initiate the process and the Clear Screen will serve dual roles. In addition to its clear screen function, the cmdClear_Click() event will function to complete adding the record to the database.

   a. Open the file Ex6-5.vbp from the Chapter6 folder on your Student Disk, and then save the project as Ex6-5a.vbp. Save any forms and modules as part of the new project.

b. Modify the cmdClear_Click() event as follows:
   1. Copy the existing event code to the Clipboard.
   2. Rename the command button to cmdAction.
   3. Paste the code from the Clipboard to the cmdAction_Click() event.
   4. Modify the code to examine the Caption property to determine whether the clear subroutine should be executed.

c. Modify the Edit menu to contain the Maintain menu item following the Select menu item. Create an Add submenu item subordinate to the Maintain menu. Assign appropriate access and shortcut keys.

d. Code the mnuEditMaintainAdd_Click() Event procedure using the following pseudocode guidelines:
   1. Disable and hide the Data control.
   2. Prompt the user for a Customer Number.
   3. Valid Customer Numbers are numbers between 100 and 150, inclusive. Verify that a Customer Number was entered and is valid. Remember to restore the Data control to the form if the Customer Number is invalid, send an appropriate message, and then exit the subroutine.
   4. Verify that the record is *not* in the database. If the Customer Number currently exists, restore the Data control, send an appropriate message, and then exit the subroutine.
   5. Change the cmdAction.Caption property to "Add Record".
   6. Make the database updatable for adding a record.
   7. Clear fields and set focus to Customer Number.
   8. Place the Customer Number on the screen, and disable the text box.

e. Modify the cmdAction_Click() event to examine the caption and to add the record to the database without editing the fields in the database.

f. Make sure that the database is not updatable, and reset the form to enable browsing.

g. Save and run the program, and then add a record.

h. Create an executable file named Ex6-5a.exe.

Exercise 6.6 ▶

The Melanie's Mall application was updated to include an Edit menu and an Add submenu item. However, if you execute the program and attempt to add a record, the program abends. In this exercise, you will examine the mnuEditAdd_Click() event and fix the code so the database is updated to include the record while the program is executing.

a. Open the file Ex6-6.vbp from the Chapter6 folder on your Student Disk, and then save the project as Ex6-6a.vbp. Save any forms and modules as part of the new project.

b. Run the application and click Add on the Edit menu. The program terminates abnormally with a database error. Examine the code window at the point of the error, and then end the application.

c. Examine the mnuEditAdd_Click() event code, and make necessary changes so the program will add a record. (*Hint:* Use a command button, cmdAddRecord, activated in the mnuEditAdd procedure to allow the user time to enter data. This command button should use the Update property to update the database and reset the ReadOnly property to False.)

d. Notice that the added record appears at the end of the database. Use the Refresh method (perhaps from a menu item on the File menu) to reorganize the records in the database by store code.

e. When you are satisfied that the program executes successfully, create an executable file named Ex6-6a.exe.

Updating Records

To change the information in an existing record, you must make the required record editable. The **Edit method** places information from the current record into a temporary storage area in memory called the **copy buffer**. Changes that you make to the record are made only in the copy buffer until the Update method explicitly saves those changes to the database.

The code shown in Example 6-2 is simple. Data entered in the copy buffer are written to the database automatically by the Update method, regardless of content. You will see a more thorough routine for maintaining data integrity in the cmdUpdate_Click() Event procedure.

Syntax ▶	*object*.**Edit**
Example 6-2 ▶	`frmEmpeMaint!datTempEmpe.Recordset.Edit` `frmEmpeMaint!datTempEmpe.Recordset.Update`

Exercise 6.7 ▶

In this exercise you will use the Edit and Update Recordset methods to code a procedure to allow the user to update existing records in the Coffee Haus database.

    a. Open the file Ex6-7.vbp from the Chapter6 folder on your Student Disk, and then save the project as Ex6-7a.vbp. Save any forms and modules as part of the new project.

    b. Add the Update submenu item to the Maintain menu on the Edit menu. Assign an appropriate access key and shortcut key.

    c. Code the mnuEditMaintenanceUpdate_Click() Event procedure using the following pseudocode guidelines:

      1. Disable and hide the Data control.

      2. Prompt the user for a Customer Number.

      3. Verify that the record is in the database. If the record does not exist, send an appropriate message, and then exit the subroutine.

      4. Make the database updatable using the Edit method.

      5. Set the focus to the Customer Name text box.

      6. Display "Update Record" in the cmdAction Caption property.

      7. Disable the Customer Number text box.

    d. Edit the cmdAction_Click() event to include the "Update Record" option that requires the program to issue the Recordset Update method and restore the screen to its original form.

    e. Save and run the program, and then update a record.

    f. When you are certain that the program functions correctly, create an executable file named Ex6-7a.exe.

Exercise 6.8 ▶

In this exercise you will debug the Melanie's Mall application so that the update function works. Do not use store names containing apostrophes.

    a. Open the file Ex6-8.vbp from the Chapter6 folder on your Student Disk, and then save the project as Ex6-8a.vbp. Save any forms or modules as part of the new project.

    b. Run the application, choose the Update menu item on the Edit menu, and then edit a record by changing the store name.

    c. Use the Data control to check the update. Notice that the update did not take place.

    d. Exit the program and examine the code to learn why the screen is not restored to its original form.

e. Make the necessary corrections to restore the screen to its original form.

f. Run the program to verify that the application executes successfully.

g. When you are certain that the program functions correctly, create an executable file named Ex6-8a.exe.

Deleting Records

You use the **Delete method** to delete an existing record from the database.

Syntax ▶   *object*.**Delete**

The Delete method removes the corresponding row from the underlying database table. The information from the deleted record still appears in the text boxes on the form. To complete the delete process for the user, you should follow the Delete method statement with the MoveNext method. The **MoveNext method** displays the next record in sequence in the database so the user sees that the correct record was deleted. The code in Example 6-3 shows the Delete method followed by the MoveNext method.

Example 6-3 ▶
```
frmEmpeMaint!datTempEmpe.Recordset.Delete
frmEmpeMaint!datTempEmpe.Recordset.MoveNext
```

Exercise 6.9 ▶

In this exercise you will use the Delete and MoveNext Recordset methods to code a procedure that lets the user delete existing records from the Coffee Haus database.

a. Open the file Ex6-9.vbp from the Chapter6 folder on your Student Disk, and then save the project as Ex6-9a.vbp. Save any forms and modules as part of the new project.

b. Add the Delete submenu item to the Maintain menu on the Edit menu, and code the mnuEditMaintainDelete_Click() Event procedure to delete Coffee Haus records from the database using the following pseudocode guidelines:

1. Disable and hide the Data control.
2. Prompt the user for a Customer Number.
3. Set the ReadOnly property to False and refresh the database.
4. Verify that the record is in the database. If the record does not exist, send an appropriate message, and then exit the subroutine.
5. Store the search string in the txtCustNum control and disable this control.
6. Set the focus to the Customer Name text box.
7. Display "Delete Record" in the cmdAction Caption property.
8. Disable the mnuEdit menu control.

c. Edit the cmdAction_Click() event to include the "Delete Record" option that requires the program to issue the Recordset Delete and MoveNext methods and restore the screen to its original form. The Delete action also should send a message indicating that a record was deleted.

d. Save and run the program, and then delete a record.

e. When you are certain that the program functions correctly, create an executable file named Ex6-9a.exe.

Exercise 6.10 ▶

In this exercise you will debug the application so controls are appropriately disabled and restored based on database maintenance function processing for the Melanie's Mall database. Look for incorrect or missing statements and subroutines that might never be activated.

a. Open the file Ex6-10.vbp from the Chapter6 folder on your Student Disk, and then save the project as Ex6-10a.vbp. Save any forms and modules as part of the new project.

b. Run the application and examine the interface for the following processing considerations:

1. During the Add process, the Edit and Find menus should be disabled until the process is complete.

2. During the Update process, the Edit and Find menus should be disabled until the process is complete.

3. During the Delete process, the Edit and Find menus should be disabled until the process is complete.

4. Upon completion of a maintenance function process, the Edit and Find menus should be enabled.

5. During any maintenance function process, the Data control should be disabled and made invisible.

6. Upon completion of a maintenance function, the Data control should be enabled and made visible.

7. Upon completion of a maintenance function, a message should be sent indicating that the current maintenance function has been completed.

c. Correct the application so it complies with the processing considerations list.

d. Save and run the application, and test your changes.

e. When you are certain that the program functions correctly, create an executable file named Ex6-10a.exe.

Writing Code for the frmMaster Interface

Figure 6-1 shows the frmMaster interface, which is the first screen in the Temporary Employee Management System (TEMS). The frmMaster interface provides initial access to the TEMS processes of data management, report printing, and database backup capabilities. You will develop the report printing procedures in Chapter 7 and database backup procedures in Chapter 8.

The user can choose a processing option in two ways: by clicking the command button or by clicking a menu item on the File menu. If the user chooses a menu item from the File menu, a call is made to the associated command button Event procedure. In this way, the same code is executed regardless of how the user accessed it. If you need to alter the code, you only need to make a change in one place, which optimizes the maintenance function.

The cmdDataManagement_Click() Event Procedure

You can access the data management processes using a command button Event procedure or a menu item Event procedure. The menu item Event procedure calls the command button Event procedure code. Figure 6-6 shows that access to data management procedures is preceded by a call to the PassWordCheck procedure. The entered password determines the level of access to the database. The Hide and Show methods are used to remove the frmMaster form from the screen and to display the frmEmpeMaint form on the screen. The Shely system uses the Hide and Show methods instead of the Load and Unload statements so that the forms can remain in memory during processing. Remember that the Show method will load the frmEmpeMaint form into memory, if necessary, as is the case the first time the frmEmpeMaint form is required.

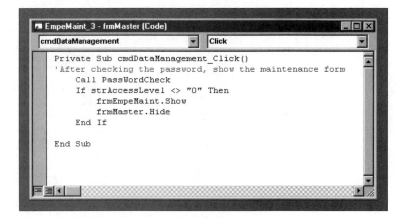

Figure 6-6: The cmdDataManagement_Click() event

The frmEmpeMaint Form

The enhanced SSTER interface shown in Figure 6-2 contains the necessary command buttons to browse, add, update, delete, and search the database. The level of access is determined by the access code computed in the PassWordCheck subroutine. Access levels to the various maintenance options are:

- 2 = browse and search only
- 4 = browse, search, add, and update only
- 8 = full, including browse, search, add, delete, update, and backup

Anyone logging on to the application will have an access level of at least 2, enabling them to browse and search the data. Anyone with an access level greater than 2 will be able to browse, search, add, and update the data. Only those with an access level of 8 will be able to perform all of the events available. To accomplish this, a simple check is added to each of the maintenance functions to verify user access.

The command buttons that appear on the interface are controlled by the ActivateButtonsAndMenus() and DeactivateButtonsAndMenus() Sub procedures shown in Figure 6-7.

```
Sub ActivateButtonsAndMenus()

'Clear and reset maintenance form fields

'(de-)activate menus and command objects

  With frmEmpeMaint

    !mnuFile.Enabled = True

    !mnuMaintenance.Enabled = True

    !cmdBrowse.Enabled = True

    !cmdAdd.Enabled = True

    !cmdUpdate.Enabled = True

    !cmdDelete.Enabled = True

    !cmdClear.Enabled = True

    !cmdReturn.Enabled = True

  End With

End Sub
```

Figure 6-7: The ActivateButtonsAndMenus() and DeactivateButtonsAndMenus() Sub procedures

```
Sub DeactivateButtonsAndMenus()

'Use Enabled property to make menu items and command buttons

'unavailable for update

  With frmEmpeMaint

    !mnuFile.Enabled = False

    !mnuMaintenance.Enabled = False

    !cmdBrowse.Enabled = False

    !cmdAdd.Enabled = False

    !cmdUpdate.Enabled = False

    !cmdDelete.Enabled = False

    !cmdClear.Enabled = False

    !cmdReturn.Enabled = False

  End With

End Sub
```

Figure 6-7: The ActivateButtonsAndMenus() and DeactivateButtonsAndMenus() Sub procedures (continued)

Figure 6-8 shows the interface as it appears when the frmEmpeMaint form first appears on the screen.

Figure 6-8: Initial frmEmpeMaint form

Exercise 6.11 ▶

Modify the existing Coffee Haus application to use user-defined Sub procedures more efficiently.

    a. Open the file Ex6-11.vbp from the Chapter6 folder on your Student Disk, and then save the project as Ex6-11a.vbp. Save any forms and modules as part of the new project.

b. Examine the mnuEditMaintainAdd(), mnuEditMaintainDelete(), and mnuEditMaintainUpdate() Event procedures for repeated code. Also examine the cmdAction_Click() event.

c. Create the following Sub procedures: RestoreScreen to enable previously disabled command buttons, and DisableControls to disable appropriate controls.

d. Replace the Event procedure embedded code that performs the restore and deactivate functions with subroutine calls.

e. Save, run, and test the application. Remember to test the Clear Screen function.

f. When you are certain that the program functions correctly, create an executable file named Ex6-11a.exe. (If you receive an error message that your disk is full, delete any previously created executable files and then try again.)

Exercise 6.12 ▶

The Melanie's Mall application has been modified to include the use of Sub procedures to enable previously disabled command buttons (MMRestore) and to disable appropriate controls (MMDisable). The Sub procedures MMRestore and MMDisable contain the appropriate code. However, the application does not currently use these subroutines. In this exercise, you will remove, disable, and restore code from the mnuEditAdd(), mnuEditDelete(), and mnuEditUpdate() Event procedures and replace this code with the appropriate Sub procedure call. In addition, you must modify the cmdAction() Event procedure to use the appropriate Sub procedure call.

a. Open the file Ex6-12.vbp from the Chapter6 folder on your Student Disk, and then save the project as Ex6-12a.vbp. Save any forms and modules as part of the new project.

b. Modify the application to use the MMRestore and MMDisable subroutines.

c. Save, run, and test the application.

d. When you are certain that the program functions correctly, create an executable file named Ex6-12a.exe.

The cmdBrowse_Click() Event Procedure

You can access the cmdBrowse_Click() event from the File menu or by using the command button. Figure 6-9 shows the cmdBrowse_Click() Event procedure code.

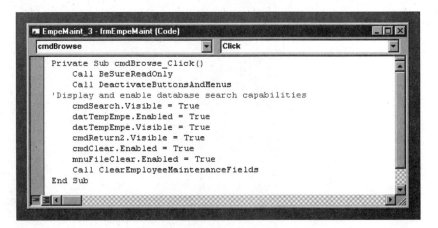

Figure 6-9: The cmdBrowse_Click() event

The first two statements in the Browse procedure establish the database as ReadOnly and deactivate all maintenance functions that might alter the data in the database. Then the Search button and Data control become active and visible for database access. The Data control is enabled. The Search button functions as it did in Chapter 5 using the SelectEmployee subroutine. The Data control arrows are used in place of the Find commands from Chapter 5. Figure 6-10 shows the employee maintenance form in Browse mode.

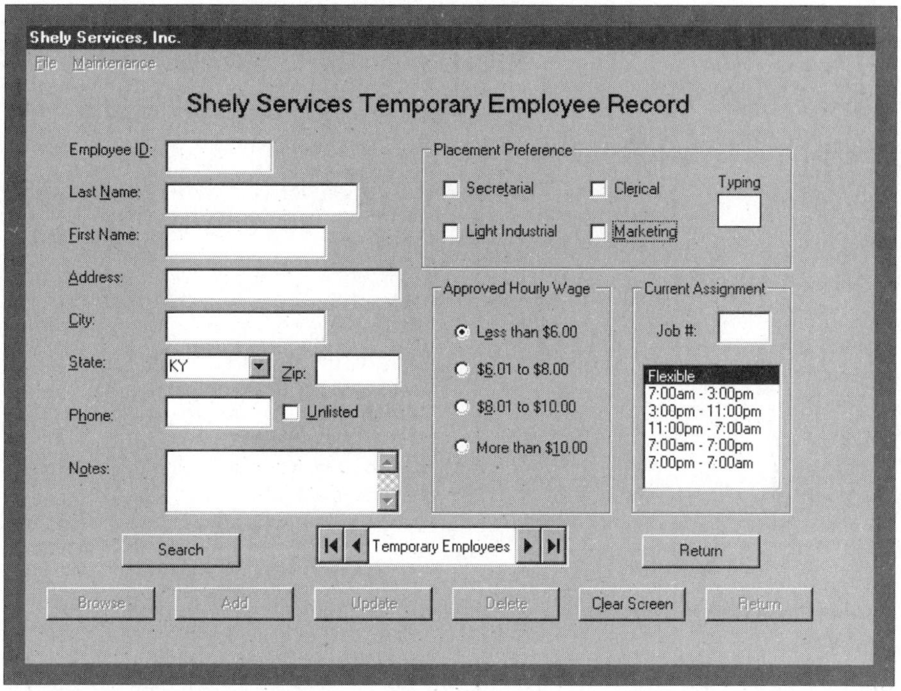

Figure 6-10: Employee maintenance form in Browse mode

When you click the Return command button next to the Data control, the process initiated by the Browse procedure is reversed. The ActivateButtonsAndMenus subroutine restores the form to its initial state. The Data control, search, and return controls become invisible and the Data control is disabled. The ClearEmployeeMaintenanceFields subroutine is called to remove all data from the form.

The cmdAdd_Click() Event Procedure

Figure 6-11 shows the cmdAdd_Click() event. To add records to the Shely database, the user must have an access level of 4 or 8. If the access level is 2, an error message reminds the user that add access is denied and returns the user to the frmEmpeMaint form in its current state.

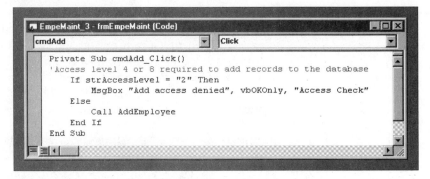

Figure 6-11: The cmdAdd_Click() event

If the access level is 4 or 8, control transfers to the AddEmployee subroutine found in the DataBaseProcessing code module. Then the code proceeds as follows:

1. Make sure that data is protected. (In this project this check will be made more often than is really necessary for clarity.) The code to ensure data protection is `Call BeSureReadOnly`.

2. Get a valid employee ID. The GetEmployeeID Function procedure will return "000" if the employee ID is invalid and the subsequent If statement will be bypassed. The code to validate the employee ID is as follows:

```
strSearchID = GetEmployeeID(strSearchID)
If strSearchID <> "000" Then
    [valid ID processing instructions]
End If
```

The GetEmployeeID function discussed in Chapter 5 is used to prompt the user for an employee ID and validate it to make sure that the ID is within the accepted range (from 100 to 499).

3. Make sure that the employee ID does not already exist in the database because the primary key must be unique. Clear all fields and exit if employee ID exists. The code to do this is:

```
'Get the employee ID and verify that the ID is not currently used
  strSearchID = GetEmployeeID(strSearchID)
  If strSearchID <> "000" Then
    strSearchString = "EmployeeID = '" + strSearchID + "'"
    frmEmpeMaint!datTempEmpe.Recordset.FindFirst _
      strSearchString
    If frmEmpeMaint!datTempEmpe.Recordset.NoMatch Then
'Employee does not exist
      [processing instructions continue]
    Else
'Employee already exists
      intResponse = MsgBox("Employee already exists", _
      vbOKOnly, "Add Employee")
      Call ClearEmployeeMaintenanceFields
    End If
```

A valid search string is used with the FindFirst method to search the database for the existence of the ID entered. The NoMatch method is used to check for the existence of the employee ID. If the NoMatch method returns a value of True, the employee ID does not currently exist in the database and processing instructions to add the employee can continue. If the employee ID already exists, then the data entry fields are cleared, a message notifies the user that this employee ID exists, and then the subroutine terminates.

4. The employee ID entered does not currently exist in the database. Set the database ReadOnly property to False using the following code: `Call OpendatTempEmpe`. The statement `ReadOnly = False` in the OpendatTempEmpe subroutine removes the ReadOnly attribute from the database so that changes can be made.

5. Tell the database that you are adding a new record using the following code:

```
frmEmpeMaint!datTempEmpe.Recordset.AddNew
```

The AddNew method creates a new record for the updatable Recordset object associated with the datTempEmpe database. This method sets the database fields to default values. If no default values are specified, then the fields are set to Null.

6. Initialize the employee ID in the Employee ID text box, and then place the insertion point in the Last Name field using the following code:

```
frmEmpeMaint!txtEmpeID.Text = strSearchID
frmEmpeMaint!txtLName.SetFocus
```

7. Disable all menus and command buttons using the following code:

```
Call DeactivateButtonsAndMenus
```

8. Change the Activate button caption to "Click to ADD" and make it visible using the following code:

```
frmEmpeMaint!cmdActivate.Caption = "Click to ADD"
frmEmpeMaint!cmdActivate.Visible = True
```

9. Enter the data. (**Note:** If the record with the lowest employee ID in the database has a check in the Secretarial Placement Preference check box, the GetWordsPerMinute subroutine will execute each time a record is added or updated. This problem will be corrected by a process that you add in Chapter 8.)

10. Process the request. When the user clicks the Click to ADD command button, the ProcessRequest() Sub procedure shown in Figure 6-12 is performed.

The ProcessRequest Subroutine

The cmdActivate Caption property contains a caption that indicates whether the request is an add, update, or delete. The Windows standard of mixed case letters using book title capitalization is altered in these captions for emphasis. The Select Case form of the selection structure is used to determine the next processing action. Regardless of the maintenance function, the DoubleCheck function (see Figure 6-13) is called to verify that the user wants to complete the database action.

```
Public Sub ProcessRequest()
  Dim intUserResponse As Integer
'Based on the maintenance function,
'verify that the user wishes to continue
'If the user wishes to continue, update the database
  Select Case frmEmpeMaint!cmdActivate.Caption
    Case "Click to ADD", "Click to UPDATE"
      If DoubleCheck(intUserResponse) = vbYes Then
        If CheckData(intUserResponse) <> vbNo Then
          frmEmpeMaint!datTempEmpe.Recordset.Update
        If frmEmpeMaint!cmdActivate.Caption = _
          "Click to ADD" Then
          MsgBox "Record added", , "Database Action"
        Else
            MsgBox "Record updated", , "Database Action"
        End If
        Else
          Exit Sub
        End If
      Else
        frmEmpeMaint!datTempEmpe.Recordset.CancelUpdate
      End If
    Case "Click to DELETE"
      If DoubleCheck(intUserResponse) = vbYes Then
        frmEmpeMaint!datTempEmpe.Recordset.Delete
        frmEmpeMaint!datTempEmpe.Recordset.MoveNext
        MsgBox "Record deleted", , "Database Action"
      End If
End Select

'Reset ReadOnly property and activate maintenance buttons and menus
  Call BeSureReadOnly
  frmEmpeMaint!cmdActivate.Visible = False
  Call ActivateButtonsAndMenus
  Call ClearEmployeeMaintenanceFields
  frmEmpeMaint!cmdActivate.Caption = ""

End Sub
```

Figure 6-12: ProcessRequest() Sub procedure

```
Public Function DoubleCheck(ByVal intResponse)
'Verify that the user wants to ADD, DELETE, or UPDATE
  Select Case frmEmpeMaint!cmdActivate.Caption
    Case "Click to ADD"
      DoubleCheck = _
            MsgBox("Do you want to ADD this employee?", _
            vbYesNo, "ADD check")
    Case "Click to UPDATE"
      DoubleCheck = _
            MsgBox("Do you want to UPDATE this employee?", _
            vbYesNo, "UPDATE check")
    Case "Click to DELETE"
      DoubleCheck = _
            MsgBox("Do you want to DELETE this employee?", _
            vbYesNo, "DELETE check")
  End Select
End Function
```

Figure 6-13: DoubleCheck function

A "No" response returned from the DoubleCheck function results in execution of the CancelUpdate method. The **CancelUpdate method** cancels any pending updates for the Recordset object. Control is transferred to the statement following the End Select. The Refresh method forces a complete repaint of the frmEmpeMaint form.

If the user wants to continue the update with a "Yes" response to the DoubleCheck function, the CheckData function is called to verify the presence of all required fields. The CheckData Function procedure introduced in Chapter 3 has been modified to accommodate database processing requirements as follows:

■ The code to validate the employee ID has been removed.
■ The zip code is further validated by checking for a length of 5 and verifying that data entered is numeric.

To verify that entered data is numeric, you use the IsNumeric function.

Syntax ▶   **IsNumeric**(*expression*)

In this syntax, *expression* is a Variant containing a numeric expression or string expression. The function returns a Boolean value. A value of True indicates that the expression can be evaluated as a number.

If the required entries were made, the Update method saves the contents of the copy buffer to the updatable Recordset object. A message to the user indicates that the record was added, updated, or deleted, depending on the requested action.

You complete the ProcessRequest function in the same manner regardless of responses from the DoubleCheck or CheckData functions. The BeSureReadOnly Sub procedure code sets the database to ReadOnly and then refreshes the database using the Refresh method. The cmdActivate command button is hidden and its caption removed and the ActivateButtonsAndMenus and ClearEmployeeMaintenanceFields Sub procedures are executed.

The cmdDelete_Click() Event Procedure

Figure 6-14 shows the cmdDelete_Click() event. Event processing depends on an access level of 8. If the access level is 8, control transfers to the DeleteEmployee subroutine and processing proceeds with verification that the database record exists using the mentioned GetEmployeeID function.

```
EmpeMaint_3 - frmEmpeMaint (Code)

cmdDelete                          Click

Private Sub cmdDelete_Click()
'Access level 8 required to delete records from the database
    If strAccessLevel <> "8" Then
        MsgBox "Delete access denied", vbOKOnly, "Access Check"
    Else
        Call DeleteEmployee
    End If
End Sub
```

Figure 6-14: The cmdDelete_Click() event

The record pointer must point to the record to be deleted. The ReadOnly property of the data object must be set to False before the record is located with the FindFirst method. If the user decides not to delete the record, the ReadOnly property must be reset to True before any other action is taken against the database. Otherwise, the contents of the record will be lost.

The user must be given an opportunity to confirm that the record should be deleted. The procedure is followed as in the AddEmployee subroutine. After the user confirms a decision to delete the record, the Delete method removes the current record from the updatable Recordset. Then the current record becomes inaccessible. As records are deleted, the database does not actually delete the record. The record is marked as inactive and is not readily available. You must compress the database occasionally in Visual Basic or Microsoft Access using the CompactDatabase method to eliminate unwanted records.

Moving to the next record via the MoveNext method ensures that the deleted record cannot become current. Subsequent references to a deleted record in a Recordset are invalid and produce an error.

Figure 6-15 shows the DeleteEmployee() Sub procedure.

```
Public Sub DeleteEmployee()

   Dim strSearchID As String

   Dim strSearchString As String

'Set the ReadOnly property to True

   Call BeSureReadOnly


'Get the Employee ID and verify that the record exists

   strSearchID = GetEmployeeID(strSearchID)

   If strSearchID <> "000" Then

      Call OpendatTempEmpe

      strSearchString = "EmployeeID = '" + strSearchID + "'"

      frmEmpeMaint!datTempEmpe.Recordset.FindFirst _

         strSearchString

      If Not frmEmpeMaint!datTempEmpe.Recordset.NoMatch Then

'Employee exists, prompt for delete

         Call DeactivateButtonsAndMenus

'Establish maintenance function as a DELETE function

         frmEmpeMaint!cmdActivate.Caption = "Click to DELETE"

         frmEmpeMaint!cmdActivate.Visible = True

      Else

'Employee does not exist

         intResponse = MsgBox("Employee does not exist", _

            vbOKOnly, "Delete Employee")

         Call BeSureReadOnly

         Call ClearEmployeeMaintenanceFields

      End If

   Else

      Call BeSureReadOnly

      Call ClearEmployeeMaintenanceFields

   End If

End Sub
```

Figure 6-15: The DeleteEmployee() Sub procedure

The cmdUpdate_Click() Event Procedure

Figure 6-16 shows the cmdUpdate_Click() event. The record update function involves making changes to existing records in the database. Users with access codes of 4 or 8 can update records in the Shely database. If the user's access level is 2, then an error message reminds the user that Update access is denied and returns the user to the frmEmpeMaint form in its current state.

```
EmpeMaint_3 - frmEmpeMaint (Code)                              _ □ ×
cmdUpdate                    ▼    Click                          ▼
    Private Sub cmdUpdate_Click()
    'Access level 4 or 8 required to update records in the database
        If strAccessLevel = "2" Then
            MsgBox "Update access denied", vbOKOnly, "Access Check"
        Else
            Call UpdateEmployee
        End If
    End Sub
```

Figure 6-16: The cmdUpdate_Click() event

If the access level is not 2, control is transferred to the UpdateEmployee subroutine found in the DataBaseProcessing code module. The Update routine finds a record, copies its contents to the form, and then rewrites it with any changes back to the database table. As in the DeleteEmployee procedure, the OpendatTempEmpe subroutine sets the ReadOnly property to False before the record pointer is set and the program proceeds to verify that the entered employee ID corresponds to an existing record.

If the requested record exists in the database, the record is presented to the user for changes. The Recordset Edit object makes the current record updatable in the Recordset object. The remaining code functions as in the AddEmployee routine substituting the caption "Click to UPDATE" in place of "Click to ADD" in the cmdActivate caption. Figure 6-17 shows the UpdateEmployee subroutine.

```
Public Sub UpdateEmployee()

  Dim strSearchID As String

  Dim strSearchString As String

  Dim strResponse As String
'Set ReadOnly property to True

  Call BeSureReadOnly


'Get the employee ID and verify that the record exists
  strSearchID = GetEmployeeID(strSearchID)

  If strSearchID <> "000" Then
'Set ReadOnly property to False

      Call OpendatTempEmpe


      strSearchString = "EmployeeID = '" + strSearchID + "'"

      frmEmpeMaint!datTempEmpe.Recordset.FindFirst _
        strSearchString
```

Figure 6-17: UpdateEmployee subroutine

```
'Employee exists, make Recordset updateable

    If Not frmEmpeMaint!datTempEmpe.Recordset.NoMatch Then

        frmEmpeMaint!datTempEmpe.Recordset.Edit

        Call DeactivateButtonsAndMenus


        frmEmpeMaint!cmdActivate.Caption = "Click to UPDATE"

        frmEmpeMaint!cmdActivate.Visible = True

    Else

'Employee does not exist

        intResponse = MsgBox("Employee does not exist", _

        vbOKOnly, "Update Employee")

        Call BeSureReadOnly

        Call ClearEmployeeMaintenanceFields

    End If

  Else

'Employee ID is "000"

    Call BeSureReadOnly

    Call ClearEmployeeMaintenanceFields

  End If

End Sub
```

Figure 6-17: UpdateEmployee subroutine (continued)

Return Events

The cmdReturn_Click() event appears as a command button with the caption "Return" and functions to interchange the frmEmpeMaint form for the frmMaster form using the form's Hide and Show methods, respectively (see Figure 6-18). This Return command button is functional when the frmEmpeMaint form first appears. The control is unavailable when the application is in Browse mode or any of the database maintenance modes (add, delete, or update).

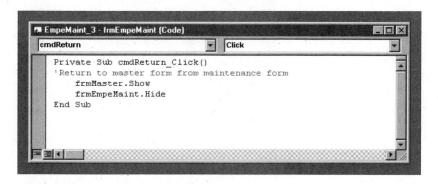

Figure 6-18: The cmdReturn_Click() event

The cmdReturn2_Click() event also appears as a command button with the caption "Return." This command button is visible only during Browse mode and exists for the purpose of returning the form to its initial state after the browse operation is completed (see Figure 6-19).

```
EmpeMaint_3 - frmEmpeMaint [Code]                          _ □ X
cmdReturn2                       ▼    Click                        ▼
    Private Sub cmdReturn2_Click()
    'Return to maintenance form initial structure
        Call ActivateButtonsAndMenus
        datTempEmpe.Visible = False
        datTempEmpe.Enabled = False
        cmdSearch.Visible = False
        cmdReturn2.Visible = False
        Call ClearEmployeeMaintenanceFields
    End Sub
```

Figure 6-19: The cmdReturn2_Click() event

The ControlBox property of the frmEmpeMaint form should be set to False, which forces the user to return to the main form before exiting and before the project can shut down. Should there be any unload processes in the project, setting this property to False ensures that they were completed.

The Secretary Check Box and Words Per Minute

In Chapter 3, each time the Secretary Placement Preference check box was checked, the user was prompted to enter the employee's typing speed. Beginning in Chapter 4, this event was commented out of the code to avoid having the input box appear as data were being read in from the database. Data were not being added or updated to the database, so the removal of the code was not a problem.

With the ability to add and update records in the database, the call to the GetWordsPerMinute subroutine from the chkPlacement_Click(Index As Integer) event must be reinstated for *only* the add and update processes. The code in Figure 6-20 checks the cmdActivate Caption property for "Click to ADD" or "Click to UPDATE" and the chkPlacement(0) Value property for 1. If both condition tests evaluate to True, the code then prompts the user to enter a typing speed, otherwise the typing speed is set to "0". The typing speed is examined using the IsNumeric function. If the IsNumeric function evaluates to False, the lblTypingSpeed Caption property is set to "0", otherwise the words per minute are stored as entered.

```
EmpeMaint_3 - DataEditing [Code]                            _ □ X
(General)                        ▼    GetWordsPerMinute              ▼
    Public Sub GetWordsPerMinute()
    'For ADD or UPDATE and secretarial placement preference,
    'get the typing speed
        Dim strWordsPerMinute As String
        If frmEmpeMaint!cmdActivate.Caption = "Click to ADD" Or _
            frmEmpeMaint!cmdActivate.Caption = "Click to UPDATE" Then
            If frmEmpeMaint!chkPlacement(0).Value = 1 Then
                strWordsPerMinute = InputBox("Enter typing speed", _
                    "Words Per Minute")
                If IsNumeric(strWordsPerMinute) = False Then
                    frmEmpeMaint!lblTypingSpeed.Caption = "0"
                Else
    'Store the typing speed as entered
                    frmEmpeMaint!lblTypingSpeed.Caption = _
                    strWordsPerMinute
                End If
            Else
                frmEmpeMaint!lblTypingSpeed.Caption = "0"
            End If
        End If
    End Sub
```

Figure 6-20: The GetWordsPerMinute subroutine

SUMMARY

The TEMS system for maintaining temporary employees' records in a database is complete. The system in its current form allows for new employee data entry, browsing, updating, and deleting records from the database. You addressed all data integrity and security concerns.

The TEMS system uses subroutine and function calls that make maintaining the system more efficient. Figure 6-21 shows the Explorer window for the TEMS system in its current form. You should examine each module carefully noting the grouping of subroutines together by function.

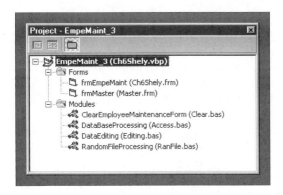

Figure 6-21: Explorer window for TEMS system

PROGRESSIVE PROJECTS

1. Bean County Plumbing Inventory System (BCPIS)

In this chapter, your project will start to take its final shape. Along with the maintenance routines for the MastPart table, you need to complete two new tables and their respective maintenance forms—one for the Master Location table (MastLoc) and one for the Master Inventory table (MastInv). It is also necessary to generate an introductory form, similar to the one in the text. (*Hint:* A good logo always helps a project.) You also need to move the password check to the introductory form. In order to focus efforts on moving the project through this stage, the best way might be to work through the material in this chapter carefully so that it is clearly understood. Make any initial changes, and then use the code for the various subroutines (add, delete, and update) as a starting point. The subroutines should be coded so they can virtually stand alone with only a few calls to other subroutines. Once the maintenance form is functioning, you can complete the other two subroutines. It will save time to cut, paste, and edit your code—however, make sure that routines in the various modules reference the form from which they are called using the *form!object.property* convention.

Make sure that you set up all the forms so users will move from one to another in a controlled manner. For example, no user should be able to exit the program in the middle of an update routine or go to another form in the middle of a delete check. Make sure that you coordinate menus and buttons. There are a lot of little things that go wrong with a program if activities are not controlled carefully.

The special challenge in this project is to develop routines to protect the integrity of all three tables. A part or a location ID should not be entered into the MastInv table unless it exists in its respective table. Conversely, no part or location ID should be deleted if it is referenced in the MastInv table. Consider Figure 1-15 carefully before beginning to write code. Go slow and test one subroutine at a time.

After you finish these steps in the project, there should be a database (BCPISdb.mdb) with three tables (MastLoc, MastInv, and MastPart), and a Visual Basic project (BCPIS.vbp) with an entry form and three maintain forms—one for each table. Test the code and the add routines carefully. Remember to make a backup copy of your work.

2. Single Parents Public Service Library (SPLIB)

Because the material in this chapter is dependent upon the code being performed in a very set sequence, study the material in the chapter carefully. Using the material in the chapter as a reference, create subroutines that add, delete, and update data for the MastItem table. Add password routines as indicated in the Shely project so that forms and events are appropriately controlled. This is also a good time to examine the form's layout and colors, and to reset the form so that it covers the entire screen.

Create a special introductory screen by including a logo and easy-to-understand menus and processes. Make sure that you check the subroutines.

Remember the user should never be able to create a situation in which the program fails to execute properly. Test and retest the logic on the forms to see if it is possible to fool the program. Make sure that the add routine works as expected and that all of the data are written to the database correctly. Make sure that the delete command deletes only one record at a time and that records are actually deleted. Remember to make a backup copy of your work.

When you finish this project in this chapter, the project (SPLIB.vbp) will have all its forms (MastItem and MastUser in the SPLIBdb.mdb) established, and the user can move correctly between the forms. Also, make sure that all of the data maintenance functions (browse, add, update, and delete) function correctly. The user might add or update using incorrect data, but the program always must maintain its integrity. No one should be able to enter a user ID in the MastItem table unless it exists in the MastUser table, and no one should be able to delete a user ID in the MastUser table if it exists in the MastItem table. Review Figure 1-25 carefully.

3. Short Cut Lawn Service (SCLS)

So far, your project has one table (UnitInv) in its database (SCLSdb.mdb) and a form that displays the table's contents. You need to add the Customer table (CustData) and a corresponding form, and there needs to be an introductory form similar to the one in the Shely project.

First, restructure the UnitInv form so that it fills the screen, remove the call to the password check, and complete the other housekeeping chores (like cleaning up the Unload subroutine). Then, after studying the material in the chapter, use the add, delete, and update subroutines in the chapter as models for creating similar routines for this form. Work carefully and check each routine before going on to the next one. If there is trouble, it is usually with the add routine. Make sure that data are not added if the user decides not to continue adding data. Name the project SCLS.vbp.

Wait until the form maintaining the UnitInv table is complete before creating the Customer table (CustData) and form. Use cut, paste, and editing to make these tasks go faster. Again, check everything carefully—make sure that data integrity is maintained. The unit ID must exist in the UnitInv table before it is entered into the CustData table. Also, the unit ID must not be removed from the UnitInv table if it exists in the CustData table. Examine Figure 1-35 carefully.

Create the introduction form with a logo, menus, and buttons that accurately control the user's access to the forms. You can add the password check after everything else works. The user must not be able to activate events at will, especially not in the middle of an add, update, or delete routine. When this part of the project is complete, with everything working correctly, it should be impossible for the user to activate an event that generates unexpected results. Remember to make a backup copy of your work.

INDEPENDENT PROJECTS

1. Wally's Phone Companion

Wally doesn't like to answer telephone calls from solicitors. He has a telephone device that displays the phone number of the caller, and if he doesn't recognize the phone number, he doesn't answer the call. The problem is that Wally can't remember the phone numbers of his friends, so he is not sure if the number displayed on the device is a solicitor.

Wally wants a program that will allow him to enter, update, and delete the phone numbers of his friends. Then, when someone calls, he can enter the phone on the screen and retrieve the name of the person who is calling.

Create a table in a database for the names and phone numbers of Wally's friends. Then complete a project for managing Wally's data and for his need to check phone numbers. You will receive extra credit for a password to keep Wally's roommate from accessing the numbers. Save the form, project, and database as Ch6IP1.

2. Barbara's Phone Companion

Barbara keeps a personal phone book next to her phone in which she keeps the names, addresses, phone numbers, and birthdays of her friends and family. Over the years, Barbara has inserted scraps of paper with information that she never entered into her personal phone book. Barbara needs a program to manage this pile of data.

Create a program that will permit Barbara to add, update, and delete data about her friends and family. Store the data in a database table using the person's phone number as the primary key. (For extra credit, search on the last name, whereby the name will have to be padded to match the size of the field in the table exactly.) Make sure that the final project is easy to use. Save the form, project, and database as Ch6IP2.

3. Dee's Book Locator

As a lawyer, Dee receives many legal resource books. But she is never sure where a book is—at home, in the staff library, in the staff workroom, or in her office. Dee wants a program so she or any of her staff can find the general location of her books quickly. She is not interested in a complete cataloguing system, but rather, a quick reference tool for *sets* of books.

Create a database table for Dee's books. Use fixed-length primary keys (for example, OhioLegCode + blanks) and limit book title to names of sets. Dee's staff should be able to add, relocate, and delete sets of books. Create an attractive form with a logo and appropriate menus and buttons. Save the form, project, and database as Ch6IP3.

Reporting Information

Introduction ▶ The Shely Services Temporary Employee Record (SSTER) interface (frmEmpeMaint) is complete. In Chapter 6, you added a master form (frmMaster) to the project to control initial access to data management, corporate reports, and database backup procedures. In this chapter, you will combine a master form and its associated SSTER interface with a temporary employee reports form (frmPrint).

You will update the TEMS system in this chapter to produce a detail report, an exception report, and a control break report using the Printer object. You will learn about Crystal Reports and create an additional detail report. Data for these reports will depend on direct database access as opposed to database access through the data object. You will use standard SQL statements to generate the data. Figure 7-1 shows the temporary employee reports interface (frmPrint).

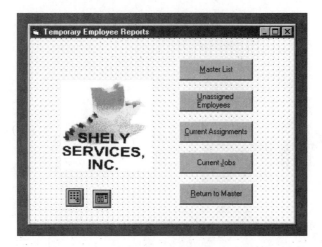

Figure 7-1: Temporary Employee Reports interface

Creating Reports

The TEMS system currently focuses on viewing information for a single employee through a well-designed form that makes the user interface easy to use. An alternative to viewing data from individual records online is to produce reports that summarize the data in some way. These reports should be available for viewing online as well as in printed form.

A well-designed report makes the report easy to read and understand. In general, a report layout should contain the following specifications:

- A **report header**, which contains a minimum of the report title, current date, page number, and report source
- **Detail lines**, which contain data organized by columns with column headings that describe information in the column
- A **report footer**, which indicates that the generated report is complete
- Spacing to allow for equal left and right margins, uniform spacing between columns, and decimal-aligned data

The TEMS System Reports

The Master List of Temporary Employees report is a detail report that lists the employee ID, name, address (including data from the address, city, state, and zip fields in the database), and phone number for each employee. A **detail report** is a report that contains data from each record in the database, but the report might not include all of the data from a single record. For example, the Master List of Temporary Employees report contains only a subset of the record data. Figure 7-2 shows the layout for the temporary employees detail report. All TEMS system reports are designed using the Courier New font.

```
Mon ##, ####                    Shely Services Human Resource System                Page: ##
                                  Master List of Temporary Employees


Empe
 ID              Name                              Address                           Phone

###        xxxxxxxxxxxxxxxxx        xxxxxxxxxxxxxxxxxxxxxxxxxxxxxxxxxxxxxxxxxx      (###) ###-####

###        xxxxxxxxxxxxxxxxx        xxxxxxxxxxxxxxxxxxxxxxxxxxxxxxxxxxxxxxxxxx      (###) ###-####

###        xxxxxxxxxxxxxxxxx        xxxxxxxxxxxxxxxxxxxxxxxxxxxxxxxxxxxxxxxxxx      (###) ###-####

###        xxxxxxxxxxxxxxxxx        xxxxxxxxxxxxxxxxxxxxxxxxxxxxxxxxxxxxxxxxxx      (###) ###-####

###        xxxxxxxxxxxxxxxxx        xxxxxxxxxxxxxxxxxxxxxxxxxxxxxxxxxxxxxxxxxx      (###) ###-####


                             End of Master List of Temporary Employees
```

Figure 7-2: Record layout for Master List of Temporary Employees report

The Unassigned Temporary Employees report is an exception report. An **exception report** is a report that only lists data from records that match a specific criterion. This criterion is the "exception" that generates only certain records for the report. The exception report for the TEMS system lists records for employees who are available for job placement. These records are exceptions because the employees are not assigned to a current job. The detail lines for the report include the employee ID, employee name, placement preference, and typing speed, if applicable, for each employee. Figure 7-3 shows the layout for the available employees' exception report for each unassigned employee.

```
Mon ##, ####                    Shely Services Human Resource System                Page: ##
                                   Unassigned Temporary Employees


                                                        Availability                   Typing
Employee        Employee                                                                WPM
   ID             Name          Secretary  Clerical  Industrial  Marketing

  ###      xxxxxxxxxxxxxxxxxxxxxxxxx           *                                          ##
  ###      xxxxxxxxxxxxxxxxxxxxxxxxx           *          *                               ##
                             End of Available Temporary Employees
```

Figure 7-3: Record layout for Unassigned Temporary Employees report

The Current Job Assignments for Temporary Employees report is a control break report. A **control break report** is a report that summarizes data for a specified field(s). This type of report determines how the summary line(s) are printed based on a change in the value or content of a **control field**. The control field for this control break report is the job ID field. The report lists employee job assignments by job ID. Figure 7-4 shows the layout for the TEMS current job assignments. For each job, the job ID and job title are printed. Within each job, the employee ID and name for all employees assigned to the job are listed. When there is a change in a job ID, the total number of employees assigned to the previous job is printed.

```
Mon ##, ####              Shely Services Human Resource System              Page: ##

                     Current Job Assignments for Temporary Employees


                          XXX  XXXXXXXXXXXXXXXXXXXXXXXXXXXXXX
                                XXX   XXXXXXXXXXXXXXXXXXXXXXXXX
                                XXX   XXXXXXXXXXXXXXXXXXXXXXXXX

                                                  Number of Employees = 2

                          XXX  XXXXXXXXXXXXXXXXXXXXXXXXXXXXXXX
                                XXX   XXXXXXXXXXXXXXXXXXXXXXXXX

                                                  Number of Employees = 1

                                                         Total Number = 3

                          End of List of Temporary Employees Job Assignments
```

Figure 7-4: Record layout for Current Job Assignments for Temporary Employees report

You will create the detail, exception, and control break reports using Visual Basic code and SQL statements to retrieve data directly from the database. But first you will create a Crystal Report to list current jobs and sort them by job ID.

Creating Reports with Crystal Reports

Crystal Reports is a Visual Basic add-in program that can simplify the task of creating printed reports. Designing and adding a report to the project using Crystal Reports is a two-step process. First, you use the Crystal Report program custom control to design the report. You design the report on the Visual Basic screen, but it is in reality a stand-alone program that you can use with other Microsoft programs. The second step is to add the CrystalReport control to the project that will permit the program to call and execute the report.

You access Crystal Reports through the Report Designer on the Add-Ins menu. (If the Crystal Reports Registration form appears, click the Done button.) From the Crystal Reports Pro form menu, you click New on the File menu to begin creating a report. Figure 7-5 shows the Create New Report dialog box. You will use the Listing expert to create the TEMS system report. If you are using Visual Basic 6.0, you might need to find CRYSREPT in the Common\Tools\VB folder on the installation CD-ROM. Execute the file to make Crystal Reports available in the Program Files\Microsoft Visual Studio\Common\Tools\Reports folder. You must then move the contents of the folder to the Program Files\Microsoft Visual Studio\VB98\Reports folder. (Your file locations might be different.) Now Crystal Reports should appear on the Add-Ins menu. The MS Data Report Designer 6.0 is also available on the References menu. However, in this text, you will use Crystal Reports.

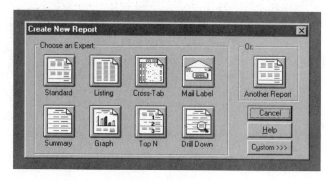

Figure 7-5: Create New Report dialog box

The first step in the Create Report Expert is to define the tables used to create the report. A list of current jobs for the TEMS system is created using the ShelyTemps.mdb database file. Figure 7-6 shows the selection in the Choose Database File dialog box.

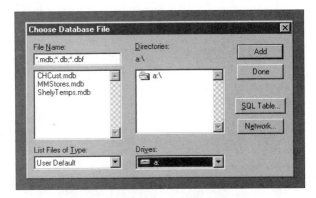

Figure 7-6: Choose Database File dialog box

The second step in the Create Report Expert asks you to specify any links between tables that are required to create the report. No links are required for the listing of current jobs.

Figure 7-7 shows the Fields tab in the Create Report Expert dialog box, which is the third step in the report generation process. The JobID and the JobTitle are selected from the CurrentJobs table. Clicking the Preview Report button lets you preview the report.

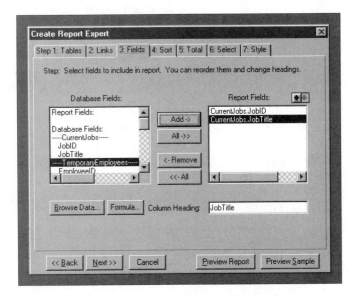

Figure 7-7: Create Report Expert dialog box Fields tab

Figure 7-8 shows a preview of the report after clicking Zoom on the Report menu. You should save the report using the File menu prior to enhancing the report design.

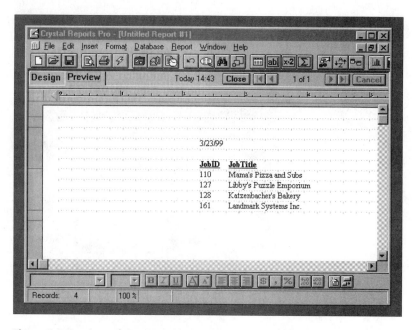

Figure 7-8: Preview of the Crystal Reports Pro generated report

You can use the Design tab to redesign and preview the report layout until you are satisfied with its appearance and decide that it is complete. The Job Listings report needs a title, and you need to sort the current jobs in order by JobID. Figure 7-9 shows the dialog box that opens after clicking the A-Z button on the toolbar. You add a sort field to the report by selecting the field and then clicking the Add button. You can sort the field in ascending or descending order.

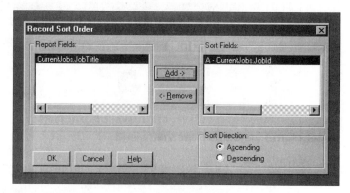

Figure 7-9: Record Sort Order dialog box

There are many options available for improving the existing report design. Experience in this case is definitely the best teacher. You can practice generating reports in the exercises for this section. Figure 7-10 shows the Format Date dialog box that opens when you click the Change Format command on the shortcut menu found by right-clicking the date in its current form.

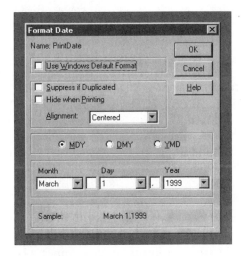

Figure 7-10: Format Date dialog box

Remember that the date field is an object that you might need to resize. Figure 7-11 shows the report, which includes a report title. Moving the objects on the screen changes their field locations.

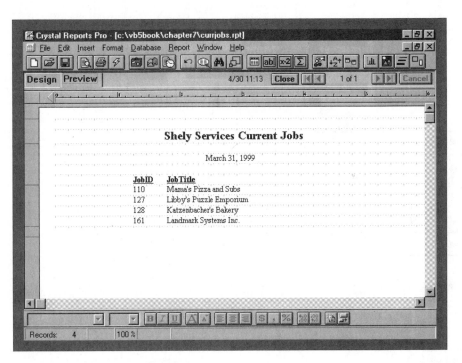

Figure 7-11: Shely Services Current Jobs report

In order to add this report to the TEMS system, you must add the CrystalReport control to the Toolbox using the Components command on the Project menu. As with any object, the CrystalReport control has properties that you can set at run time. The control is added to the frmPrint form. The Crystal Report icon will not be visible at run time.

The properties required to generate the Current Jobs report are ReportFileName, Destination, DiscardSavedData, and Action, which are described next.

The **ReportFileName** property contains the filename of the report to be printed.

Syntax ▶	*object.***ReportFileName** = *value*

In this and all subsequent syntax statements, the *object* is the Crystal Report icon (crptPrint). The *value* is a character string that indicates the path to the .rpt file. Example 7-1 shows the command.

Example 7-1 ▶	`crptPrint.ReportFileName = "A:\CurrJobs.rpt"`

The **Destination property** determines where the report is printed. One of four constants is used to control the report's destination: 0—crptToWindow prints the report to a window on the screen; 1—crptToPrinter prints the report to the printer; 2—crptToFile prints the report to a file on a disk; and 3—crptMapi sends the report to another person on your network via MAPI Email (Microsoft Mail). If you use the crptToFile property, you must set the **PrintFileName property** to a file location.

Syntax ▶	*object.***Destination** = *value*

In this syntax, the *value* is the constant designation (crptToWindow, crptToPrinter, crptToFile, or crptMapi). Example 7-2 shows the code to send the report to the printer.

Example 7-2 ▶	`crptPrint.Destination = crptToPrinter`

The **DiscardSavedData property** contains a Boolean value that indicates whether the data in the report file is saved.

Syntax ▶	*object.***DiscardSavedData** = *value*

In this syntax, a *value* of True indicates that the data in the report file should not be saved. The default value is False. Example 7-3 shows the command to ignore the data in the report file.

Example 7-3 ▶	`crptPrint.DiscardSavedData = True`

The **Action property** is a run-time property that triggers printing the report. The *value* is set to 1 to print the report in response to a user event, in this case the Current Jobs (cmdCurrentJobs) command button. Example 7-4 shows the code to print the report.

Syntax ▶	*object*.**Action** = *value*

Example 7-4 ▶	`crptPrint.Action = 1`

Figure 7-12 shows the code window for the cmdCurrentJobs_Click() Event procedure.

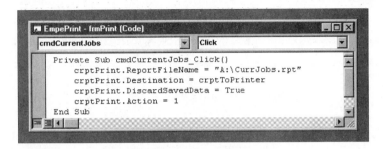

Figure 7-12: The cmdCurrentJobs_Click() Event procedure

Exercise 7.1 ▶

Coffee Haus requires a detailed report listing all customers sorted by customer name. The report should contain the customer name, customer number, owner name, and phone number. You will generate the report using Crystal Reports.

  a. Open the file Ex7-1.vpb from the Chapter7 folder on your Student Disk, and then save the project as Ex7-1a.vbp. Save any forms and modules as part of the new project.

  b. Complete the following steps to generate the report:

    1. Choose Report Designer from the Add-Ins menu. If the Crystal Reports Registration dialog box opens, click the Done (or Cancel) button to go to the Crystal Reports Pro interface.

    2. Choose New from the File menu and select the Listing expert.

    3. Choose Data File in the Create Report Expert dialog box to open the Choose Database File dialog box. Select the CHCust.mdb file that you moved to the root directory of drive A, and then click the Add button to select the Customer and Order tables. Click the Done button to finish the process.

    4. On the Fields tab of the Create Report Expert dialog box, select the fields required for the report using the record layout in Figure 7-13.

    5. Select Preview Report and edit the design from the Design tab to incorporate the report title and field names listed in the record layout. Use the shortcut menu to edit the column heading text and date in the format presented. Use the Preview tab and Design tab to examine the results of report edits.

    6. Save the report in the root directory of drive A as Ex7-la.rpt.

    7. Close Crystal Reports Pro.

  c. Complete the following steps to add the report to the Ex7-1a project:

    1. Using the Components command on the Project menu, add the CrystalReport control to the Toolbox.

    2. Place the CrystalReport control in the upper-left corner of the frmCustData form. Name the control crptCHList.

    3. In the mnuFileRepCust_Click Event procedure, use assignment statements to set the ReportFileName, Destination, DiscardSavedData, and Action properties. The ReportFileName should indicate the path to the file. Destination is crptToPrinter, DiscardSavedData is True, and Action is equal to 1.

d. Save and run the project. Print the report.

e. When you are satisfied that the program executes successfully, create an executable file named Ex7-1a.exe.

```
                    Coffee Haus Wholesale Distributors
                        Master List of Customers

                            May 31, 1999

    Customer Name              Cust #              Owner                Phone

XXXXXXXXXXXXXXXXXXXXXXXXXXXXXXXXXX    ###    XXXXXXXXXXXXXXXXXXXXXXXX    (###) ###-####

XXXXXXXXXXXXXXXXXXXXXXXXXXXXXXXXXX    ###    XXXXXXXXXXXXXXXXXXXXXXXX    (###) ###-####

XXXXXXXXXXXXXXXXXXXXXXXXXXXXXXXXXX    ###    XXXXXXXXXXXXXXXXXXXXXXXX    (###) ###-####
```

Figure 7-13: Coffee Haus Wholesale Distributors Master List of Customers report

Exercise 7.2 ▶

Melanie's Mall requires a detailed report listing store information sorted by store code. Figure 7-14 provides a record layout for the needed report. You will generate the report using Crystal Reports.

a. Open the file Ex7-2.vbp from the Chapter7 folder on your Student Disk, and then save the project as Ex7-2a.vbp. Save any forms and modules as part of the new project.

b. From the Report Designer option on the Add-Ins menu, create the report using your knowledge of Crystal Reports to meet the record layout specifications.

c. Create the title as part of the page header using the Insert–Text Field menu item.

d. Add the report page number using the Insert–Special Field menu item.

e. Remember that all fields in design and preview modes are objects that you can move and resize. Move and resize fields until your design matches the specifications in the record layout (see Figure 7-14).

f. Save the report as Ex7-2a.rpt in the root directory of drive A, and then close the Crystal Reports Pro program.

g. Add the CrystalReport control to the project.

h. In the mnuFileRepStoreList_Click() Event procedure, add the code necessary to generate the report to the printer.

i. When you are satisfied that your program executes successfully, print the report and create an executable file named Ex7-2a.exe.

```
Mon ##, ####            Melanie's Mall Master List of Stores          Page #
Store Code          Store Name           Location         Contact           Extension

   ###      XXXXXXXXXXXXXXXXXXXXXXXXXXXXXX       ##     XXXXXXXXXXXXXXXXXXXXXXXXXXXXX       ####

   ###      XXXXXXXXXXXXXXXXXXXXXXXXXXXXXX       ##     XXXXXXXXXXXXXXXXXXXXXXXXXXXXX       ####

   ###      XXXXXXXXXXXXXXXXXXXXXXXXXXXXXX       ##     XXXXXXXXXXXXXXXXXXXXXXXXXXXXX       ####
```

Figure 7-14: Melanie's Mall Master List of Stores report

Creating Reports with the Printer Object

There are several ways to print text and graphics in Visual Basic. One of the simplest methods is to use the PrintForm method. The **Printer object** enables you to communicate with a system printer (initially the default system printer) and provides additional control over print options. The Printers collection contains each of the printers defined on your system. A **collection** is an object that contains a set of related objects.

You also can use the Printer object and its associated properties and methods to control how output prints on the page. Remember that properties control the appearance and behavior of an object. Figure 7-15 shows the properties that were used to generate the TEMS reports.

Syntax ▶   **Printer.**_property_ = _value_

Property	Description
CurrentX	Returns or sets the horizontal coordinates for the next printing or drawing method. Not available at design time. The value is zero at an object's left edge.
CurrentY	Returns or sets the vertical coordinates for the next printing or drawing method. Not available at design time. The value is zero at an object's top edge.
FontBold, FontItalic, FontStrikethrough, FontName, FontSize, FontUnderline	Returns or sets font styles in the following formats: **bold**, _italic_, ~~strikethrough~~, and underline. The FontBold, FontItalic, FontStrikethrough, and FontUnderline properties are included for use with the CommonDialog control and for compatibility with earlier versions of Visual Basic. The new Font object properties provide for additional functionality.
ScaleHeight	Returns or sets the number of units for the vertical measurement of the interior of an object when using graphics methods or positioning controls.
ScaleLeft	Returns or sets the horizontal coordinates for the left edge of an object when using graphics methods or positioning controls.
ScaleTop	Returns or sets the vertical coordinates for the top edge of an object when using graphics methods or positioning controls.
ScaleWidth	Returns or sets the number of units for the horizontal measurement of the interior of an object when using graphics methods or positioning controls.

Figure 7-15: Printer properties

The Printer methods used in the TEMS system reports are the Print, EndDoc, TextHeight, and TextWidth methods. You should remember that a _method_ is a predefined Visual Basic procedure. The Print method is the method most frequently used by the Printer object.

Syntax ▶	[*object*].**Print** *outputlist*

In this syntax, the *object* can be a form, the printer, or the Immediate window. The default object is the form. The *outputlist* describes the text to be printed and formatting criteria for the text. The syntax for the *outputlist* is:

Syntax ▶	[**Spc**(*number*) I **Tab**(*number*)] *expression* [*character-position*]

In this syntax, the *expression* represents the data to print. Data can be a text string, a variable, or a reference to a property of an object. If the **Spc** argument is included, space characters will be inserted in the output *before* the *expression* is printed. The *number* argument specifies the number of characters to insert after the previously printed characters. You could use the Spc argument to insert a fixed number of spaces between the column titles in a report.

If the **Tab** argument is included, the *expressionlist* will be inserted at the absolute column number specified by the *number* argument. You could use the Tab argument to align detail data in the correct column. Using Tab or Spc is a matter of personal preference; this text uses the Tab argument.

The *character-position* argument specifies the insertion point for the next *expression*. If you use a semicolon as the *character-position* argument, the insertion point of the next *expression* immediately follows the last character displayed. The default *character-position* is the first absolute column on a new line, meaning that a carriage return and line feed are inserted. Example 7-5 shows the code to print the statement "Total Number = *x*", where *x* is the number of employees, at a tab setting of 60.

Example 7-5 ▶	`Printer.Print Tab(60); "Total Number = " & intNumberOfEmployees`

Syntax ▶	**Printer.EndDoc**

When the Printer object contains the output you want to print, use the EndDoc method to send the output directly to the default printer for the application. The Print method does not automatically send information to the printer immediately. The information is stored in the **printer buffer**, which is an area of the computer's memory that holds printed output before sending it to the printer. The EndDoc method ends a print operation that uses the Printer object and sends the document to the printer. The Page property of the Printer object automatically is reset to 1 when the EndDoc method is called.

Exercise 7.3 ▶

Coffee Haus staff have established a standard report header for all reports. The report header layout appears in Figure 7-16. In this exercise, you will use the Printer object to generate the required report header.

    a. Open a new project and save the form and project as Ex7-3a.vbp.

    b. Add a command button to the project. Name the control cmdPrint and set the caption property to Print Header.

    c. Create a Sub procedure named CHStandardHeader. Save the module as Ex7-3a.bas. Name the module CHHeader.

    d. Use the Printer object to code the subroutine to generate the standard header in Figure 7-16.

    e. The report header contains two blank lines at the top.

f. The subroutine will require the use of the following Printer properties described in Figure 7-15: Print, FontSize, ScaleLeft, CurrentX, ScaleWidth, TextWidth, and Page. The ScaleWidth and TextWidth properties are used to compute the CurrentX location prior to printing the header title and the page number. Center the header title. Print the page number at the top-right margin.

g. Use the EndDoc method to release the header to the printer.

h. In the cmdPrint_Click event, call the Sub procedure CHStandardHeader.

i. Save and run the program. Print the standard header.

j. When you are satisfied that the header is correct, create an executable file named Ex7-3a.exe.

```
Mon ##, ####        Coffee Haus Wholesale Distributors      Page: ##
```

Figure 7-16: Coffee Haus standard report header layout

The Melanie's Mall application requires a standard report header for all of its reports. The report header layout appears in Figure 7-17. In this exercise, you will use the Printer object to generate the required report header.

a. Open a new project and save the form and project as Ex7-4a.vbp.

b. Add a command button to the project. Name the control cmdPrint and set the caption property to Print Header.

c. Create a Sub procedure named MMStandardHeader. Save the module as Ex7-4a.bas. Name the module MMHeader.

d. Use the Printer object to code the subroutine to generate the standard header shown in Figure 7-17.

e. The report header contains two blank lines at the top.

f. The subroutine will require the use of the following Printer properties as described in Figure 7-15: Print, FontName, FontBold, FontSize, ScaleLeft, CurrentX, ScaleWidth, TextWidth, and Page. The ScaleWidth and TextWidth properties are used to compute the CurrentX location prior to printing the header title and the page number. Center the header title. Print the page number at the top-right margin.

g. Use the EndDoc method to release the header to the printer.

h. In the cmdPrint_Click event, call the Sub procedure MMStandardHeader.

i. Save and run the program. Print the standard header.

j. When you are satisfied that the header is correct, create an executable file named Ex7-4a.exe.

```
##/##/####                  Melanie's Mall                  Page: ##
```

Figure 7-17: Melanie's Mall standard report header layout

Using the CommonDialog Control for Printing

The **CommonDialog control** is a control that you can use to display six standard dialog boxes. Figure 7-18 shows the methods to display each dialog box and its associated functions.

Dialog box	Method	Description
Color	ShowColor	Displays a dialog box that lets the user select a color from a color palette or to create and select a custom color.
Font	ShowFont	Displays a dialog box that lets the user select a font by specifying a font size, color, and style.
Help	ShowHelp	Runs Winhlp32.exe and displays the Help file specified.
Open	ShowOpen	Displays a dialog box and lets the user select a file to be opened by specifying the drive, directory, filename, and filename extension.
Print	ShowPrinter	Displays a dialog box and lets the user specify how to print the output.
Save As	ShowSave	Displays a dialog box and lets the user select a file to save by specifying the drive, directory, filename, and filename extension.

Figure 7-18: Standard dialog boxes

You must place the CommonDialog control on the form before you can use it in your program. The CommonDialog control does not appear on the form at run time so its position on the form is not important. If the CommonDialog control does not currently exist in the Toolbox, you can add it by clicking the Components command on the Project menu and then selecting Microsoft CommonDialog Control 5.0 on the Controls tab. The TEMS system only uses the ShowPrinter and ShowHelp methods.

Syntax ▶   *object*.**ShowPrinter**

In this syntax, the *object* is the name of the CommonDialog control (dlgPrint). Figure 7-19 shows the default dialog box that opens using the code dlgPrint.ShowPrinter.

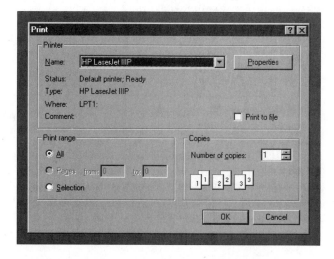

Figure 7-19: Print dialog box with default settings

The Print dialog box lets the user select the printer, print range, number of copies, paper orientation, and other options. Figure 7-20 lists a subset of properties associated with the Print dialog box. A complete list is available in online Help.

Property	Description
CancelError	Boolean value indicating whether an error is generated when the user clicks the Cancel button in the Print dialog box. (You will activate the CancelError property when you learn about error routines in Chapter 8.)
Copies	Sets a value indicating the number of copies to print. The default value is 1.
DialogTitle	Sets a string indicating the text in the title bar of the Print dialog box. The default value is "Print."
Flags	Sets the options for the Print dialog box. Figure 7-19 shows the default options.
PrinterDefault	Boolean value sets an option that determines if the user's selections in the Print dialog box are used to change the system's default printer settings. The default value is True, which means that any selection(s) the user makes in the Properties window or through code are used to change the printer settings in the user's WIN.INI file. ***Be sure to set the default to False in the Properties window to avoid rewriting the Win.ini file.***

Figure 7-20: Print dialog box properties

The TEMS system uses the CommonDialog control's Flags property to set the options for the dialog box.

Syntax ▶

object.**Flags** [= *value*]

In this syntax, the *object* is the name of the CommonDialog control and *value* is a constant specifying the options for the Print dialog box. The value is determined by adding together associated intrinsic constants.

Example 7-6 shows the code used in the TEMS system that disables and hides the Print to file check box and that disables the Pages and Selection option buttons. In Example 7-6, the cdl prefix in the intrinsic constant indicates that the constant is referring to the CommonDialog control and PD indicates that the Flags setting relates to the Print dialog box. Figure 7-21 shows the resulting Print dialog box.

Example 7-6 ▶

```
dlgPrint.Flags = cdlPDDisablePrintToFile + _
    cdlPDHidePrintToFile + cdlPDNoPageNums + _
    cdlPDNoSelection
```

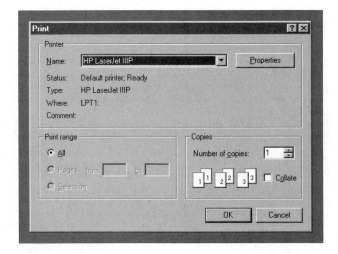

Figure 7-21: Print dialog box with Flags settings

Figure 7-22 shows the code window for the cmdDetailReport_Click() Event procedure. The report header, detail, and footer code appears in user-defined subroutines that
you will see in the "Writing Code" section of this chapter. Pay particular attention here
to the placement of the Flags property settings, ShowPrinter method, and the EndDoc
method statements. You must set the Flags property settings before using the
ShowPrinter method to display the Print dialog box. The underscore character is used
to continue a statement to the next line. You send data to the printer *only after* the Print
dialog box opens. At this point in the processing, the report will print regardless of
whether the user clicked the OK or Cancel button in the Print dialog box. In Chapter 8,
you will activate the CancelError property to let the user cancel the print process.

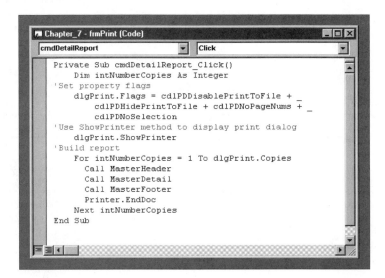

Figure 7-22: The cmdDetailReport_Click() Event procedure

Sending a Report to the Screen

Sometimes you need to see the results of report processing immediately on the
screen. The TEMS system lets the user generate the Unassigned Employees exception
report for processing to the screen or to the printer. Instead of using the Printer

object, all report data are sent to the screen by replacing the Printer object with the name of the form. The MsgBox function lets the user see results on the screen or route the report to the printer. The MsgBox function statement is executed in the cmdExceptionReport_Click() Event procedure when the user clicks the Unassigned Employees command button.

Using the SELECT Statement

In Chapters 5 and 6, you used the Data control to access all records in the database. When you accessed a single record, you saw all data for that record. Sometimes you might need to process only a subset of the database, such as a subset of record data from the entire database or a subset of database records. When you are using large databases with multiple tables, the Data control approach to subsets of data is usually not the best option.

You use the SELECT statement to retrieve a subset of data from the database, such as a set of records from a single table or set of records from multiple tables or queries. The SELECT statement instructs the Microsoft Jet database engine to return information from the database as a set of records. You can think of the Microsoft Jet database engine as a data manager component of a database management system that retrieves data from and stores data in user and system databases.

Syntax ▶

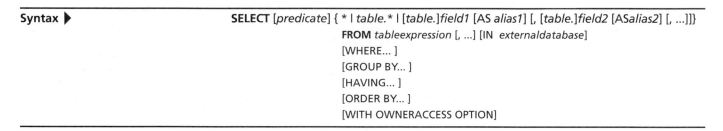

```
SELECT [predicate] { * | table.* | [table.]field1 [AS alias1] [, [table.]field2 [ASalias2] [, ...]]}
        FROM tableexpression [, ...] [IN externaldatabase]
        [WHERE... ]
        [GROUP BY... ]
        [HAVING... ]
        [ORDER BY... ]
        [WITH OWNERACCESS OPTION]
```

In this syntax, the *predicate* restricts the number of records returned. Acceptable predicates include ALL, DISTINCT, DISTINCTROW, or TOP. The default is ALL. The asterisk (*) selects all fields from the specified table or tables. *Table* is the name of the table containing the fields from which records are selected. *Field1, field2...* are the names of the fields containing the data you want to retrieve. If more than one field is included, the program retrieves the fields in the order listed. *Alias1* and *alias2* replace the original column names in a table with "alias" column headers. *Tableexpression* is the name of the table or tables containing the data you want to retrieve. *Externaldatabase* is the name of the database containing the tables in *tableexpression* if they are not in the current database.

To perform this operation, the Microsoft Jet database engine searches the specified table or tables, extracts the selected columns, selects rows that meet the criterion, and then sorts or groups the resulting rows into the order specified. The minimum syntax for a SELECT statement is SELECT *fields* FROM *table*. You use the other syntax expressions to define the query further. Example 7-7 shows a SELECT statement that retrieves all records from the TemporaryEmployees table and then sorts them by last name. Then the retrieved data is used to create the Master List of Temporary Employees detail report. Note that the statement ends with a semicolon.

Example 7-7 ▶

```
SELECT * FROM TemporaryEmployees ORDER BY LastName;
```

The SELECT statement does not change data in the database; it is used to create a new Recordset. Creating a new Recordset from the SQL SELECT statement requires the use of the OpenDatabase and OpenRecordSet methods.

The OpenDatabase method opens a specified database in a Workspace object and returns a reference to the Database object that represents it. If necessary, make sure that you select the Microsoft object library from the References command on the Project menu.

Syntax ▶

Set *database = workspace.***OpenDatabase** *(dbname, options, read-only, connect)*

In this syntax, *database* is an object variable that represents the Database object that you want to open. An **object variable** is a variable that references an object (`Dim dbsCurrent As Database`). *Workspace* is an optional object variable that represents the existing Workspace object that will contain the database. If no workspace is provided, OpenDatabase uses the default workspace. *Dbname* is a string that is the name of an existing Microsoft Jet database file. *Options* is a variant that sets various options for the database. *Read-only* is an optional Boolean value that is True if you want to open the database with read-only access or False (default) if you want to open the database with read-write access. *Connect* is an optional string that specifies connection information, including passwords. For a more detailed explanation, see online Help. Example 7-8 shows the database object, dbsCurrent, which uses the ShelyTemps.mdb database and the default workspace.

Example 7-8 ▶

```
Dim dbsCurrent As Database
Set dbsCurrent = OpenDatabase("A:\ShelyTemps.mdb")
```

The OpenRecordset method creates a new Recordset object and appends it to the Recordset collection. A Recordset collection contains all open Recordset objects in a Database object.

Syntax ▶

Set *recordset = object.***OpenRecordset** *(source, type, options, lockedits)*

In this syntax, *recordset* is an object variable that represents the Recordset object you want to open. *Object* is an object variable that represents an existing object from which you want to create the new Recordset. *Source* is a string specifying the source of the records for the new Recordset. The source can be a table name, a query name, or a SQL statement that returns records. *Type* is an optional constant that indicates the type of Recordset to open; *options* is an optional combination of constants that specify characteristics of the new Recordset; and *lockedits* is an optional constant that determines the locking for the Recordset. You will find more information about these arguments under Settings in online Help for the Open Recordset method. Example 7-9 shows the code necessary to create the Recordset rstNewTable as a selection of records from the ShelyTemps.mdb database ordered by employee's last name.

Example 7-9 ▶

```
Dim strQuery As String
Dim dbsCurrent As Database
Dim rstNewTable As Recordset
Set dbsCurrent = OpenDatabase("A:\ShelyTemps.mdb")
strQuery = "SELECT * FROM TemporaryEmployees ORDER BY LastName;"
Set rstNewTable = dbsCurrent.OpenRecordset(strQuery)
```

After creating the new Recordset, which is a subset of the original database, you can process the table using the Recordset methods you learned in Chapters 4 and 5. Figure 7-23 shows code from the MasterDetail subroutine that builds and prints the detail lines for the Master List detail report. You use the semicolon to indicate that variables in subsequent Printer.Print statements will appear on the same line as a previous Printer.Print statement. If a semicolon does not appear, the Printer object inserts a carriage return and line feed.

```
'Move to the first record in the Recordset
'For each record in the Recordset,
'store database fields as variables
'Build and print the detail line
  rstNewTable.MoveFirst
  Do While Not rstNewTable.EOF
    strEmployeeID = rstNewTable!EmployeeID
    strLastName = rstNewTable!LastName
    strFirstName = rstNewTable!FirstName
    strAddress = rstNewTable!Address
    strCity = rstNewTable!City
    strState = rstNewTable!State
    strZip = rstNewTable!Zip
    Listed = rstNewTable!Listed
    If Listed = True Then
        strPhone = "  (unlisted)"
    Else
        strPhone = rstNewTable!Phone
    End If
    Printer.Print strEmployeeID;
    Printer.Print Tab(5); strLastName + ", " + strFirstName;
    Printer.Print Tab(30); strAddress + ", " + strCity + _
        ", " + strState + ", " + strZip;
    Printer.Print Tab(90); strPhone
    rstNewTable.MoveNext
  Loop
```

Figure 7-23: Building and printing detail lines

The query retrieves each field for the report from the new Recordset object (rstNewTable) and assigns its value to a variable. Then the Print method of the Printer object prints the data. A sample detail line prints as follows:

```
186 Ambry, Sue Ann   862 Edgewater Lane, Riverview, WV, 68943   (405) 555-5476
```

When the program finishes using the table, the table is deleted.

Syntax ▶   *object.***Close**

In this syntax, the *object* placeholder is an object variable that represents an open database. Closing an open object removes it from the collection to which it is appended. The program ignores an attempt to close the default workspace. Example 7-10 shows the code to close the current database.

Example 7-10 ▶   `dbsCurrent.Close`

Exercise 7.5 ▶

Coffee Haus requires an exception report that lists the coffee flavor preferences for its flavored coffee customers. Figure 7-24 shows the required report detail. In this exercise, you will use the Printer object and the SQL SELECT statement to generate the detail report.

  a. Open the file Ex7-5.vbp from the Chapter7 folder on your Student Disk, and then save the project as Ex7-5a.vbp. Save any forms and modules as part of the new project.

  b. Add the CHHeader.bas module from the Chapter7 folder on your Student Disk to the project.

  c. In the mnuFileRepFlavor_Click Event procedure, complete the following:

    1. Declare variables of the Database and Recordset data type as well as string variables to hold the query and report title.

    2. Generate the standard report header by calling the CHStandardHeader Sub procedure.

    3. Format and print the report title.

    4. Using the record layout in Figure 7-24, design and generate code to print the report column headings. Remember to use the Tab function to position output.

    5. Open the database and create a query to select records from the database in CustName order.

    6. Create a Recordset using the created query.

    7. Move to the first record in the Recordset.

    8. While there are records in the Recordset, generate and print the customer name, phone number, and flavored coffee preferences for customers who have indicated a preference for purchasing flavored coffee.

    9. Close the database and send the report to the printer.

  d. Save and run the program. Print the report.

  e. Examine the report and make any necessary tab adjustments until the report looks like the record layout in Figure 7-24.

  f. When you are satisfied that the report is successfully generated, create an executable file named Ex7-5a.exe.

```
Mon ##, ####                Coffee Haus Wholesale Distributors                    Page: ##
                                  Coffee Flavor Preferences

          Customer                                                    Flavor Preference
           Name                              Phone               Mocha  Hazelnut  Amaretto
xxxxxxxxxxxxxxxxxxxxxxxxxxxxxxxxxxxxxxx   (###) ###-####            *        *         *

xxxxxxxxxxxxxxxxxxxxxxxxxxxxxxxxxxxxxxx   (###) ###-####            *

xxxxxxxxxxxxxxxxxxxxxxxxxxxxxxxxxxxxxxx   (###) ###-####                     *

xxxxxxxxxxxxxxxxxxxxxxxxxxxxxxxxxxxxxxx   (###) ###-####                               *
```

Figure 7-24: Coffee Flavor Preferences report

Exercise 7.6 ▶

Melanie's Mall requires a report that will generate a list of stores from one of the four sections of the mall. These sections are identified as A, B, C, or D in the first position of the location field. In this exercise, you will generate an exception report based on the section code indicated by the user in an input box. A portion of the code is saved on your Student Disk.

    a. Open the file Ex7-6.vbp from the Chapter7 folder on your Student Disk, and then save the project as Ex7-6a.vbp. Save any forms and modules as part of the new project.

    b. Run the program and select the Stores by Section menu item from the Reports menu to print the existing exception report.

    c. In the mnuFileRepSection_Click() Event procedure, add the code necessary to generate the store name and location for stores in the required section (strCode). Center and double space the report body under the existing column headings. You might need to move the code that prints the standard header to avoid printing the header more than once.

    d. Save, run, and print the report.

    e. When you are satisfied that the report is correct, create an executable file named Ex7-6a.exe.

Writing Code

You learned about the frmMaster interface for the TEMS system in Chapter 6. In this chapter, you completed the event code associated with printing reports; now you can print reports from the frmPrint interface. You can use the cmdPrintReports() Event procedure from the File menu or use the Print Reports command button. Figure 7-25 shows the code window for the cmdPrintReports_Click() Event procedure.

Figure 7-25: The cmdPrintReports_Click() Event procedure

The cmdPrintReports_Click() Event Procedure

The cmdPrintReports_Click() Event procedure uses the PassWordCheck subroutine to verify that the user has print access to the reports. Print access is based on the access code calculated and stored in a data array. If access is denied, then the user returns to the frmMaster interface. If access is granted, the frmPrint interface appears using the Show method. The first time frmPrint is displayed, the form must be retrieved from the disk. All subsequent occurrences of the frmPrint.Show statement will display the form on the screen from memory. The form is superimposed on the frmMaster interface.

Code Modules for Printing

Three code modules exist for generating required reports using the Printer object. PrintMasterList is the user-defined code module used to create the Master List of Temporary Employees detail report shown in Figure 7-26. The code module consists of three subroutines: MasterHeader, MasterDetail, and MasterFooter. **Modularization**, or the process of dividing a task into multiple subtasks, is an integral part of application development for the TEMS system. Dividing the detail report into these three subroutines simplifies the debugging process by allowing the programmer to focus on fewer lines of code at once. Several of the subroutines, for example the header subroutines, could be combined. The subroutines are kept separate here for clarity.

```
March 28, 1999            Shely Services Human Resource System            Page: 1
                          Master List of Temporary Employees


Empe
 ID       Name                          Address                           Phone

 186   Ambry, Sue Ann       862 Edgewater Lane Riverview, WV, 68943      (405) 555-5476

 182   Danier, Debra        616 Main St., Manorton, OH, 54277           (612) 555-8733

 143   DeLaney, Sara        9532 Overbrook Dr., Columbine, KY, 66872     (668) 555-7732

 117   Jamison, Mariam      816 Pine Street, Riverview, WV 68943           (unlisted)

 114   Kingsley, MariBeth   6532 Shannon Court Apt. 14, Riverview, WV 68943  (405) 555-3654

 124   Kingstanley, Roberta 7733 Lane Road, Manorton, OH, 54277         (606) 555-0123

 142   Lancer, Caroline     827 Oak Rd., Columbine, KY, 66872            (688) 555-7644

 118   Masters, Lawrence    873 Bookwood Lane, Riverview, WV, 11234        (unlisted)

 131   Mathews, Lora        1927 April Lane, Riverview, WV, 68943        (668) 555-5512

 183   Mayberry, Kenneth    183 Pinebrook Terrace, Columbine, KY 66872   (668) 555-2763

 146   McCumber, Janice     1414 Coastal Lane, Columbine, KY 66872         (unlisted)

 166   Noble, Wandra        818 College Ave., Riverview, OH, 68943       (405) 555-5543

 108   Rogers, Berry        1220 Main St., Apt. 17, Columbine, KY, 66872 (668) 555-9954


                       End of Master List of Temporary Employees
```

Figure 7-26: Master List of Temporary Employees report

Figure 7-27 shows the MasterHeader subroutine used to generate the heading lines on the detail report. The heading lines include the report header (date, system, and page number), report title, and column headings. This subroutine uses the Printer object and its associated properties as defined in Figure 7-15. You use the ScaleLeft and CurrentX properties to place the insertion point at the left margin. The program code computes a new CurrentX position by subtracting the

TextWidth from the ScaleWidth and dividing by two to get the midway point for printing the report header in the center of the page. In a similar fashion, the program prints the page number at the right edge of the page by computing a new CurrentX as ScaleWidth minus TextWidth. You change the font, style, and size using the FontBold, FontName, FontSize properties. After the insertion point placement is established, the Printer.Print *variable*[;] form of the Print property prints the data. When the semicolon is used, the variable is printed without appending a carriage return and line feed.

```
Public Sub MasterHeader()
'Declare variables
   Dim strHeader As String, strPageNumber As String
   Dim strTitle As String
'Set font and font size
   Printer.FontName = "Courier New"
   Printer.FontSize = 10
'Print 2 blank lines
   Printer.Print
   Printer.Print
'Print the date at the left margin
   Printer.CurrentX = Printer.ScaleLeft
   Printer.Print Format(Date$, "mmm dd, yyyy");
'Center and print the standard report header
   strHeader = "Shely Services Human Resource System"
   Printer.CurrentX = _
      (Printer.ScaleWidth - Printer.TextWidth(strHeader)) / 2
   Printer.Print strHeader;
'Print the page number at the right margin
   strPageNumber = "Page: " + Format$(Printer.Page, "###")
   Printer.CurrentX = _
      Printer.ScaleWidth - Printer.TextWidth(strPageNumber)
   Printer.Print strPageNumber
   Printer.Print
'Set the font size and style, center the report title
   Printer.FontSize = 14
   Printer.FontBold = True
   strTitle = "Master List of Temporary Employees"
   Printer.CurrentX = _
      (Printer.ScaleWidth - Printer.TextWidth(strTitle)) / 2
'Print report title
   Printer.Print strTitle
```

Figure 7-27: The MasterHeader subroutine

```
'Set font size, reset style to regular for column headings

  Printer.FontBold = False

  Printer.FontSize = 9

  Printer.Print

  Printer.Print

  Printer.Print Tab(1); "Empe";

  Printer.Print

  Printer.Print Tab(2); "ID";

  Printer.Print Tab(11); "Name";

  Printer.Print Tab(46); "Address";

  Printer.Print Tab(95); "Phone";

End Sub
```

Figure 7-27: The MasterHeader subroutine (continued)

The code for the footer subroutines and header subroutines for the exception and control break reports use the same Printer properties to accomplish the desired effect. You can view this code by opening the completed Ch7Shely.vbp project from the Chapter7 folder on your Student Disk.

Figure 7-28 shows the code module for the MasterDetail subroutine. After creating an instance of a database object (dbsCurrent) and a Recordset object (rstNewTable), the OpenDatabase and OpenRecordset methods create a table of all employee records sorted by last name. Code within a Do While loop is executed to retrieve data from the new table until the end of file condition is raised. Within the loop, each field in the table is stored in a string variable and subsequently printed using the Tab method and the concatenation operator. The MoveNext method retrieves the next record prior to the Loop statement. The Close method closes the open database when it reaches the end of the new table file.

```
Public Sub MasterDetail()

'Declare variables

  Dim strEmployeeID As String, strLastName As String

  Dim strFirstName As String

  Dim strAddress As String, strCity As String

  Dim strState As String

  Dim strZip As String, strPhone As String

  Dim dbsCurrent As Database

  Dim rstNewTable As Recordset

  Dim strQuery As String

  Dim Listed As Boolean
```

Figure 7-28: The MasterDetail subroutine

```
'Set detail font and size
  Printer.FontName = "Courier New"
  Printer.FontSize = 9
  Printer.Print
  Printer.Print
'Create a Recordset of database data sorted by last name
  Set dbsCurrent = OpenDatabase("A:\ShelyTemps.mdb")
  strQuery = _
    "SELECT * FROM TemporaryEmployees ORDER BY LastName;"
  Set rstNewTable = dbsCurrent.OpenRecordset(strQuery)
'Move to the first record in the Recordset
'For each record in the Recordset,
'store database fields as variables
'Build and print the detail line
  rstNewTable.MoveFirst
  Do While Not rstNewTable.EOF
    strEmployeeID = rstNewTable!EmployeeID
    strLastName = rstNewTable!LastName
    strFirstName = rstNewTable!FirstName
    strAddress = rstNewTable!Address
    strCity = rstNewTable!City
    strState = rstNewTable!State
    strZip = rstNewTable!Zip
    Listed = rstNewTable!Listed
    If Listed = True Then
      strPhone = "  (unlisted)"
    Else
      strPhone = rstNewTable!Phone
    End If
    Printer.Print strEmployeeID;
    Printer.Print Tab(5); strLastName + ", " + strFirstName;
    Printer.Print Tab(30); strAddress + ", " + strCity + _
      ", " + strState + ", " + strZip;
    Printer.Print Tab(90); strPhone
    rstNewTable.MoveNext
  Loop
    dbsCurrent.Close
End Sub
```

Figure 7-28: The MasterDetail subroutine (continued)

PrintAvailableList is the user-defined code module that creates the Unassigned Temporary Employees exception report shown in Figure 7-29. The code module consists of three subroutines: AvailableHeader, AvailableDetail, and AvailableFooter.

```
March 28, 1999            Shely Services Human Resource System            Page: 1


                            Unassigned  Temporary  Employees


   Employee   Employee                        Availability                        Typing
      ID        Name       Secretary   Clerical   Industrial   Marketing          WPM

      182    Danier, Debra      *                                     *            55

      124    Kingstanley, Roberta   *                   *                          20

      142    Lancer, Caroline              *

      118    Masters, Lawrence             *

      166    Noble, Wandra      *                       *             *            84

      108    Rogers, Berry                 *


                        End of Available Temporary Employees
```

Figure 7-29: Sample unassigned Temporary Employees report

Figure 7-30 shows the code for the AvailableDetail subroutine. As an exception report, the AvailableDetail subroutine needs to filter the database and capture only those records where the JobID is 000. The SELECT statement accomplishes this task and stores the data in the new Recordset object.

```
Public Sub AvailableDetail()
'Declare variables
  Dim dbsCurrent As Database
  Dim rstNewTable As Recordset
  Dim strQuery As String
'Create a Recordset of database data where JobID = 000
  Set dbsCurrent = OpenDatabase("A:\ShelyTemps.mdb")
  strQuery = "SELECT * From TemporaryEmployees WHERE JobID = '" & "000" & "' ORDER BY LastName;"
  Set rstNewTable = dbsCurrent.OpenRecordset(strQuery)
'Move to the first record in the Recordset
'For each record in the Recordset,
'build and print the detail line
'Use asterisks to indicate placement preference
  rstNewTable.MoveFirst
  Do While Not rstNewTable.EOF
    Printer.Print "   " & rstNewTable!EmployeeID;
    strName = rstNewTable!LastName + ", " + rstNewTable!FirstName
    Printer.Print "   " & Left$(strName, 25);
```

Figure 7-30: The AvailableDetail subroutine

```
      If rstNewTable!Secretarial Then

         Printer.Print Tab(34); "*";

      End If

      If rstNewTable!Clerical Then

         Printer.Print Tab(44); "*";

      End If

      If rstNewTable!Industrial Then

         Printer.Print Tab(54); "*";

      End If

      If rstNewTable!Marketing Then

         Printer.Print Tab(64); "*";

      End If

      If rstNewTable!Typing = 0 Then

         Printer.Print

      Else

         Printer.Print Tab(70); rstNewTable!Typing

      End If

      rstNewTable.MoveNext

   Loop

   dbsCurrent.Close

End Sub
```

Figure 7-30: The AvailableDetail subroutine (continued)

The Unassigned Temporary Employees report detail requires the employee ID, employee name, placement preference availability, and typing speed where indicated. You use an asterisk to record an available employee's placement preference. You use multiple If statements instead of the Select...Case structure because an employee might have more than one placement preference. The Do While loop performs detail record processing until the end of file condition is raised.

PrintJobListing is the user-defined code module used to create the Current Job Assignments for Temporary Employees control break report shown in Figure 7-31. The code module consists of three subroutines: JobHeader, PrintControlBreak, and JobFooter.

```
March 28, 1999              Shely Services Human Resource System           Page: 1
                     Current Job Assignments for Temporary Employees


                           110 Mama's Pizza and Subs


                             114 Kingsley, Maribeth
                             183 Mayberry, Kenneth



                                                            Number of Employees = 2



                           127 Libby's Puzzle Emporium


                             186 Ambry, Sue Ann
                             117 Jamison, Mariam
                             146 McCumber, Janice



                                                            Number of Employees = 3



                           128 Katzenbacher's Bakery
                                  (Unassigned)


                           161 Landmark Systems, Inc.


                             143 DeLaney, Sara
                             131 Mathews, Lora



                                                            Number of Employees = 2


                                                                Total Number = 7

                    End of List of Temporary Employees Job Assignments
```

Figure 7-31: Current Job Assignments for Temporary Employees report

Figure 7-32 shows the PrintControlBreak subroutine. This control break report uses the CurrentJobs and the TemporaryEmployees tables to report employees located at each job assignment. You use nested repetition structures based on the number of control fields to perform control break processing. The control field for the Current Job Assignments report is the JobID. When there is a change in JobID in the CurrentJobs table, the total number of employees associated with the old JobID is printed.

```
Public Sub PrintControlBreak()

'Declare variables

  Dim dbsCurrent As Database

  Dim rstJobTable As Recordset

  Dim rstNewTable As Recordset

  Dim strJobQuery As String

  Dim strEmployeeQuery As String

  Dim intNumberOfEmployees As Integer

'Set font and size, print two blank lines

  Printer.FontName = "Courier New"

  Printer.FontSize = 12

  Printer.Print

  Printer.Print

'Create a Recordset of database data ordered by Job ID

  Set dbsCurrent = OpenDatabase("A:\ShelyTemps.mdb")


  strQuery = "SELECT * FROM CurrentJobs ORDER BY JobID"

  Set rstJobTable = dbsCurrent.OpenRecordset(strQuery)


'Move to the first record in the Recordset

  rstJobTable.MoveFirst

'For each record in the Recordset,

'Print the Job ID and Job Title

  Do While Not rstJobTable.EOF

    Printer.Print Tab(25); rstJobTable!JobID & " ";

    Printer.FontUnderline = True

    Printer.Print rstJobTable!JobTitle

    Printer.FontUnderline = False

    Printer.Print

'The following line of text builds the employee query,

'selecting the required data fields

'and should be keyed in on one line

    strEmployeeQuery = "SELECT EmployeeID, LastName, FirstName FROM
TemporaryEmployees WHERE JobID = '" & rstJobTable!JobID & "' ORDER
BY LastName;"
```

Figure 7-32: The PrintControlBreak subroutine

```
        Set rstNewTable = _
            dbsCurrent.OpenRecordset(strEmployeeQuery)
    'If there are no records for the current job, print Unassigned
            If rstNewTable.RecordCount = 0 Then
                    Printer.Print Tab(37); "(Unassigned)"
                    GoTo Continue
            End If


            rstNewTable.MoveFirst
    'For each record in the Recordset until the Job ID changes
    'print the assigned employee data
            Do While Not rstNewTable.EOF
                Printer.Print Tab(32); rstNewTable!EmployeeID;
                Printer.Print Tab(37);
                Printer.Print rstNewTable!LastName & ", ";
                Printer.Print rstNewTable!FirstName
                rstNewTable.MoveNext
            Loop
    'When there is a change in Job ID, print the total
    'number of employees assigned to the job
            Printer.Print
            Printer.Print Tab(50);
            Printer.Print "Number of Employees = ";
            Printer.Print rstNewTable.RecordCount
            intNumberOfEmployees = _
                intNumberOfEmployees + rstNewTable.RecordCount
    Continue:
            Printer.Print
            rstNewTable.Close
            rstJobTable.MoveNext
      Loop
    'At the end of the Recordset, print the total
    'number of employees for the last Job ID
        Printer.Print Tab(60);
        Printer.Print "Total Number = " & intNumberOfEmployees
        dbsCurrent.Close
    End Sub
```

Figure 7-32: The PrintControlBreak subroutine (continued)

The first Do While structure processes the JobID data. For each new job, the program prints the JobID and JobTitle. Then a SELECT statement builds a table from the TemporaryEmployees table that contains the EmployeeID, LastName, and FirstName of all employees with the current JobID. If there are no employees assigned to the current JobID, then the program prints the "(Unassigned)" message.

The second (internal) Do While structure processes the detail information from the newly created Recordset object for the current job. When this table has been completely processed, the program prints the total number of employees for that JobID, closes the Recordset, and obtains a new record from the CurrentJobs table. Processing continues in this way until all jobs in the CurrentJobs table have been processed. When the program reaches the end of the CurrentJobs table, it prints the total number of employees using the RecordCount property.

Syntax ▶   *object.***RecordCount**

In this syntax, *object* is the name of the Recordset object. The **RecordCount property** returns the number of records accessed in a Recordset object. Example 7-10 uses the RecordCount property to store the number of records in the intNumberOfEmployees variable.

Example 7-11 ▶   `intNumberOfEmployees = rstNewTable.RecordCount`

Exercise 7.7 ▶

Coffee Haus staff require a control break report listing customers by state code. When there is a change in state code, the report should print the total number of customers in the previous state. Figure 7-33 shows the report layout. In this exercise, you will create the control break report.

  a. Open the file Ex7-7.vbp from the Chapter7 folder on your Student Disk, and then save the project as Ex7-7a.vbp. Save any forms and modules as part of the new project.
  b. Use the following pseudocode to code the mnuFileRepCustbyState_Click() event:
    1. Declare Database and Recordset variables.
    2. Declare strings to contain the query, report title, saved state code, and control break message.
    3. Declare an integer variable to contain the customer count.
    4. Call the Sub procedure CHStandardHeader to print the report header.
    5. Print the report title and column headings.
    6. Open the database and create the query.
    7. While there are records in the Recordset, save the state, initialize the customer count, and print the state code for each state.
    8. Within the previous repetition structure, create an inner loop to print the detail if the Recordset state code equals the saved state code.
    9. When there is a change in state, print customer totals.
    10. Close the database and release the report to the printer.
  c. Save and run the program. Examine the report and include Printer.Print statements in the code where necessary to allow for spacing indicated in the record layout.
  d. When you are satisfied that the program executes successfully, create an executable file named Ex7-7a.exe.

```
Mon ##, ####              Coffee Haus Wholesale Distributors              Page: ##
                                   Customers by State
              Customer Name                   Owner                   Phone
State Code: xx

xxxxxxxxxxxxxxxxxxxxxxxxxxxxxxxxxxxx     xxxxxxxxxxxxxxxxxxxxxxxxxx      (###) ###-####


xxxxxxxxxxxxxxxxxxxxxxxxxxxxxxxxxxxx     xxxxxxxxxxxxxxxxxxxxxxxxxx      (###) ###-####


                                                             Number of customers = #


State Code: xx

xxxxxxxxxxxxxxxxxxxxxxxxxxxxxxxxxxxx     xxxxxxxxxxxxxxxxxxxxxxxxxx      (###) ###-####


xxxxxxxxxxxxxxxxxxxxxxxxxxxxxxxxxxxx     xxxxxxxxxxxxxxxxxxxxxxxxxx      (###) ###-####


xxxxxxxxxxxxxxxxxxxxxxxxxxxxxxxxxxxx     xxxxxxxxxxxxxxxxxxxxxxxxxx      (###) ###-####


xxxxxxxxxxxxxxxxxxxxxxxxxxxxxxxxxxxx     xxxxxxxxxxxxxxxxxxxxxxxxxx      (###) ###-####


                                                             Number of customers = #
```

Figure 7-33: Coffee Haus Customers by State report

Exercise 7.8 ▶

Melanie's Mall requires a Mall Store Locations report that prints the stores in order by location. After viewing the report found in Ex7-8.vbp, your employer requests that you modify the report to indicate the stores by section, preceded by a "Stores in Section X" message, and include a summary of the number of stores by section. You should remember that the section code is found in the first position in the location field. If necessary, use online Help to learn how to use the Left function. The record layout provided in Figure 7-34 indicates the placement of the control header and total data. In this exercise, you will modify the code to include the control header and total data.

    a. Open the file Ex7-8.vbp from the Chapter7 folder on your Student Disk, and then save the project as Ex7-8a.vbp. Save any forms and modules as part of the new project.

    b. In the mnuFileRepLocation_Click() Event procedure, add the code necessary to include control header and total data as required by your employer.

    c. Save and run the application. Print the report.

    d. When you are satisfied that the control header and totals are appropriately placed, create an executable file named Ex7-8a.exe.

```
##/##/####                        Melanie's Mall                        Page: ##

                                 Mall Store Locations

        Location                    Store Name                      Contact

Stores in Section X

           xx              xxxxxxxxxxxxxxxxxxxxxxxxxxxxx       xxxxxxxxxxxxxxxxxxxxx

           xx              xxxxxxxxxxxxxxxxxxxxxxxxxxxxx       xxxxxxxxxxxxxxxxxxxxx

           xx              xxxxxxxxxxxxxxxxxxxxxxxxxxxxx       xxxxxxxxxxxxxxxxxxxxx


                                                             Number of stores = #


Stores in Section X


           xx              xxxxxxxxxxxxxxxxxxxxxxxxxxxxx       xxxxxxxxxxxxxxxxxxxxx

           xx              xxxxxxxxxxxxxxxxxxxxxxxxxxxxx       xxxxxxxxxxxxxxxxxxxxx


                                                             Number of stores = #
```

Figure 7-34: Melanie's Mall Mall Store Location report

SUMMARY

This chapter adds a mechanism for generating reports for the TEMS system. You used the SQL SELECT statement to filter the database and to create a new table for each report that contains only the necessary data. You generated detail, exception, and control break reports using Visual Basic's Printer object. You used the Crystal Reports add-in to generate a current jobs report. The Unassigned Employees report is available for the screen. The TEMS system continues to use subroutine calls for efficiency. Figure 7-35 shows the Project Explorer window for the TEMS application in its current form. Make sure that you examine each module carefully and note the grouping of subroutines together by function. Run the Ch7Shely.vbp file and validate the performance of the system.

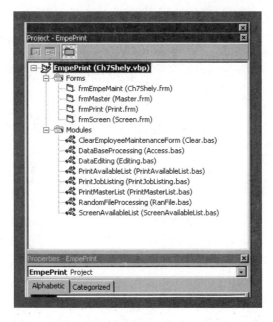

Figure 7-35: Project Explorer window for the TEMS system

Exercise 7.9 ▶

Coffee Haus staff would like to have access to the Print dialog box that is available with all of their other Windows standard applications. In this exercise, you will modify each of the Coffee Haus reports to show the Print dialog box prior to printing the report. The user should not be allowed to print the report to a file, include page numbers, or choose the Selection option.

   a. Open the file Ex7-9.vbp from the Chapter7 folder on your Student Disk, and then save the project as Ex7-9a.vbp. Save any forms and modules as part of the new project.

   b. Add the CommonDialog control to the frmCustData form. Name the control dlgPrint.

   c. Set the dlgPrint control's PrinterDefault property to False to avoid resetting the Win.ini file.

   d. In the menu Event procedures for each report, set the Flags property for the dlgPrint CommonDialog control to hide and disable the Print to file option, disable page number printing, and disable the Selection option. Use online Help to discover the appropriate constants.

   e. Insert the ShowPrinter method in the menu event for each of the reports.

   f. Save and run the application.

   g. When you are satisfied that the CommonDialog control is functioning properly for each report, create an executable file named Ex7-9a.exe.

Exercise 7.10 ▶

Employees working the Information Desk at Melanie's Mall would like to have the option of printing the Stores by Section report to the screen in order to help customers locate a store immediately. In this exercise, you will add code to the Sub procedure ScreenPrint to print the report to the screen when requested. A portion of the code is saved on your Student Disk.

   a. Open the file Ex7-10.vbp from the Chapter7 folder on your Student Disk, and then save the project as Ex7-10a.vbp. Save any forms and modules as part of the new project. The form frmScreen has been added to the project for use in displaying the report on the screen.

   b. Examine the mnuFileRepSection_Click() Event procedure. Code has been added to the routine to ask the user if they would like to print the report to the screen. In addition, the code to print the section report has been moved to a Sub procedure named PrintSectionReport in the SectionReport module.

   c. Code the ScreenPrint Sub procedure in the ScreenPrinter module to print the report to the frmScreen form. (*Hint*: The code to print the report to the printer already exists. This code can be copied to the ScreenPrint Sub procedure and modified to print the report to the form. Replace the call to MMHeader with MMHeader code and modify the code to print the header to the form.) Remember to use the Show method to display the frmScreen form.

   d. Save and run the application.

   e. When you are satisfied that the program executes successfully, create an executable file named Ex7-10a.exe.

PROGRESSIVE PROJECTS

1. Bean County Plumbing Inventory System (BCPIS)

BCPIS needs three printed reports using the header and footer formats and the detail lines shown in the chapter for the Shely project. (These reports are described in Chapter 1.) When you are testing column headings, you can save paper by sending the output to a form first. When you are satisfied with the alignment of data on the form, you can send the output to the printer.

For the third report, consider beginning with the MastInv table, and retrieving data from the other two tables as needed. Use internal Do While structures.

Because many people will see and use the printed reports, they must be designed with care—a report is always a reflection upon its designer. Save the report as Ch7BCPIS in the Chapter7 folder on your Student Disk. Use descriptive names for the new Sub procedures you create. Remember to maintain a backup copy of your work.

2. Single Parents Public Service Library (SPLIB)

SPLIB needs three reports and special display forms using the header and footer formats and the detail lines shown in the chapter for the Shely project. (These reports are described in Chapter 1.) Each of the three reports follows the respective formatting and programming structures for the reports described in this chapter. Make sure that you design each report carefully and professionally so it will be easy for the user to understand its information. SPLIB wants to be proud of its system.

Volunteers also must be able to display data on the screen. You must make provisions for volunteers to enter an item ID and then have the program display the name of the member or guest who currently has the item if it is out. A volunteer also should be able to enter a member or a guest's identification number and have a list of all items borrowed by that person displayed on the screen (the second report). Make sure that you test the code for accurate results. Save the project as Ch7SPLIB in the Chapter7 folder on your Student Disk. Use descriptive names for the new Sub procedures that you create. Remember to maintain a backup copy of your work.

3. Short Cut Lawn Service (SCLS)

SCLS needs three reports and two special forms with Help menus. (These reports are described in Chapter 1. You will learn about Help menus in Chapter 9.) Each report must be professional in appearance and must print the data accurately. Because the spacing for the column headings might be a little difficult to program on the first pass, you should test reports on a form before directing the output to the printer. The formatting and programming for each of the reports is outlined in this chapter.

SCLS also requires two forms with logos. When an employee enters the identification of a unit, the data for that unit will display on the screen. The Notes field will appear as a scrollable object. Employees also must be able to enter the identification for a unit and have the names of the clients assigned to that unit displayed (the third report). Make sure that the data displayed are absolutely correct. Save the project as Ch7SCLS in the Chapter7 folder on your Student Disk. Use descriptive names for the new Sub procedures that you create. Remember to maintain a backup copy of your work.

INDEPENDENT PROJECTS

For each of the independent projects, you will develop a small database. If necessary, add the Project\References\Microsoft 2.5\3.5 Compatibility Library to the project.

1. Jim's Bronze Collection

Jim collects antique bronze items, from old locks to ship's bells. He wants a list of his items and a list of items with a value of more than $500, printed in incremental values of $500. He wants to define each item by using an identification number, a name, a description (note), a measure of size (small, medium, or large), and a value. The first report must include all details. The second report should list the ID, name, and value for each item, along with unit and total values. Save the form, project, and database as Ch7IP1.

2. Libby's Cup and Saucer Collection

Libby collects a certain type of antique cups and saucers. Over the years, Libby's collection has grown in size, but the cups and saucers now are difficult to find. Libby wants a list of the items in her collection and a list of the more valuable and rare items so that she can trade less valuable items for items with greater value. Each set has an identification number based on the imprint on the set (J001 through J999, and G001 through G999), a description (note), the quality (excellent, good, or fair), and an estimated value.

Create a database and develop the two reports. The second report must list a total value, with breaks and subtotals for dollar values for $0 to $10.99, $11.00 to $25.99, $26.00 to $50.99, $50.00 to $75.99, and $76.00 and over. Save the form, project, and database as Ch7IP2.

3. Jen's Cat Collection

Jen collects miniature cat figures, some of which are valuable. Jen wants a list of all cats, sorted by type, with control breaks and subtotals. She would also like a list of all figures with a value over $10 and grand total value for her collection.

Create a database with an identification code for each figure (xnnn), where x is the figure type (p for porcelain, b for bronze, c for coal, etc.) and nnn is a number from 001 to 999. The database also should contain a brief description, a full description (note), and an estimated value for each figure. Save the form, project, and database as Ch7IP3.

Advanced Visual Basic Topics

Introduction ▶ Now that you have completed the Shely Services Temporary Employee Record (SSTER) interface and generated the required reports, you need to complete the final steps in the project. There is an old saying among systems analysts that you can complete 90% of a project in 90% of the allotted time, but completing the last 10% of the project might take another 90% of your allocated time. Hopefully, this will not be the case here.

You will update the TEMS system in this chapter to trap errors that could occur as a result of user actions. The TEMS system makes extensive use of file processing. Numerous errors might occur if user actions are not accomplished in the appropriate order. For example, an error will occur if the disk containing the appropriate files is not located in drive A as specified in the program code. You must plan for this problem and many other errors by trapping such errors.

In this chapter you will generate the corporate database from the sequential file you created in Chapter 3 and provide a routine to back up the ShelyTemps.mdb database. Finally, you will learn about ActiveX controls, which now are known as COM or component object modules.

Processing Errors

In its current form, the TEMS system uses methods available within Visual Basic for trapping and processing errors. In the DataEditing module, for example, code was added to ensure that all data were entered. Passwords identify secure entry to the database. You have used the MsgBox function extensively to inform the user of processing errors. For example, Figure 8-1 shows the message box that appears if the user fails to enter a valid password when requested or enters an invalid password.

Figure 8-1: MsgBox for invalid password

When you are developing a Visual Basic application, you most likely will encounter programming errors along the way. A **programming error** is any error in a program that causes the program to end abnormally or produce unexpected results. Different types of programming errors include syntax errors, compile-time errors, run-time errors, and logic errors.

You have most likely encountered syntax errors in your programs. A **syntax error** occurs when you are writing the code. The **syntax** of a programming language is the set of rules that specifies the proper way to use the statements in the programming language. A syntax error occurs when a programmer enters a line of code that Visual Basic cannot understand. If you misspell a reserved word, such as Open, or incorrectly build an instruction, such as the assignment statement, Visual Basic issues a warning that you entered the statement incorrectly. You find syntax errors as you enter the code or when you compile a program. For example, the message box shown in Figure 8-2 indicates that the expression you entered is not complete. The statement `intCallingPoint = intCallingPoint *` needs an additional variable to complete the expression. This error, although indicated as a compile error, results during design time.

Figure 8-2: MsgBox for invalid expression syntax error

Compiling the program is the process of converting Visual Basic statements into statements that the computer can understand. When you encounter a syntax error, the message box that opens might be informative. For example, Figure 8-3 shows a message box that opens if a variable is not defined when the program is executed. Usually these errors are self-explanatory. Syntax and compile-time errors appear immediately and inform the programmer that any subsequent program execution will not be successful. In this example, after you click the OK button, a window displays, as shown in Figure 8-4, the line of code that contains the error in the associated message box.

Figure 8-3: MsgBox for variable not defined compile error

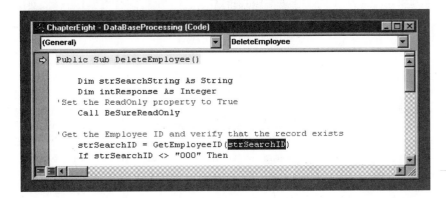

Figure 8-4: Code window identifying variable not defined

A **run-time error** occurs when your program is running and encounters an instruction that results in an invalid operation or an instruction that it cannot execute. Examples of instructions that result in an invalid operation include attempting to perform arithmetic with character data, trying to divide a number by zero, or trying to store too large a number into an integer variable. For example, the statement shown in Example 8-1 results in a run-time error because the programmer failed to convert the character data entered in the TextBox controls to numeric data using the Val function. If the user enters character data, the program fails.

Example 8-1 ▶

```
lblTotal.Caption = txtQuantity.Text * txtPrice.Text
```

To correct this error, use the following statement:
```
lblTotal.Caption = Val(txtQuantity.Text) * Val(txtPrice.Text)
```

The code shown in Example 8-2 does not guarantee that the user will enter a value in the input box. If the user does not enter a value, execution of the program will attempt to divide the value in intTotal by zero, the value that is a result of applying the Val function to a null string. You cannot divide by zero.

Example 8-2 ▶

```
intResponse = _
        Val(InputBox("Enter an integer:", "Divide By Zero Test"))
lblAverage.Caption = intTotal / intResponse
```

The programmer should use the If statement to verify that the value in intResponse is not zero prior to executing the calculation by using the following code:

```
If intResponse <> 0 Then
        lblAverage.Caption = intTotal / intResponse
End If
```

In Example 8-3, the programmer is attempting to store the value 100,000 in an integer variable, which will generate an overflow at run time. Integer variables can store only numbers in the range -32,768 to 32,767. The variable intPopulation should be declared as the Long data type as follows: `Dim lngPopulation As Long`.

Example 8-3 ▶

```
Dim intPopulation as Integer
intPopulation = 100000
```

The second type of run-time error occurs when instructions cannot be executed. These run-time errors might occur as the result of the user attempting events that the program code doesn't anticipate. For example, attempting to access a file on drive A when there is no disk in the drive or attempting to access a file that has been deleted results in a run-time error. The programmer must anticipate these types of errors.

Logic errors occur when the program produces incorrect results. For example, a logic error occurs when you intend to compute the sum of two numbers but inadvertently use the multiplication operator instead of the addition operator. If this operation results in a value that is too large for the receiving variable, then the logic error results in a run-time error. However, usually program execution continues and incorrect results are reported. When incorrect results are reported, the programmer must identify and correct the logic error.

In a business environment, there are absolutely no perfect programs. There are just too many possible permutations in a data set and a dynamic business changes too quickly for a programmer to anticipate everything that might happen. Consequently, the programming function does not end when a program is distributed to its user. Programs require maintenance, and the maintenance function is costly. One of the secrets to limiting program costs is to anticipate as many errors as possible. In addition, good documentation can minimize the time and the cost of program maintenance.

It is the programmer's responsibility to minimize the risk of a program terminating abnormally after it has been distributed to the user. The term used in industry to describe this abnormal termination is **ABEND**, which stands for **AB**normal **END**. A well-written and tested program rarely ABENDs. In the following sections you will learn how to program for errors that could result in the abnormal termination of a program.

Detecting File Processing Errors

When Visual Basic encounters a file error or a data error during program execution, it normally will send an error message to the terminal and then terminate the program. The programmer can use error-trapping mechanisms to intercept an error and instruct the program how to handle the error and continue processing. **Error**

trapping is the process of interrupting and handling a run-time error. You use Visual Basic's On Error statement to include error trapping in your code. The **On Error statement** enables an error-handling routine and specifies the location of the error-handling routine within a procedure. Normally, you should place the On Error statement at the beginning of the code procedure.

Syntax ▶   **On Error GoTo** *line/label*

In this syntax, the error-handling routine that starts at the location *line/label* is executed. The line argument is any line label or line number. If a run-time error occurs, control branches to *line/label* and the subsequent code is executed. The specified *line/label* must be in the same procedure as the On Error statement. The TEMS system makes use of the **On Error GoTo** *label* form of the statement.

Syntax ▶   **On Error Resume Next**

In this syntax, control goes to the statement immediately following the statement where the error occurred. Execution continues as if no error occurred.

Syntax ▶   **On Error GoTo 0**

In this syntax, any enabled error handler is disabled in the current procedure.

Failure to use an On Error statement causes any run-time error that occurs to be fatal. A **fatal error** is an error that results in an error message and termination of program execution.

In normal practice, you would have added the **On Error GoTo** *label* form of the On Error statement to the SequentialFileProcessing module created in Chapter 3 to trap any system-generated errors. These errors might result from the failure to find the specified file on the disk in drive A or because there is no disk in drive A. Figure 8-5 shows the modification to the OpenSequentialAppend subroutine code from Chapter 3.

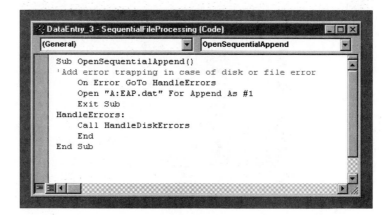

Figure 8-5: Use of the On Error statement

In this subroutine, any system-generated error causes control to pass to the HandleErrors: label and the HandleDiskErrors subroutine is called. The colon is required to indicate a line label. After the call to the subroutine in Figure 8-5 is executed, control returns to the line following the call to the subroutine and the program terminates. The attempt to open the EAP.dat file raises the error condition. The Open statement has been bypassed by the On Error GoTo statement.

Err Object and Error Function

When a run-time error occurs, the properties of the **Err object** are assigned data that uniquely identify the error and information that can be used to handle the error. The Err object is an object predefined by Visual Basic. The information stored in the Err object properties includes the:

- **Description property:** a short description of the error
- **Number property:** a numeric value representing the error
- **Source property:** the name of the object or program that generated the error

The **Error function** returns the error message that corresponds to a given error number.

Syntax ▶   **Error[(*errornumber*)]**

In this syntax, the optional *errornumber* argument can be any valid error number. If *errornumber* is a valid error number but is not defined, the Error function returns the string "Application-defined or object-defined error." When *errornumber* is omitted, the message corresponding to the most recent run-time error is returned. If no run-time error has occurred or *errornumber* is zero, the Error function returns a zero-length string (" ").

The return value of the Error function corresponds to the Description property of the Err object. You can find information about error numbers and messages in the Help system, or in system manuals (manuals for dedicated programs), such as Access. In this section, you will introduce a limited number of checks on the program to make sure that it generates the correct error messages. You will add error-handling checks that anticipate the types of errors that users might generate. Figure 8-6 shows the results of executing a program if there is no disk in drive A. The program reports the error number ('71') and an error description (Disk not ready). Figure 8-7 shows a method for anticipating and trapping this and other system errors.

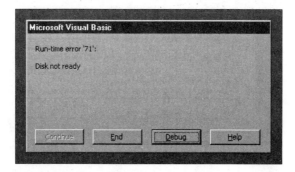

Figure 8-6: Disk not ready run-time error

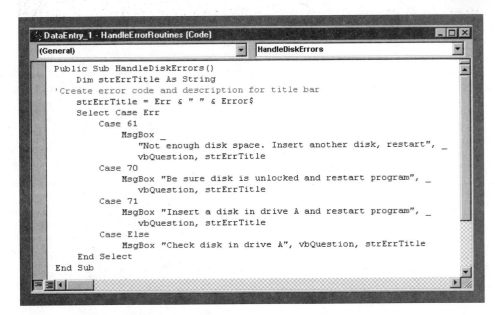

Figure 8-7: Trapping system errors

As a result of the code in Figure 8-7, the program does not abnormally terminate if there is no disk in the drive. The program uses the MsgBox statement to inform the user of the problem and instructs the user to restart the program. Figure 8-8 shows the message box that occurs.

Figure 8-8: MsgBox for Disk not ready error

There are other kinds of errors that can occur once the file is open and the program is running. What happens if someone takes the disk out of the disk drive and then tries to write a record? Probably nothing for the first record because Visual Basic only writes to the disk after the buffer attached to the file is full. Eventually, however, Visual Basic will try to write the records and then a system error screen will open to request that the user insert a disk or terminate the program by pressing the Esc key.

There is not much the programmer can do under normal programming circumstances that will work on all systems. If the system is caught in the middle of an operation and needs direction, the user either will have to reinsert the disk or terminate the program. If the user reinserts the disk, the program writes the records and continues. If the program is terminated, all data from the time of the last save will be lost. You should add a warning to the documentation that you provide to users so they know how to proceed when this type of error occurs.

The Resume Statement

Rather than having the program terminate, you may want to prompt the user to correct a trapped error and then continue program execution. The **Resume statement** resumes execution after an error-handling routine finishes. There are three forms of the Resume statement: Resume [0], Resume Next, and Resume *line*. You can explore the Resume [0] and Resume *line* using online Help. One form is the Resume Next statement.

Syntax ▶   **Resume Next**

The **Resume Next statement** is issued to cause the execution of the program to resume with the next executable statement. If the error occurred in the same procedure as the error handler, execution resumes with the statement immediately following the statement that caused the error. If the error occurred in a called procedure, execution resumes with the statement immediately following the statement that last called out of the procedure containing the error-handling routine. In the code shown in Figure 8-9, program control returns to the statement following the call to the OpenSequentialAppend() subroutine. The program tests the error code so that the program can continue executing. Note the use of Exit Sub to bypass the HandleErrors: label.

```
Sub OpenSequentialAppend()

    On Error GoTo HandleErrors

    Open "A:EAP.dat" For Append As #1

'processing would continue here

    Exit Sub

HandleErrors:

    Call HandleDiskErrors

    Resume Next

End Sub
```

Figure 8-9: Alternate error processing for the OpenSequentialAppend() subroutine

The Error Statement

Sometimes it is useful to generate your own errors to see if applications have completed as you expected. For example, opening a file for random access creates the file if it doesn't exist. In the case of the Shely application, the password array would contain no data. An error needs to be generated indicating that the array data was not loaded. The **Error statement** simulates the occurrence of an error.

Syntax ▶   **Error** *errornumber*

In this syntax, the required *errornumber* can be any valid error number or, as in this case, a user-generated error.

Figure 8-10 shows that Error 200 is generated if the array is not loaded. Execution of the program terminates so the user can supply a disk that contains the password data file. The number 200 has no meaning itself except that it is not one of the numbers assigned in the error number table in the Help system. You can view this code in the SetUpArray subroutine of the RandomFileProcessing module, which is in the Ch8Shely.vbp.

```
'Check the array for data
'If no data exists, generate error 200
    If strArray(1, 1) = "" Then
        Error 200
        GoTo HandleErrors
    End If
    Exit Sub  'bypass the error routine
HandleErrors:
    Select Case Err
        Case 70, 71  'missing data file
            frmMaster!lblMissingPasswords.Caption = _
                "Exit program, check file folder, restart program"
            frmMaster!lblMissingPasswords.Visible = True
        Case 200     'no data in file
            frmMaster!lblMissingPasswords.Caption = _
                "No passwords available" + vbNewLine + _
                "Exit program, check file, restart program"
            frmMaster!lblMissingPasswords.Visible = True
        Case Else    'generate error message
            frmMaster!lblMissingPasswords.Caption = _
                "Error:  Problem loading passwords," + vbNewLine + _
                "Check file and restart program"
            frmMaster!lblMissingPasswords.Visible = True
    End Select
```

Figure 8-10: Using a user-generated error

Since you don't want the program to display a message box and then end the program as shown in Figure 8-10, you can add a label named lblMissingPasswords, to the main form where messages can be displayed. The Label's properties are set so that the background color matches the form and the font is set to red.

As an alternative to the process described, you could write more extensive code to request the user to insert the proper disk. After a specified number of invalid attempts, the program could be terminated. In either case, the user needs to know what has happened and how to correct the problem.

Exercise 8.1 ▶

The Coffee Haus application needs a method for having the program capture and process an error when the user fails to insert the disk in drive A. Use the On Error statement to capture the error. In this exercise, you will add an On Error statement to capture the processing error when the disk is not in the drive.

    a. Open the file Ex8-1.vbp from the Chapter8 folder on your Student Disk, and then save the project as Ex8-1a.vbp. Save any forms and modules as part of the new project.

    b. Examine the ErrorHandler Sub procedure for the trappable errors captured by the Err object. When the program encounters one of these errors, the program should call the ErrorHandler Sub procedure. After displaying the MsgBox message, the program should terminate.

    c. Run the application. Notice that the program encounters a run-time error and the program terminates abnormally. End the application.

    d. In the Form_Load() Event procedure, code the On Error statement to go to the label DiskError. Examine the line of code that opens a file named NotThere for Input on drive A.

    e. Place the DiskError: label at the end of the code before the End Sub statement. Call the HandleError Sub procedure and add the End statement to end the application. Place an Exit Sub statement prior to the line label to bypass the error code for normal processing.

    f. Save and run the application.

    g. When you are satisfied that the program executes successfully, create an executable file named Ex8-1a.exe.

Exercise 8.2 ▶

The Melanie's Mall application needs a method for having the program capture and process the error when the user fails to insert the disk in drive A. Use the On Error statement to capture the error. In this exercise, you will add an On Error statement to capture the processing error when the disk is not in the drive.

    a. Open the file Ex8-2.vbp from the Chapter8 folder on your Student Disk, and save the project as Ex8-2a.vbp. Save any forms and modules as part of the new project.

    b. Run the application without placing a disk in drive A. Notice that the program encounters a run-time error and the program terminates abnormally. End the application.

    c. In the Form_Load() Event procedure, code the On Error statement to go to the label DiskError.

    d. Place the DiskError: label at the end of the code before the End Sub statement. To complete error handing, complete the following processing:

        1. Add a label control named lblMsg to the bottom of the screen, immediately to the left of the Data control. Set the AutoSize property to True, the Visible property to False, the Forecolor property to red, the Font property to Bold, and add a Caption of "Disk error, insert disk in drive and restart program."

        2. Following the DiskError: label, insert code to hide the Data control and display the label message.

        3. Add an Exit Sub statement prior to the line label to bypass the error code for normal processing.

        4. Make sure that the files MMStores.mdb and Ex7-2a.rpt are in the root directory on your Student Disk.

    e. Save and run the application without placing the disk in the drive.

    f. When you are satisfied that the program executes successfully, create an executable file named Ex8-2a.exe.

Trapping Special Errors

Another type of error occurs when objects generate their own errors that the program can ignore or handle. In Chapter 7, you added a CommonDialog control to use with print routines. You used the ShowPrinter method to display the CommonDialog control's Print dialog box. When the user clicked the Cancel button, the Cancel event was ignored and the report printed anyway. Using the CancelError property, the programmer can control program processing even more.

The **CancelError property** returns or sets a value indicating whether an error occurs when the user clicks the Cancel button. The default for the CancelError property is False. If the CancelError property is set to True, a run-time error occurs when the user clicks the Cancel button. The code shown in Figure 8-11 for the cmdDetailReport_Click() Event procedure causes execution to transfer to the HandleErrors: label when the user clicks the Cancel button. As a result, the detail report is not generated and the subroutine ends.

```
Private Sub cmdDetailReport_Click()

  Dim intNumberCopies As Integer
'If the user clicks the Cancel button in the
'print dialog box, exit the subroutine
  On Error GoTo HandleErrors
'Set property flags
  dlgPrint.Flags = cdlPDDisablePrintToFile + _
     cdlPDHidePrintToFile + cdlPDNoPageNums + _
     cdlPDNoSelection
'Use ShowPrinter method to display print dialog box
  dlgPrint.ShowPrinter
'Build report
  For intNumberCopies = 1 To dlgPrint.Copies
     Call MasterHeader
     Call MasterDetail
     Call MasterFooter
     Printer.EndDoc
  Next intNumberCopies
  Exit Sub
HandleErrors:
  Exit Sub
End Sub
```

Figure 8-11: Error handling for the CancelError property

The Ch8Shely.vbp program contains the enhanced Shely application that traps and handles anticipated errors. Examine the code carefully prior to executing the program.

Exercise 8.3 ▶

The Coffee Haus application uses the CommonDialog control to open the Print dialog box when the user prints reports. There is currently no mechanism for allowing the user to discontinue a print selection. In this exercise, you will enable the CommonDialog control's CancelError property and enter error processing to allow the user to cancel the print request.

a. Open the file Ex8-3.vbp from the Chapter8 folder on your Student Disk, and then save the project as Ex8-3a.vbp. Save any forms and modules as part of the new project.

b. In the Properties window for the CommonDialog control, dlgPrint, set the CancelError property to True.

c. In the menu event for each report found in the Reports menu item of the File menu, code the On Error statement at the beginning of the procedure to go to the HandleError: label.

d. Place the HandleError: label at the end of each print procedure and before the End Sub statement. The program should execute the Exit Sub statement if it encounters an error.

e. Place an additional Exit Sub prior to the HandleError: label to bypass the HandleError code when there is no error.

f. Save and run the application. Test the Print dialog box Cancel button for each report to verify that the print request was canceled.

g. When you are satisfied that the program executes successfully, create an executable file named Ex8-3a.exe.

Exercise 8.4 ▶

The Melanie's Mall application should allow the user to cancel any of the three print requests. In order to satisfy this requirement, you must add the CommonDialog control to the project, enable the CancelError property, and then code error-trapping routines for each of the reports.

In addition you will set the CommonDialog control's Flags property to Hide and disable the Print to file check box, remove the Page number option, and disable the Print selection option. You might need to use the Help system to verify the constants needed to set the Flags property.

a. Open the file Ex8-4.vbp from the Chapter8 folder on your Student Disk, and then save the project as Ex8-4a.vbp. Save any forms and modules as part of the new project.

b. Examine the CommonDialog control named dlgPrint to the frmMall form, and set the CancelError property to True.

c. For each of the menu events associated with report creation, set the Flags property as required, and include the dlgPrint.ShowPrinter statement to show the Print dialog box.

d. Turn on error trapping in each of the report creation events to go to the HandleError: label when the user clicks the Cancel button.

e. Add the necessary code to exit the subroutine when the program encounters an error.

f. Add the necessary code to bypass the HandleError: label and its associated code.

g. Save and run the application. Test the Cancel button in the Print dialog box for each report to verify that the print request was canceled.

h. When you are satisfied that the program executes successfully, create an executable file named Ex8-4a.exe.

Backing Up the Database

To avoid the possibility of lost or damaged data, you must back up your database files on a routine basis by making a copy of records from the ShelyTemps.mdb database. These backup copies capture the current state of the database. If any damage occurs to records in the database, you could use the backup to restore the database to a specific point in time.

The backup routines for the Shely Services project copy records from the ShelyTemps.mdb database and write them to a sequential file on drive A. Then you can use Windows file operations to move the files to the appropriate location for processing.

The name of the file includes the current date. If you back up the database more than once on the same day, then the last backup will be available. If you discover processing errors, then you can restore the data from the appropriate backup file based on the date by modifying DBLoad.vbp introduced later in this chapter. You can construct the filename using the following code:

```
Dim strFileName As String
Dim strNow As String
strNow = Format$(Date, "mmddyy")
strFileName = "A:\Shely" & strNow & ".dat"
Open strFileName For Output As #1
```

The result of processing this code is a file with the name and extension Shely010199.dat if the processing occurs on January 1, 1999. You will modify this filename format in Chapter 9.

After this processing, the database is opened and a table is generated to hold all records in the database file. The sequential file records are copied and written to the sequential file. Figure 8-12 shows the complete backup subroutine.

```
Public Sub BackUpRoutine()

  On Error GoTo HandleErrors

'Declare variables

  Dim strFileName As String

  Dim strNow As String

  Dim dbsCurrent As Database

  Dim rstNewTable As Recordset

  Dim strQuery As String


'Build query string on the Mainform


  strNow = Format$(Date, "mmddyy")

  strFileName = "A:\Shely" & strNow & ".dat"

  Open strFileName For Output As #1


  Set dbsCurrent = OpenDatabase("A:\ShelyTemps.mdb")


'Build query string and fetch the data


  strQuery = "SELECT * FROM TemporaryEmployees"

  strQuery = strQuery & "ORDER BY EmployeeID"
```

Figure 8-12: BackUpRoutine subroutine

```
      Set rstNewTable = dbsCurrent.OpenRecordset(strQuery)


   rstNewTable.MoveFirst


'Move through the records and write all fields


   Do While Not rstNewTable.EOF
     Write #1, _
       rstNewTable!EmployeeID, _
       rstNewTable!LastName, _
       rstNewTable!FirstName, _
       rstNewTable!Address, _
       rstNewTable!City, _
       rstNewTable!State, _
       rstNewTable!Zip, _
       rstNewTable!Phone, _
       rstNewTable!Listed, _
       rstNewTable!Shift, _
       rstNewTable!Secretarial, _
       rstNewTable!Clerical, _
       rstNewTable!Industrial, _
       rstNewTable!Marketing, _
       rstNewTable!Typing, _
       rstNewTable!OptValues, _
       rstNewTable!Notes, _
       rstNewTable!JobID
     rstNewTable.MoveNext
   Loop


   rstNewTable.Close
   dbsCurrent.Close
   MsgBox "Backup complete", vbOKOnly, "Database Backup"
   Exit Sub
HandleErrors:
   Call HandleErrorRoutines
End Sub
```

Figure 8-12: BackUpRoutine subroutine (continued)

An alternative process might be to add code to extend the filename to include versions so that more than one backup could occur each day. Or a warning might be given that a current file exists and will be overwritten. In this case, users might be prompted as to whether they want to continue.

Exercise 8.5 ▶

The staff at Coffee Haus needs to backup the current database on a weekly basis. In this exercise, you will add a Backup menu item to the File menu and create the code necessary to create a backup file as a sequential file on drive A. The filename should consist of the string "CH", the current date in the format MMDDYY, and the .dat file extension.

a. Open the file Ex8-5.vbp from the Chapter8 folder on your Student Disk, and then save the project as Ex8-5a.vbp. Save any forms and modules as part of the new project.

b. Add the Backup menu item to the File menu.

c. Using the BackUpRoutine in Figure 8-12 as a model, complete the code necessary to back up the CHCust.mdb database.

d. Save and run the application. Examine the sequential file backup created on drive A.

e. When you are satisfied that the backup routine executes successfully, create an executable file named Ex8-5a.exe.

Exercise 8.6 ▶

The Melanie's Mall application requires a procedure to back up the current Stores database on a weekly basis. In this exercise, you will add a Backup menu item to the File menu and create the code necessary to create a backup file as a sequential file on drive A. The filename should consist of the string "MM", the current date in the format MMDDYY, and the .dat extension.

a. Open the file Ex8-6.vbp from the Chapter8 folder on your Student Disk, and then save the project as Ex8-6a.vbp. Save any forms and modules as part of the new project.

b. Add the Backup menu item to the File menu.

c. Using the BackUpRoutine in Figure 8-12 as a model, complete the code necessary to back up the MMStores.mdb database.

d. Save and run the application. Examine the sequential file backup created on drive A.

e. When you are satisfied that the backup routine executes successfully, create an executable file named Ex8-6a.exe.

Hiding the Password Using the Log In Dialog Form

The MsgBox statement used in the subroutine for checking passwords does not provide an option for hiding the password. While you were developing the program, it was helpful to see what was happening, and the MsgBox statement provided an easy method for testing routines. Now that the program is complete, you need to hide passwords as users enter them.

Visual Basic provides a number of completed forms that you can add to existing applications. You can add the Log In Dialog form to the Shely project using the Add Form command on the Project menu. Figure 8-13 shows the Log In Dialog form.

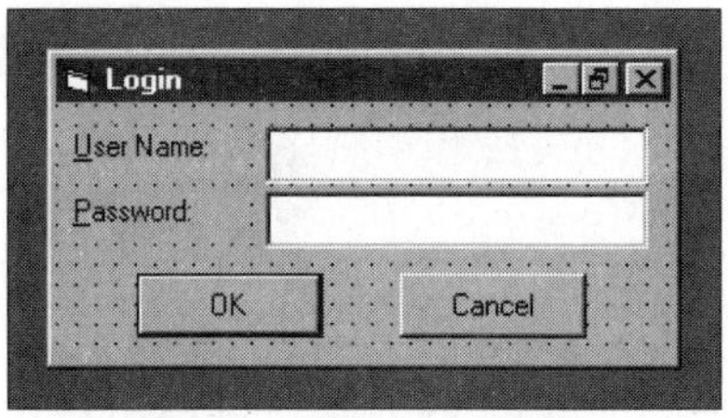

Figure 8-13: Log In Dialog form

The form comes complete with control names and routines for the cmdOK_Click() and cmdCancel_Click() events. You can modify the existing code as needed for the application.

There are three controls on the frmMaster form with events that call the PassWordCheck subroutine in the DataEditing module. You will modify these controls to show the login form and at the same time save a value identifying the event that called the PassWordCheck subroutine. You will identify the Data Management command button as 1, the Print Reports command button as 2, and the Back Up command button as 3. The value will be stored in the variable intCallingPoint declared in the General Declarations section of the PassWordCheck subroutine. Once the calling point value is stored, the Login dialog box appears on the screen using the following code:

```
Private Sub cmdDataManagement_Click()
        intCallingPoint = 1
        frmLogin.Show
End Sub
```

You must modify the code provided with the Log In Dialog form to use the PassWordCheck subroutine you created previously. Figure 8-14 shows the modified code for the Shely project.

```
'Store origination of call and show the login form

'********** Logon [frmLogon (Logon.frm)] **********

'

Option Explicit


Private Sub cmdCancel_Click()

  txtUserName = ""

  txtUserName.SetFocus

  txtPassword = ""

  Me.Hide

End Sub


Private Sub cmdOK_Click()
'Check for correct password
```

Figure 8-14: The frmLogin Code

```
      If txtUserName <> "" And txtPassword <> "" Then
'PassWordCheck subroutine is in the DataEditing Module
    Call PassWordCheck
  Else
    If txtUserName = "" Then
       MsgBox "User name required", vbOKOnly, "Login"
       txtUserName.SetFocus
    Else
      If txtPassword = "" Then
          MsgBox "Password required", vbOKOnly, "Login"
          txtPassword.SetFocus
      End If
    End If
  End If
End If
```

Figure 8-14: The frmLogin Code (continued)

The cmdCancel_Click() Event procedure uses the Me keyword to hide the form. The **Me keyword** behaves like an implicitly declared variable; it is available automatically to every procedure in a class module—in this case, the form. The statement `Me.Hide` hides the current form.

The cmdOK_Click() Event procedure calls the existing PassWordCheck subroutine. The PasswordChar property in the Properties window of the txtPassword control is set to "*". This action causes any entry in the text box to be replaced with asterisks, thus hiding the password. The program receives the code as entered.

At this point, you should remove the code previously used to capture the password from the PassWordCheck subroutine and add the code to continue processing if txtPassword contains a valid value.

The password captured in the txtPassword control must replace the string previously captured using the InputBox function using the following code:

```
If strArray(intArrayPosition, 4) = frmLogin!txtPassword
    Then strAccessLevel = strArray(intArrayPosition, 3)
End If
```

Figure 8-15 shows the modified PassWordCheck subroutine. If the user enters a valid password that is associated with a valid access code, processing continues based on the value stored in the intCallingPoint variable.

```
Public Sub PassWordCheck()

  Dim intArrayPosition As Integer
  strAccessLevel = "0"

'Assign access level code:
'Only first 5 characters of Name are checked because
'the security file has extra data in the Name field
'that also identifies the employee's section

  For intArrayPosition = 1 To intArrayCounter
    If (strArray(intArrayPosition, 4) = _
      frmLogin!txtPassword) _
      And Left$(strArray(intArrayPosition, 2), 5) = _
      Left$(frmLogin!txtUserName, 5) Then
        strAccessLevel = strArray(intArrayPosition, 3)
    End If
  Next intArrayPosition

  If strAccessLevel = "0" Then
    MsgBox "Invalid Password, try again!", , "PassWord"
    frmLogin!txtUserName = ""
    frmLogin!txtUserName.SetFocus
    frmLogin!txtPassword = ""
    frmLogin.Hide
    Exit Sub
  Else
    Select Case intCallingPoint
      Case 1  'from Maintenance button
        frmLogin!txtPassword = ""
        frmLogin!txtUserName.SetFocus
        frmLogin!txtUserName = ""
        frmEmpeMaint.Show
        frmLogin.Hide
        frmMaster.Hide
```

Figure 8-15: PassWordCheck subroutine

```
           Case 2  'from Print button
              frmLogin!txtPassword = ""

              frmLogin!txtUserName.SetFocus

              frmLogin!txtUserName = ""

              frmPrint.Show

              frmMaster.Enabled = False

              frmLogin.Hide
           Case 3   'from Back Up button
              frmLogin!txtPassword = ""

              frmLogin!txtUserName.SetFocus

              frmLogin!txtUserName = ""

              If strAccessLevel <> "8" Then

                 MsgBox "Backup access denied", _

                 vbOKOnly, "Access Check"

              Else

                 Call BackUpRoutine

              End If

              frmLogin.Hide

        End Select

     End If

End Sub
```

Figure 8-15: PassWordCheck subroutine (continued)

Exercise 8.7 ▶

The Coffee Haus application requires security access in order to allow only designated employees to maintain the database and print reports. All employees have browse and select access. User IDs and passwords are stored in the CHSecFile.dat file found in the Chapter8 folder on your Student Disk. The record structure is stored in the CHSecur.bas modules found in the Chapter8 folder on your Student Disk. A Sub procedure to build an array of security data was created for you and is saved in the Chapter8 folder as BldArray.bas. In this exercise, you will add the Log In Dialog form provided by Visual Basic for validating user IDs and passwords.

    a. Open the file Ex8-7.vbp from the Chapter8 folder on your Student Disk, and then save the project as Ex8-7a.vbp. Save any forms and modules as part of the new project.

    b. Add the CHSecur.bas and BldArray.bas modules to your project from the Chapter8 folder on your Student Disk.

    c. Click Add Form on the Project menu, and then add the Log In Dialog form found in the Add New dialog box. Save the form as frmLogin8.frm.

    d. Examine the code provided with the Log In Dialog form, and then remove this code.

    e. Examine the CHSecur.bas and BldArray.bas modules to determine the format of the record structure and array. Add code to the BuildArray Sub procedure to print the array for test purposes.

    f. Add a call to the BuildArray Sub procedure in the BldArray.bas module to the Form_Load() Event procedure.

g. Use the Menu Editor to disable the mnuEditMaintainAdd, mnuEditMaintainDelete, mnuEditMaintainUpdate, mnuFileRepCustList, mnuFileRepFlavor, and mnuFileRepCustbyState menu items.

h. Using the strValidPassword variable assigned in the BldArray.bas module, code the mnuEditMaintain and mnuReports menu items to show the login form if the password equals "N".

i. Code the cmdOK_Click() event on the Log In Dialog form to verify that the combined user ID and password entered are valid. You must examine the data in the array to accomplish this task. If the user ID and password are valid, enable all previously disabled menu controls, set the strValidPassword variable to "Y", and hide the Log In Dialog form. If there is an error in either the user ID or password, then send an appropriate message, and do not hide the Log In Dialog form.

j. Code the cmdCancel_Click() event on the Log In Dialog form to hide the form and reset the strValidPassword variable to "N".

k. Save and run the application.

l. Test the application with valid and invalid passwords. With the first execution of the program, your BuildArray Sub procedure will print the array of user IDs and passwords. After the first execution of the program, you might want to disable the print array code.

m. When you are satisfied that your application executes successfully, create an executable file named Ex8-7a.exe.

Exercise 8.8 ▶

The Melanie's Mall application requires security access in order to allow only designated employees to maintain the database and print reports. All employees have browse and select access. User IDs and passwords are stored in the MMSecFile.dat file in the Chapter8 folder on your Student Disk. The record structure is stored in the MMSecur.bas modules in the Chapter8 folder. A Sub procedure to build an array of security data was created for you and is saved in the Chapter8 folder as MMBldArray.bas. In this exercise, you will modify the existing security access code.

a. Open the file Ex8-8.vbp from the Chapter8 folder on your Student Disk, and then save the project as Ex8-8a.vbp. Save any forms and modules as part of the new project.

b. Add code to the BuildArray Sub procedure in the MMBldArray.bas module that will print the array of valid user IDs and passwords.

c. Run the application. Verify that the Reports menu items and Edit menu items are disabled. Exit the application.

d. The code necessary to check the user ID and password has been added to the program. The variable strValidPassword contains a "Y" if the password is valid. Code the mnuEdit_Click() and mnuFileReports_Click() Event procedures to show the frmLogin form if strValidPassword contains a "N".

e. Save and run the application. Test the application with valid and invalid user IDs and passwords.

f. When you are satisfied that the program executes successfully, create an executable file named Ex8-8a.exe.

Building the Shely Services Database

Before delivering the project, you must develop a means for producing the corporate database from the data entered by the Shely Services staff in Chapter 3. Until now, you have developed the project using test data. You should delete existing records from the ShelyTemps.mdb database and load data from the sequential file, EAP.dat.

The program DBLoad.vbp is not a part of the Shely project, but it is a necessary starting point for delivery of the TEMS system. Remember that the data entry program in Chapter 3 was delivered as a point of entry to the TEMS system. This means that Shely staff members were given the Ch3Shely.vbp program for use in capturing data as the TEMS system was being built. Figure 8-16 shows the user interface for the DBLoad program.

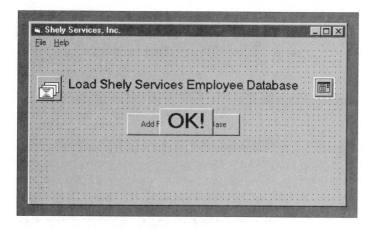

Figure 8-16: DBLoad program interface

The cmdAddRecords_Click() Event procedure in the DBLoad program calls the AddSequentialData subroutine instead of including the code directly in the Click event. Presenting the code in this manner allows for moving the code to a module at some point, if desired.

The process of building the ShelyTemps.mdb database from the EAP.dat sequential file lets you use the MousePointer property. The **MousePointer property** sets a value indicating the type of mouse pointer that appears when the user moves the mouse over a particular part of an object at run time.

Syntax ▶   *object*.**MousePointer** [= *value*]

In this syntax, *object* is a control in the interface and *value* is an integer specifying the type of mouse pointer to display. Figure 8-17 shows intrinsic constants that you can use to make the code self-documenting.

Constant	Value	Description/Icon
VbDefault	0	Default; shape determined by the object
VbArrow	1	Arrow
VbCrosshair	2	Crosshair +
VbIbeam	3	I beam I
VbIconPointer	4	Icon
VbSizePointer	5	Size ✛

Figure 8-17: Intrinsic constant values for the MousePointer property

Constant	Value	Description/Icon
VbSizeNESW	6	Size NE SW ↗
VbSizeNS	7	Size N S ↕
VbSizeNWSE	8	Size NW SE ↘
VbSizeWE	9	Size WE ↔
VbUpArrow	10	Up ↑
VbHourglass	11	Hourglass ⧖
VbNoDrop	12	No Drop ⦸
VbArrowHourglass	13	Arrow Hourglass ⧖
VbArrowQuestion	14	Arrow Question ?
VbSizeAll	15	Size All ✥
VbCustom	99	Custom icon specified by the MouseIcon property

Figure 8-17: Intrinsic constant values for the MousePointer property (continued)

Figure 8-18 shows the AddSequentialData subroutine. All required statements have been introduced and used in previous processing. Data items are converted as necessary to match the field definitions in the database exactly as is the case with the integer value placement preferences. The variable strNotes requires a blank character in the database when no note is present. The AddSequentialData subroutine processing proceeds as follows:

1. Declare the strSQL variable as a string used to build the SQL INSERT INTO statement necessary to enter records into the ShelyTemps.mdb database.
2. Declare sequential file data fields used to store fields from the EAP.dat file for each record.
3. Declare dbsCurrent as a Database object.
4. Use the On Error statement to establish a label to handle error processing.
5. Set the MousePointer property to an hourglass while the database is being loaded.
6. Open the sequential file for input.
7. Verify that the user has selected the ShelyTemps.mdb file as the file to load.
8. While the sequential file EAP.dat contains records:
   a. Read a record from the sequential file.
   b. Convert the placement preference variables to strings.
   c. If strNotes contains the null string, insert a space.
   d. Build the SQL INSERT statement.
   e. Use the Execute method to add the record to the database.
9. Close the database, display a message, show the OK button, and then restore the mouse pointer to an arrow.

```
Private Sub AddSequentialData()


'Declare variables
  Dim strSQL As String
  Dim strMess As String


'Sequential file data fields
  Dim strEmpeID, strLName, strFName As String
  Dim strAddress As String
  Dim strCity, strState, strZip, strPhone As String
  Dim strListed, strTyping, strNotes As String
  Dim strShift, strOpts, strJobID As String
  Dim intSecretary, intClerical As Integer
  Dim intMarketing, intIndustrial As Integer


'Boolean values for placement preferences
'Read in as strings
  Dim strBoSecretary, strBoClerical As String
  Dim strBoMarketing, strBoIndustrial As String


  Dim dbsCurrent As Database


  On Error GoTo HandleErrors


  frmLoadDataBase.MousePointer = 11


  Open "A:EAP.dat" For Input As #1


'Do not forget to add the compatible library


  If dlgDialog.filename <> "A:\ShelyTemps.mdb" Then
    lblMessages = "Incorrect file selected"
    Exit Sub
  End If


'Open the database
```

Figure 8-18: AddSequentialData subroutine

```
    Set dbsCurrent = OpenDatabase(dlgDialog.filename)


  Do While Not EOF(1)
    Input #1, strEmpeID, strLName, strFName, strAddress, _
      strCity, strState, strZip, strPhone, strListed, _
      intSecretary, strTyping, intClerical, intMarketing, _
      intIndustrial, strJobID, strShift, strOpts, strNotes


'Convert data read-in to match the database


    strBoSecretary = CStr(intSecretary)

    strBoClerical = CStr(intClerical)

    strBoMarketing = CStr(intMarketing)

    strBoIndustrial = CStr(intIndustrial)


    If strNotes = "" Then strNotes = " "


'Build the SQL INSERT statement to insert the sequential file
'record into the file


    strSQL = "INSERT INTO TemporaryEmployees "

    strSQL = strSQL + "(EmployeeID, LastName, FirstName, "

    strSQL = strSQL + "Address, City, State, Zip, Phone, "

    strSQL = strSQL + "Listed, Shift, Secretarial, "

    strSQL = strSQL + "Clerical, Industrial, Marketing, "

    strSQL = strSQL + "Typing, OptValues,"

    strSQL = strSQL + "Notes, JobID) "
'The following lines of code should be entered as a single line
    strSQL = strSQL + "Values ('" + strEmpeID + "','" +

    strLName + "','" + strFName + "','" + strAddress + "','"

    + strCity + "','" + strState + "','" + strZip + "','"

    + strPhone + "','" + strListed + "','" + strShift

    + "','" + strBoSecretary + "','" + strBoClerical + "','"

    + strBoMarketing + "','" + strBoIndustrial + "','"

    + strTyping + "','" + strOpts + "','" + strNotes + "','" + strJobID + "')
    ;"
'Write the record to the database


    dbsCurrent.Execute strSQL
```

Figure 8-18: AddSequentialData subroutine (continued)

```
  Close #1


  dbsCurrent.Close

  lblMessages.Caption = _

    "The Temporary Employee database has been loaded"

  cmdAddRecords.Visible = False

  cmdOK.Visible = True

  frmLoadDataBase.MousePointer = 0

  Exit Sub


HandleErrors:

  Call HandleErrorRoutines

  End

End Sub
```

Figure 8-18: AddSequentialData subroutine (continued)

Because there are many embedded single and double quotation marks, you should enter the Values statement on one line. While this is not absolutely necessary, it saves a lot of debugging. The fields in the Values statement must correspond exactly to the location of the fields in the database.

After testing the program and checking the data in the database, you need to prepare the database for one final run. You must delete all of the records in the database, except for one record with the employee ID of "000", and you should leave all other fields blank. Make sure that the employee ID field is the primary key. When you run the DBLoad program, the database will contain all of the Shely records and the "000" record. Until now, data have been shown in the maintenance form. Whenever the data object is enabled and the pointer returns to the first record in the database, the "000" record will appear and you cannot access it. This makes the page cleaner and does not show any unexpected data. This change can, of course, affect other parts of the Shely project. In this case, only one change needs to be made: In the subroutine MasterDetail in the PrintMasterList module, you must insert the statement `rstNewTable.MoveNext` after the `rstNewTable.MoveFirst` statement. This change will bypass the "000" record.

Prior to adding the "000" record, the typing speed input box could appear when a user added or updated records. This processing would occur as the result of the first record in the database containing the secretary placement preference. The "000" record addition averts this potential error.

As a final change, this is the time to ensure that the JobID in the TemporaryEmployees table matches a JobID in the CurrentJobs table as shown in Figure 8-19.

```
'Make sure JobID exists in CurrentJobs table

'Jobs must exist to be assigned

  Dim strJobID As String * 3

  Dim strJobSrch As String


  If frmEmpeMaint!txtJobID.Text <> "000" Then
```

Figure 8-19: Final verifications

```
       If Len(frmEmpeMaint!txtJobID.Text) < 3 _

         Or frmEmpeMaint!txtJobID.Text < "100" _

         Or frmEmpeMaint!txtJobID.Text > "499" Then

         MsgBox _

         "Job numbers are from 100 to 499: 000 = unassigned", _

           vbOKOnly, "Incorrect Job ID"

         CheckJobID = vbNo
'Exit Function

     Else

         strJobID = frmEmpeMaint!txtJobID.Text

         strJobSrch = "JobID = '" + strJobID + "'"


         frmEmpeMaint!datCurrentJobs.Recordset.FindFirst strJobSrch


       If frmEmpeMaint!datCurrentJobs.Recordset.NoMatch Then

         MsgBox "Not a current Job ID", vbOKOnly, "Job ID Check"

         CheckJobID = vbNo

       Else

         CheckJobID = vbYes

       End If

     End If

   End If
```

Figure 8-19: Final verifications (continued)

This is a chance to look for possible processing errors and to devise ways to keep them from happening. For example, in the Shely project, if someone enters a last name that is longer than the field length in the database, the error "Cancel by associated object" will occur. The database is the associated object, and the last name field length is established by the database. The same thing would happen if someone entered "WVB" in the State text box. The field length for the state code in the database is set to 2. One solution to the field length problem is to set the MaxLength property for the txtLName text box control to be the same length as in the database. An alternate solution is to add a routine with a MsgBox to the data editing module that would examine the length of the data entry field and then display an error message for fields that exceed the required database field length. The Shely project uses the MaxLength property where available. The cboState combo box control does not have a MaxLength property. You should write a special routine to examine the length of the field in the data editing module.

It can almost be guaranteed that the first person to use the Shely project will find an error you missed. This is why questions were asked in Chapter 1 about how and when the project team will be available to ensure a smooth startup.

Using Custom Controls

In creating the TEMS system, you have been using controls on the Toolbox window to create program interfaces. These intrinsic controls are part of Visual Basic and are included in the executable files that Visual Basic produces.

To extend the functionality of the programming language, programmers create and use existing ActiveX controls. **ActiveX controls** are controls that are not actually part of Visual Basic, but perform as if they were. Microsoft's **Component Object Module (COM)** technology allows you to create cross-platform, language-independent controls. These controls are stored as separate files on the application disk and contain .ocx, .dll, and .exe file extensions. Like other controls you have used, you must create an instance of these controls on a form before you can use them in your program.

Without knowing it, you have used two ActiveX controls in the form of the CommonDialog and Log In Dialog controls. These controls are supplied with the Enterprise and Professional Editions of Visual Basic. Third-party vendors also sell different controls to perform specific tasks. ActiveX controls commonly are called custom controls. Custom controls are version specific and might appear only as empty containers when Visual Basic programs containing different versions of the custom controls open the programs. You need to create the custom controls for the TEMS system to further enhance the project's functionality.

Adding a Toolbar

You can enhance a program's interface by adding a toolbar. Each button on a toolbar corresponds to a menu item. For frequently used menu items, the availability of a toolbar button improves the user interface. You are probably familiar with toolbar buttons from your work with other Windows applications.

In this section, you will modify the interface shown in Figure 8-16 to include a toolbar and buttons for opening files and calling Help. The Open file button will use the CommonDialog custom control. You will create and add Help files to the TEMS system master form in Chapter 9.

The **Toolbar control** contains a collection of buttons, each of which represents a Button object. The icon displayed in a toolbar button comes from a corresponding ImageList. The Toolbar and ImageList controls are ActiveX controls that you must add to the project before you can use them. As members of Microsoft Windows Common Controls, the ImageList and Toolbar are added from the Components dialog box accessed from the Project menu. Figure 8-20 shows the Components dialog box with Microsoft Windows Common Controls 5.0 selected.

Figure 8-20: Components dialog box

At this point, you can complete the steps necessary to add the toolbar to the database load program. To do so, open the project DBLoad.vbp that your instructor will provide. Add the Microsoft Windows Common Controls component available on your system. The ImageList control now should be available for use. Other controls available with the Microsoft Common Controls component are the TabStrip, Toolbar, StatusBar, ProgressBar, TreeView, ListView, and Slider controls.

The images displayed on the toolbar buttons are not stored directly in the toolbar. These images are stored in the ImageList control. The **ImageList control** stores a collection of bitmap or icon images. The ImageList control serves as a container to locate and hold any images selected for use by other Visual Basic objects.

You need to add the ImageList control to an open area on the database load interface. The ImageList control will not appear at run time. Using the suggested prefix, "ils", name the control ilsImageList. Figure 8-21 shows the Property Pages dialog box, which you can open by right-clicking the ImageList control. On the General tab, select 16 x 16 as the size of the toolbar buttons—this is the most commonly used size.

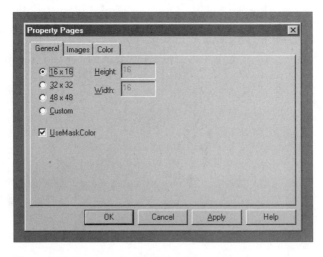

Figure 8-21: Property Pages dialog box

You use the Images tab of the Property Pages dialog box to insert and remove images from the underlying ListImages collection. You might not have these images on your system; if you don't, you can use the Open.bmp and Help.bmp files in the Chapter8 folder on your Student Disk. Visual Studio 98 contains many images available in the C:\Program Files\Microsoft Visual Studio\Common\Graphics\Bitmaps\OffCtlBr\Small\Color*.bmp file. Ask your instructor for the location of additional bitmap images used on the toolbar. To insert the pictures, you would click Insert Picture on the Images tab and then select the .bmp files in the order that they should appear on the interface (Open, Help). You should enter "Open" (without the quotation marks) as the key for the first image. The Index, 1, is supplied automatically. You can complete this process for the Help button using "Help" as the Key for the image whose Index is 2. Figure 8-22 shows the completed image list.

index for current image

item order

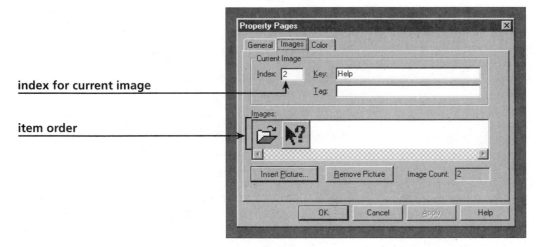

Figure 8-22: Images tab in the Property Pages dialog box

You can add the Toolbar control to the form, using the "tbr" prefix to name the control tbrToolBar. In the General tab of the Property Pages dialog box shown in Figure 8-22, you need to choose ilsImageList as the ImageList control that contains the desired buttons and choose Fixed Single as the BorderStyle. Figure 8-23 shows the completed General tab.

Buttons tab

ImageList control

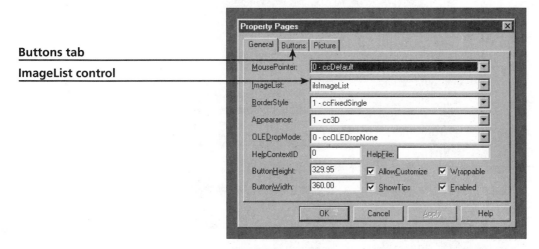

Figure 8-23: General tab in the Property Pages dialog box

The Buttons tab in the Property Pages dialog box for the ToolBar control represents a Buttons collection associated with the ilsImageList control. Figure 8-24 describes the properties for Button objects.

Property	Description
Index	Sets the location of the button on the toolbar.
Caption	Sets text that a button should contain; buttons usually do not show text.
Key	Sets a string that uniquely identifies a member in a collection.
Image	Sets the numeric index or string key of the corresponding image stored in the ListImages property of the ImageList control. Available only after the toolbar has been associated with an ImageList.
ToolTipText	Sets a string to be used as the ToolTip for the button.
Value	Sets a numeric constant indicating whether the toolbar button is unpressed, 0, or pressed, 1. The default value is 0.
Visible	A Boolean value indicating whether the toolbar button is initially available at run time. The default value is True.
Enabled	A Boolean value indicating whether the toolbar button is initially enabled at run time. The default value is True.
Style	Controls the appearance of a button and how a button interacts with other buttons on the toolbar.

Figure 8-24: Button object properties

Figure 8-25 shows the property settings for the Open button. Use this figure as a guide to add the Help button to the toolbar. The Insert Panel option adds buttons in the order that they are entered. To complete the operation of adding buttons to the ToolBar control, click the Apply button. When you close the Property Pages dialog box, the buttons will appear on the toolbar in the order of their Index.

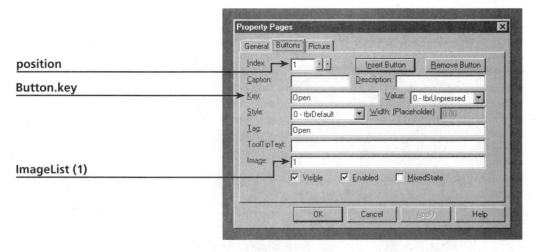

Figure 8-25: Buttons tab in the Property Pages dialog box

Adding a Status Bar

As a final step to enhance the DBLoad interface, you need to add a status bar to the bottom of the DBLoad form. The status bar is available as one of the Microsoft Common Controls. You should name the status bar stbStatus. You can adjust the height and width of the status bar using the sizing handles for the StatusBar control. In the Property Pages for the status bar, you use the Panels tab to insert panels as you need them. The panel whose Index is 1 represents the first status bar panel, which is left-aligned with no bevel and set to a width of 6000. The first status bar panel will appear invisible because it has no bevel and no content assigned to it. You might need to adjust the width for the final program. Using Figure 8-26, you can create the second panel whose Index is 2 to contain the current time. When you are finished, your completed interface should look like Figure 8-27.

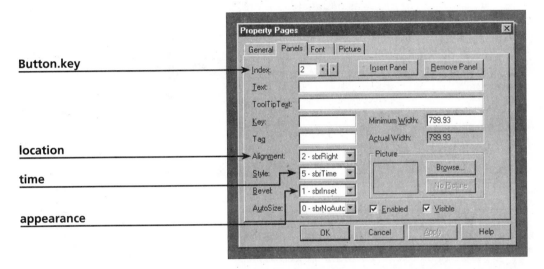

Figure 8-26: Panels tab in the Property Pages dialog box

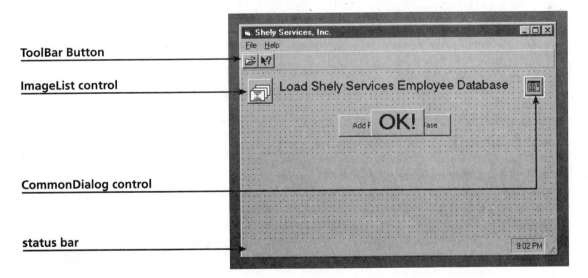

Figure 8-27: Completed DBLoad program interface

Custom Control Programming

Now that the ToolBar buttons are in place, you need to add code to make them functional. Clicking a toolbar button causes the ButtonClick() Event procedure code to be executed.

Syntax ▶   **Private Sub** *object*_**ButtonClick(ByVal** *button* **As Button)**

In this syntax, *object* is an object expression that evaluates to a ToolBar control and *button* is a reference to the clicked Button object.

To program an individual Button object's response to the ButtonClick() event, you use the value of the button argument. For example, the code in Figure 8-28 uses the Key property as designated on the ToolBar Property Pages for each Button object to determine the appropriate action.

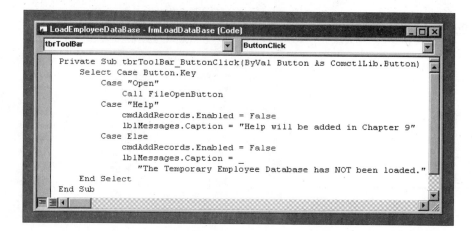

```
LoadEmployeeDataBase - frmLoadDataBase (Code)
tbrToolBar                              ButtonClick

Private Sub tbrToolBar_ButtonClick(ByVal Button As ComctlLib.Button)
    Select Case Button.Key
        Case "Open"
            Call FileOpenButton
        Case "Help"
            cmdAddRecords.Enabled = False
            lblMessages.Caption = "Help will be added in Chapter 9"
        Case Else
            cmdAddRecords.Enabled = False
            lblMessages.Caption = _
                "The Temporary Employee Database has NOT been loaded."
    End Select
End Sub
```

Figure 8-28: The tbrToolBar_ButtonClick(ByVal Button As ComctlLib.Button) event

The FileOpenButton subroutine uses the CommonDialog control to make the Open dialog box available to the application. The name of the CommonDialog control is set to dlgDialog. To treat the Cancel button as an error, you must set the CancelError property to True. The Filter property sets the filters that are displayed in the Files of Type list box of the Open dialog box.

Syntax ▶   *object*.**Filter** [= *description1* |*filter1* |*description2* |*filter2*...]

In this syntax, *object* is an object expression that evaluates to the dlgDialog control, *description* is a string expression describing the type of file, and *filter* is a string expression specifying the filename extension. In Example 8-4, the Filter property sets the Files of Type list box to contain the descriptions "Access Database (*.mdb)" and "All Files (*.*)". The corresponding filters, *.mdb and *.*, will display either files with the .mdb extension or all files based on the user's selection in the File of Type list box.

Example 8-4 ▶   dlgDialog.Filter = "Access Database (*.mdb)|*.mdb|All Files *.*|*.*"

The cmdAddRecords enabled property is initially set to False so that a file must be selected before records can be added. The ShowOpen method displays the CommonDialog control's Open dialog box. Figure 8-29 shows the FileOpenButton subroutine.

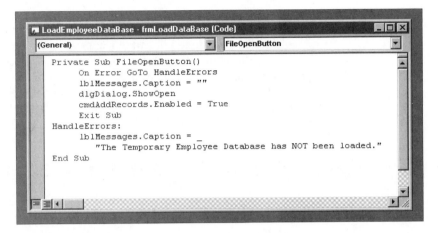

Figure 8-29: FileOpenButton subroutine

If the subroutine executes successfully, the path and filename are saved in the **FileName property** of the dlgDialog control.

Syntax ▶   *object*.**FileName** [= *pathname*]

In this syntax, *object* is an object expression that evaluates to an object in the Applies To list—in this case dlgDialog—and *pathname* is a string expression that specifies the path and filename. The FileName property containing the *pathname* is available to the program code. The FileName property is used in the AddSequentialData subroutine to verify that the user has opened the correct file as follows:

```
If dlgDialog.FileName <> "A:\ShelyTemps.mdb" Then
    lblMessages = "Incorrect file selected"
    Exit Sub
End If
```

The FileName property also is used in the AddSequentialData subroutine to open the database:

```
Set dbsCurrent = OpenDatabase(dlgDialog.FileName)
```

To complete programming for the custom controls, you can add the ToolTipText to the time panel on the status bar using the following code in the Form_Load Event procedure:

```
stbStatus.Panels.Item(2).ToolTipText = Format(Date, "mmmm dd,yyyy")
```

When the cursor pauses over the time panel, a ToolTip will display the current date. You can add ToolTips in this way to many of the objects in the Shely project, or you can initialize the ToolTip property at design time.

Now the DBLoad program is complete. You might want to complete the preceding exercises on your own by creating a new project. You can examine the DBLoad.vbp program that your instructor will provide to see the completed application.

SUMMARY

The TEMS system is now complete. In this chapter, you added routines to handle anticipated errors to the data entry program you created in Chapter 3. To view the completed program, open the Chap3Err.vbp file. You also added similar error-handling routines to the TEMS system project (which is saved as Ch8Shely.vbp). The Ch8Shely.vbp program now contains code necessary for backing up the database. In addition, you added a program to load the ShelyTemps.mdb database from the sequential file EAP.dat that you created in Chapter 3. You learned about using custom controls to create more professional applications. In Chapter 9, you will add a splash screen to the system, test the system thoroughly to make sure that all procedures work correctly, complete the Help files, and then deliver the system to the user.

PROGRESSIVE PROJECTS

You will now add error statements, backup routines, and improved password protection to the projects. After completing and testing the projects, you will load the database.

1. Bean County Plumbing Inventory System (BCPIS)

You need to add error trapping routines for the BCPISdb.mdb and the random file that you developed in Chapter 4 to the modules in which they are loaded into the project. Prior to making any changes, create a backup copy of the application. The database and random access files must be present and loaded before the user can access the system. Use the Ch3BCPIS.dat file created in Chapter 3 to load the database.

Add a label to the main screen and set its Visible property to False. Check for errors, such as no disk in the drive, files not on the disk, empty files, etc. If there are errors, display appropriate messages on the label and disable all passwords so the user can fix the problem and restart the program. You need to activate the CancelError property for the Printer object that you added in Chapter 7.

Either use the add-in password form or create a similar form so asterisks hide the password when the user enters it. Make sure that program flow moves smoothly from one event to the next. Use the Shely project discussed in this chapter to include all changes that were made to the Shely project in the Bean County project. As additional features, add a status bar and the time panel with a ToolTip to the main screen. Check where the project pauses when the database is loaded for maintenance. Then change the mouse pointer to an hourglass while the data are being loaded.

Verify that the add, update, and delete procedures accurately maintain data in the database. Print reports and examine them for accuracy. Then delete all but one record from the database (a "000" record as described in this chapter). Create a small program to copy the data from the sequential file to the BCPISdb.mdb. Examine and use the SQL statement from the Shely project. Remember everything must match perfectly. Add the backup routines. Save the form and project as Ch8BCPIS in the Chapter8 folder on your Student Disk. In Chapter 9, you will complete the project.

2. Single Parents Public Service Library (SPLIB)

Security is not a critical issue for SPLIB; however, you should change the limited password check to hide the password as the user enters it. Follow the directions in the chapter for the password add-in feature, or create a form to capture the password. The advantage of the add-in form is that the password variable is a property of the form. Set the PasswordChar property so that asterisks replace characters as the user enters them. Change the flow of the project so that events follow events as expected. Use the Shely project as a guide. Prior to making any changes, create a backup copy of the project.

Many volunteers use the main form, so its appearance must be attractive and professional. Add a status bar with the time in the lower-right corner. Use the ToolTipText property in the Form_Load event to incorporate the date as a Tooltip for the time panel. You also can display messages in the left panel using the code `StatusBar1.Panels.Item(1).Text = "A nice message"`. You also can set the panel text at design time. A clever panel might access messages from an array and change from time to time. (Check the timer object.) Change the mouse icon while the database is loaded for maintenance. The hourglass is the standard choice, but you can use any icon. This project will be highly visible, and although the management of the data is a priority, an attractive and easy-to-use project is also important.

Add error routines to the subroutines where the SPLIBdb.mdb and the random password file are loaded. Check to make sure that disk, files, and data are present. Use Ch3SPLIB.dat created in Chapter 3 to load the database. Display error messages on a label on the main form so the message remains until the user restarts the project. Make sure that you change event coding so that volunteers cannot cause events to activate if there are errors.

As a final step, you need to load the database with the data from the sequential file created in Chapter 3 and then add a backup routine. Delete all the records in the database, except the "000" record as described in this chapter. Follow the Shely project carefully, and make sure that the database fields in the SQL statement match the values exactly. Make sure that the data have been loaded correctly. Add the backup routines. Save the project as Ch8SPLIB.vbp in the Chapter8 folder on your Student Disk.

3. Short Cut Lawn Service (SCLS)

Create a form and use the code in the Shely project to add data to the SCLSdb.mdb from the sequential file created in Chapter 3, Ch3SCLS.dat. Prior to making any changes, create a backup copy of the project. You also need to remove the test data and print the contents of the database to make sure that all of the data are correct. Add a "000" record as described in the chapter.

You will add error statements to the routines that load the SCLSdb.mdb database and the contents of the random file that you created in Chapter 4. Try to anticipate everything that might go wrong and include a case statement for each, such as an incorrect disk, missing files, no data, etc. To find the error messages, use the Help system in Visual Basic, or generate the error and locate the error message and error number. Use a label on the main form to display error messages, and add code so that the user must restart the project after correcting the error.

Replace the password message box with a form. Either use the add-in password form or create one. The add-in form has strPassword as a global variable. The PasswordChar property should be set to "*". It will be necessary to check program flow and make changes similar to the ones for the Shely project; otherwise, the program will cause events to be activated incorrectly.

Add a status bar to the main form with the current time in the lower-right corner. The ToolTipText property should show the current date. Run the project. If there is a long pause when the database is opened, add statements that change the pointer icon. However, in this project, the delay might be so short that the user might not see the mouse pointer change. Try the report modules to see if more time is available.

You can use and modify the backup routine that you created for the Shely project in this project. Make sure that you open the saved file with a word processor to ensure that all of the data have been copied, especially the first and last records. Save the project as Ch8SCLS.vbp in the Chapter8 folder on your Student Disk.

INDEPENDENT PROJECTS

1. Judy's Flamingo Collection

Judy lives in Florida and collects flamingos, such as flamingo light switch plates, flamingo night lamps, flamingo Christmas tree ornaments, flamingo brooches, etc. Some of Judy's flamingos are old and quite valuable, so she took her collection to a specialist, who estimated and documented each item in her collection. However, to get insurance, she needs to have records with pictures.

Create a database with records for each item. The database should contain a field for capturing a digital image of each item. The records should include fields for item ID (0001 to 9999), a brief descriptive name, a detailed item description, a location (room), the estimated value, the date estimated, and the purchase date for each item. Create a form with buttons to locate and open the file, to print the screen, to request the item ID, and to end the program. You can use icons on the buttons or you can display text by setting the button's Text property. Use case statements to recognize which buttons have been selected. Also, use the status bar to display a message on the left and the time on the right with a date Tooltip. You can display messages by setting the Text property.

When Judy selects the button to locate an object, show an input box to get the item ID and to retrieve the data from the database. Display the data in the lower-left corner of the screen. On the right side of the screen, show the corresponding (*.gif) image for each item. (Judy will use a digital camera to capture the GIF images; you can use any GIF file on your computer as a placeholder.) You can store the location and name of the image in the database, or you can paste the image into the database field. (The first option is faster.) Make sure that the screen is neat and attractive. Save the form and project as Ch8IP1.

2. Bob's Swim Records

Note: To complete this project, you must have an Internet connection.

Bob has been a masters swimmer for 27 years, during which time he has set state, regional, and national records. Bob has kept records of all his races at regional and national championships. His events include all of the freestyle long distance events including 200, 400, 800, and 1500 meters; 400, 500, 1000, and 1650 yards; and 2 mile and 5K swims. Use the Internet to search for information about masters swimming events, and then build a test database using your search results. Search for five events and five to ten races for each event. The actual events and the times are not important because Bob can enter his own data into the database after the project is completed. The buttons can be relabeled when necessary.

Create a form with one button for each event with a label that describes the event and buttons for locating the database and exiting the program. Add a time panel in the lower-right corner of the screen, with a date ToolTip. When Bob clicks a button to select an event, display an input box requesting whether results are to be shown on the screen or printed. Using the case statements, retrieve the appropriate data from the database. If Bob selects the Print command, open the Print dialog box and then print the results with headers and totals sorted by date. If Bob selects the screen display, display the data on a scrollable form. Program the project so that Bob can only see the events associated with the selected button.

3. Melanie's Christmas Present

Note: To complete this project, you must be able to record and play a sound.

Melanie is still young, but she already likes to watch the computer screen and push the keys to see what happens. Create 26 *.wav files by recording the letters A to Z, with messages such as "This is the letter A for Apple." (If you have a scanner, scan copies of each letter from a child's first alphabet book, as a *.gif file.) Create a screen and add buttons or a series of command objects for each letter. If you use an array of command objects, place the objects on a colorful form in an attractive manner. For the buttons, any *.bmp object from the chapter will do if a letter of the alphabet is assigned to the button's Text property. Make the buttons small (8 × 8). Add the MultiMedia control (in the Components dialog box) to the form. Make it invisible (but do not disable it), and then set its properties\controls to `PlayEnabled = True`. Add the following code to formload: `MMControl1.DeviceType = "WaveAudio"`.

Each button or command will need a command (case statements are the best to use) similar to the following code:

```
MMControl1.filename = "C:\Windows\Media\Chimes.wav"
MMControl1.Command = "open"
MMControl1.Command = "play"
```

If you scanned any images, then add the appropriate file to an image object each time Melanie selects a command or button. Remember this is to be fun for Melanie so the project should be easy and fun to use.

Delivering the Project

Introduction ▶ Now the TEMS system is complete and you have loaded the ShelyTemps.mdb database from the data entry program in Chapter 3. You learned about using custom controls in Chapter 8 to create more professional-looking applications. In Chapter 8 you thoroughly tested the system to make sure that all procedures function properly. In this chapter you will prepare the system for delivery to Shely Services, Inc. You will add the copyright form shown in Chapter 1 to the project and generate a splash screen. Then you will add and test the ToolTip text and online Help files. Finally, you will use the Setup Wizard to create files for distribution to Shely Services, Inc.

Adding the Splash Screen

A splash screen is the first image that appears when a user runs an application. The splash screen contains copyright information about the application that displays while the application is being loaded. The application uses the Timer control and its associated event to hold the user's attention while the program files are being read into memory. Figure 9-1 shows the copyright screen from Chapter 1 that has been modified for use as a splash screen.

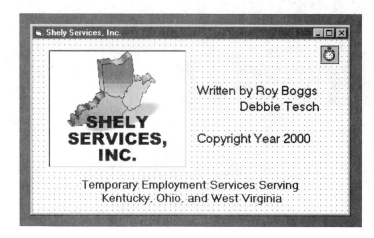

Figure 9-1: TEMS system splash screen

The copyright screen from Chapter 1 was modified to remove the Exit button and to use the Timer control to control the length of the display. In addition, the frmCopyright form is established as the **startup form**, or the form in a multiform project that automatically loads and appears when the user executes the application. The Interval property of the tmrCopyrite control is set to 20000, which represents a 20-second time period for the display. During this display period, the frmMaster, frmLogin, frmEmpeMaint, frmPrint, and frmScreen forms are loaded into memory using the Load statement.

Syntax ▶	**Load** *object*

In this syntax, the *object* represents the form to be loaded. The **Load statement** loads a form or control into memory. The properties and controls associated with each form are available to the application for reference and can be altered, even though the form is not currently visible to the user. The form is displayed when the Show method statement is executed by its associated event. In the Shely project, all forms are loaded in the Form_Load() event of the frmCopyright form. As forms are loaded, all form properties are set to their initial values and then the Load Event procedure associated with the form is executed.

When the Timer control interval expires, the tmrCopyrite_Timer() event is executed. In the Shely application, the Timer event unloads the tmrCopyright form and displays the frmMaster form using the Show method.

Adding Help Using ToolTips

A **ToolTip** is a word or phrase that describes the function of a toolbar button or other tool. The ToolTip appears when you rest the mouse pointer on an object containing a ToolTip. In Chapter 8 you used the ToolTipText property to display the current date when the user positioned the mouse pointer over the time panel on the status bar.

Syntax ▶   *object*.**ToolTipText** [= *string*]

In this syntax, *object* is an object expression and *string* is the expression that appears in a small rectangle near the object when the user's mouse pointer hovers over the object for approximately one second at run time. You can create the string expression for the ToolTip at design time by setting the ToolTipText property in the control's Properties dialog box. Figure 9-2 shows the ToolTipText properties assigned in the Shely project.

Control	ToolTipText Property Value
cmdDataManagement	"Browse and Manage Temporary Employee Data"
cmdPrintReports	"Show and Print Current Information"
cmdBackUp	"Copy Shely Database to Backup File"
cmdExit	"End the TEMS Program"

Figure 9-2: Shely project ToolTipText assignments

The ToolTipText properties for the TEMS system are assigned at design time in the Properties window for the CommandButton controls.

Microsoft Help Files

Online Help files offer an excellent resource for a user to get help while working in an application. Almost all Windows applications provide standard Help files with which most users are familiar. However, the actual online Help file is not part of the Visual Basic program; the designer creates the Help file separately from the project and then adds the file to the project. The following sections provide only a basic introduction to creating and using Help files. Complete Help files with icons, key maps, and so on are beyond the scope of this book. When developing Help files, you might consider several inexpensive third party packages that are easy to use and provide excellent results.

To create online Help files specific to the Shely project, you will use a word processor to create an .rtf file and a Help project (.hpj) text file containing compiler directions. Then you will compile the *.rtf and *.hpj files with a Help compiler to create a *.hlp file. After editing the material and recompiling as necessary, you will add the completed Help file to the Visual Basic project.

In order to create Help files, you need a Help compiler. In Visual Basic 5.0, you can use the Find command on the Windows Start menu to find the HCW compiler. Or you might need to download the Microsoft Help Workshop (Hcwsetup.exe) from Microsoft's World Wide Web site. After installing the Microsoft Help Workshop, you can find the necessary compiler in the C:\Program Files\Help Workshop\Hcw.exe file. You also can find the Hcwsetup.exe file in the Hcw folder in the Tools folder on the Visual Basic CD. For Visual Basic 6.0, the file is located at C:\Program Files\Microsoft Visual Studio\Common\Tools\Hcw.exe. The compiler comes with the professional edition, and if it is not available on your system, you can download it from Microsoft.

Creating an *.rtf File

The secret to creating an effective Help file is to plan which data you want to include in it. Then you can use a word processor to write the Help file and save it as an *.rtf file. The Help compiler only interprets codes included in an *.rtf file.

Figure 9-3 shows the content page of the online Help file created for the main form of the Shely project. The underlined phrases, which appear green in the application, are hyperlinks to other (target) pages that the user can select.

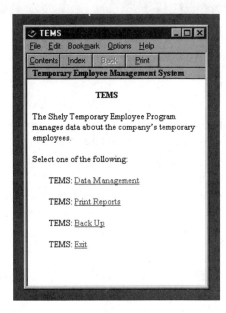

Figure 9-3: Content page of the online Help file for the Shely project

Figure 9-4 shows the *.rtf file that serves as the content page. Each option is double underlined, and the link appears as hidden text without a space. (To hide text using Microsoft Word, select the text, click Format on the menu bar, click Font, and then click the Hidden check box.) To create the content page, type the text shown in Figure 9-4 and then format the text. You might need to type a space between the option and the link so you can select the text; then after formatting the text, delete the space. In Microsoft Word, if you turn on the nonprinting characters using the Show/Hide ¶ button on the Standard toolbar, the link will appear with a dotted underline. When you are finished, save the file as ShelyHelp.rtf in the Chapter9 folder on your Student Disk.

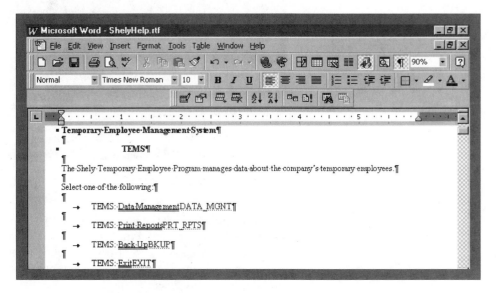

Figure 9-4: Content page *.rtf file

The second target page appears when the user selects the link to the Data Management option, as shown in Figure 9-5.

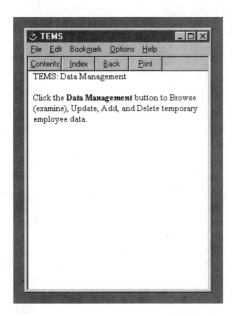

Figure 9-5: Data Management Help page

To create the target page shown in Figure 9-5 in the ShelyHelp.rtf file, you must enter a page break and then type the target page text shown in Figure 9-6.

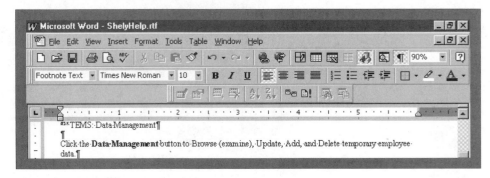

Figure 9-6: The *.rtf file for the Data Management target page

You should enter the symbols #, $, and K as footnote symbols in the document using the Footnote command on the Insert menu. The # provides the name of the link (DATA_MGMT), $ provides the name on the contents page (Data Management), and K provides the keywords for this target page, which are browse, update, add, and delete. Type a semicolon to separate the keywords, and do not type spaces between keys. Figure 9-7 shows the footnotes on the target page.

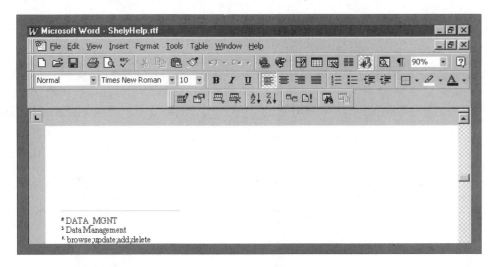

Figure 9-7: Footnotes for the Data Management *.rtf file target page

Pages three through five of the TEMS online Help system can be entered with the data for the second target page. For each target page you enter, make sure you include a page break and the footnotes to capture the name of the link, the name on the contents page, and keywords associated with the target page. Figures 9-8 through 9-10 show target pages three through five.

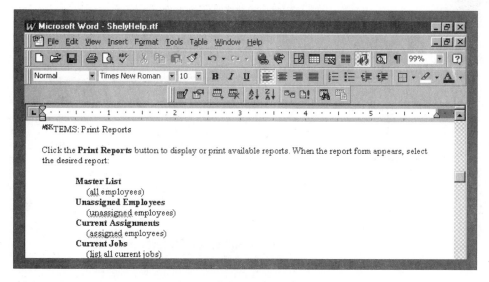

Figure 9-8: The *.rtf file for the Print Reports target page

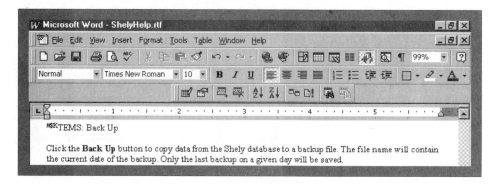

Figure 9-9: The *.rtf file for the Back Up target page

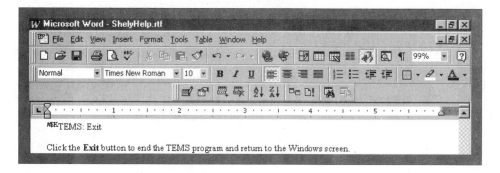

Figure 9-10: The *.rtf file for the Exit target page

Figure 9-11 shows the associated footnotes for each page. After creating these target pages, you can save the file (as ShelyHelp.rtf) and then print the document to examine it for accuracy.

Print Reports Target Page	Back Up Target Page	Exit Target Page
#PRT_RPTS	#BKUP	#EXIT
$Print Reports	$Backup	$Exit
Kreports;jobs;listings	Kbackup	Kexit;end

Figure 9-11: Footnotes for the additional target pages of the ShelyHelp.rtf file

Creating a Help Project *.hpj File

You create directions for the Help compiler using a word processor and then save the text file with the *.hpj file extension. This file describes the title for the Help files, the location of the *.rtf file, and references to the dimensions of the Help window. Figure 9-12 shows the ShelyHelp.hpj file. After you use this .hpj file to compile the ShelyHelp.rtf file, you must edit the file using the Help compiler (Hcw.exe).

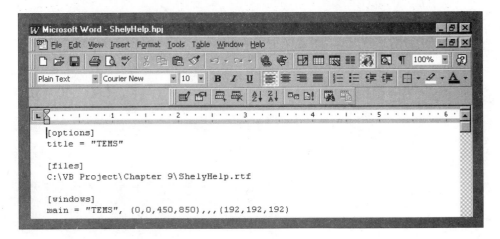

Figure 9-12: ShelyHelp.hpj file

Using the Microsoft Help Workshop

You use the Microsoft Help Workshop to compile the ShelyHelp.hpj file that uses the ShelyTemp.rtf file. Figure 9-13 shows the Microsoft Help Workshop window after opening the ShelyHelp.hpj file. Once you create the ShelyHelp.hpj file, you maintain it using the Hcw.exe file. After compiling the ShelyHelp.hpj file, you cannot modify it directly as a text file. If you need to make changes to the .hpj file, you must use the option buttons in the Help Workshop associated with the respective code.

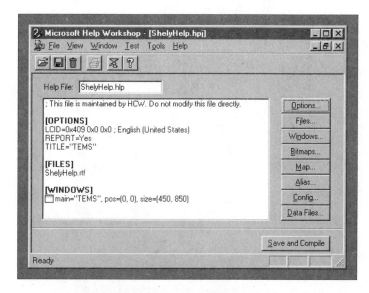

Figure 9-13: Microsoft Help Workshop containing the ShelyHelp.hpj file

You create the Help file by clicking the Save and Compile button. The Help Workshop then uses the ShelyHelp.rtf file to create the Help file. After you compile the file and correct any compile messages, you can close the result box. If you encounter any errors in the .hpj file, you should modify the file using the Help Workshop. Your result will be a standard Help file with the extension *.hlp (ShelyHelp.hlp), which is a stand-alone file that you can run from Windows Explorer. After creating the *.hlp file, you should execute and examine the file for errors. Figures 9-14 through 9-17 show the target pages for Data Management, Print Reports, Back Up, and Exit when the ShelyHelp.hlp file is executed.

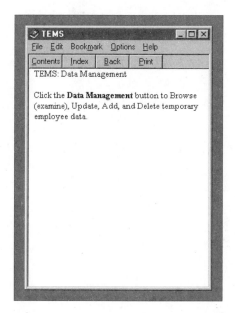

Figure 9-14: Generated Data Management Help page

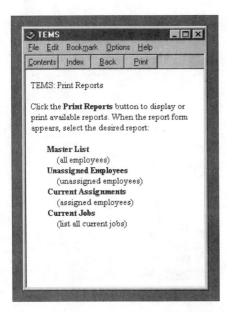

Figure 9-15: Generated Print Reports Help page

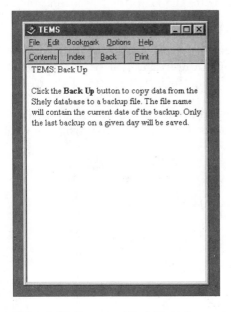

Figure 9-16: Generated Back Up Help page

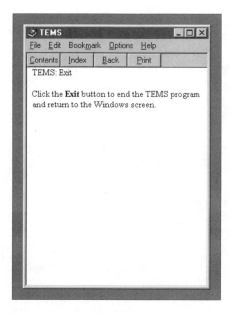

Figure 9-17: Generated Exit Help page

Figure 9-18 shows the Index using the defined keys. The Index functions in the same way as the Index for all standard Windows online Help applications. When the user selects an Index key and then clicks the Display button, the associated Help page as defined in the ShelyHelp.rtf file opens.

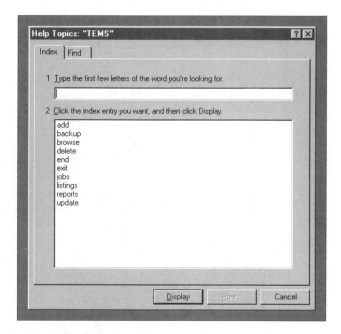

Figure 9-18: TEMS Help Index

Add the Help File to the Visual Basic Project

Now you must add the completed Help file to the Shely project. The Help file is available from the frmMaster form. The first step is to add a Help menu and a CommonDialog control named dlgDialog to the form. You can open the Property Pages dialog box for the dlgDialog by right-clicking the CommonDialog control. Then you enter the location of the Help file on the Help tab, as shown in Figure 9-19.

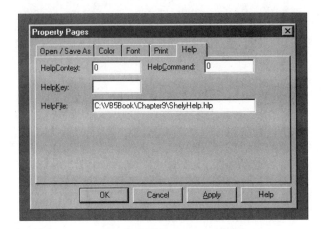

Figure 9-19: Property Pages dialog box for the dlgDialog control

To access the Help file, you must add the following code to the mnuHelp_Click() Event procedure:

```
Private Sub mnuHelp_Click()
  dlgDialog.HelpCommand = cdlHelpContents
  dlgDialog.ShowHelp
End Sub
```

When you execute the Shely project and select the Help menu, the Shely Help file will appear on the screen.

Preparing the Shely Project for Delivery

While developing this project, you have taken precautions to make it easier for you (the programmer) to move from one computer to another, such as using drive A to store data files and opening the same file from several places in the program. Both of these precautions could become problematic if left unchanged. For example, if the client loses the master data disk, then it would be difficult for another programmer to change the name and location of files if they are named in several places. To correct this, you will restructure the project to name all files in one place and store the data files on drive C.

To centralize file access, the Form_Initialize() Event procedure of the frmMaster form will assign the location of all Shely files to global variables. Figure 9-20 shows the required global variable declarations and their associated module names. The program code shown in Figure 9-20 shows that all statements that access files are replaced with the associated variable name.

Variable Declaration	Module Assignment
Public strDataBase As String	DataBaseProcessing
Public strRandomFile As String	RandomFileProcessing
Public strBackUpFile As String	BackUp
Global strCryRpt As String	CrystalRpt

Figure 9-20: Global variable assignments for the Shely files

You will store the final Shely project and all data files in a folder on drive C with the pathname C:\Program Files\Shely TEMS. By isolating file assignments in a single location, you make the maintenance function easier especially if you need to relocate the data files later. The file location assignments in the Form_Initialize() Event procedure are as follows:

```
'
'Make any changes to the location of files here.
'They are not named elsewhere in the VB code.
'
' (Note: The database is also set in the
' property box of the data objects on the
' frmEmpeMaint form.)
'
' (Note: The location of the database is also
' named in the Crystal Report file.  It can be
' changed in Crystal Reports.)
'
'**********************************************************
'*
strRandomFile = "C:\Program Files\Shely TEMS\SSicher.txt"
strDataBase = "C:\Program Files\Shely TEMS\ShelyTemps.mdb"
   Dim strNow As String
   Dim strFileName As String
   strNow = Format$(Date, "mmddyy")
   strFileName = "ShelyBkUp_" + strNow + ".dat"
strBackUpFile = "C:\Program Files\Shely TEMS\" + strFileName
dlgDialog.HelpFile = "C:\Program Files\Shely TEMS\ShelyHelp.hlp"
strCryRpt = "C:\Program Files\Shely TEMS\currjobs.rpt"
```

When you deliver the project, you must place all data files in the C:\Program Files\Shely TEMS folder. These files include the ShelyTemps.mdb, ShelyHelp.hlp, currjobs.rpt, and the SSicher.txt files.

Figure 9-21 shows the Project Explorer window and the list of forms and modules for the Shely TEMS project. Before you package the Shely project for delivery, you should thoroughly test the program one more time on a platform that simulates the Shely computer and its printer to make sure that the Shely computer has the capacity to run the executable application.

Figure 9-21: Project Explorer window for the Shely TEMS project

One problem that might occur is that the Shely printer could produce different spacing than the printer used to prepare the print modules. Many impact and ink jet printers might produce unpredictable results; a laser printer usually doesn't cause problems.

After you complete your final testing, you should create an executable file named Shely TEMS.exe in the C:\Program Files\Shely TEMS folder. The Shely TEMS folder should look like Figure 9-22.

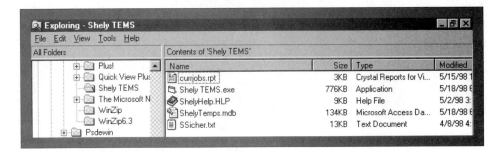

Figure 9-22: Shely TEMS folder

The Setup Wizard

Now that you have placed the completed Shely TEMS system data files in the defined application folder and created the Shely TEMS.exe file, you can take the final step of preparing to deliver the software to Shely Services. To package the software for delivery, you will use the Setup Wizard available with Visual Basic. The Setup Wizard might have a different name and location on your installation of Visual Basic, and the various screens might look different, however, the process and the steps remain much the same.

To prepare the Shely Project for moving to the Shely computer, use the following basic steps:

1. Locate the Setup Wizard. For Visual Basic 5.0 users, the location is probably C:\Program Files\DevStudio\Vb\Setupkit\Kitfil32\Setupwiz.exe. For Visual Basic 6.0 users, search for Pdcmdh.exe, called the Package and Deployment Wizard.

2. Run the Setupwiz.exe program and locate the Shely TEMS.vpb project file using the browser. Figure 9-23 shows the Select Project and Options dialog box after locating the Shely TEMS.vbp project.

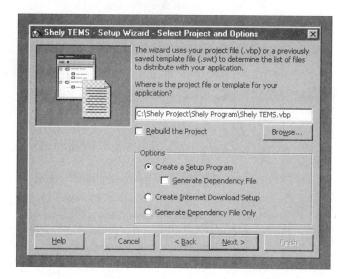

Figure 9-23: Setup Wizard – Select Project and Options dialog box

3. Proceed to the Distribution Method dialog box of the Setup Wizard. Choose the Floppy disk option as the method of distribution, as shown in Figure 9-24.

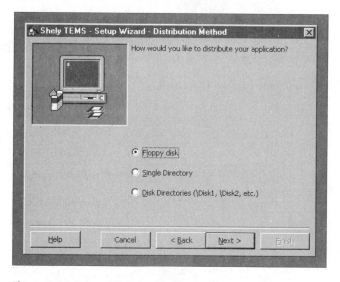

Figure 9-24: Setup Wizard – Distribution Method dialog box

4. In the Floppy Disk dialog box of the Setup Wizard, establish the floppy drive location and disk size as shown in Figure 9-25.

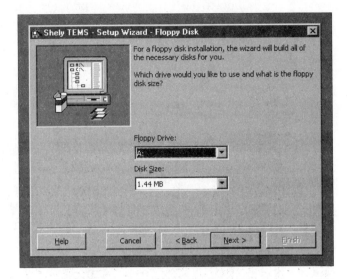

Figure 9-25: Setup Wizard – Floppy Disk dialog box

5. In the Data Access dialog box of the Setup Wizard, you are instructed to choose any of the applicable ISAM database formats. The Shely TEMS system uses only the database Jet engine. Be certain that the dbUseJet check box is checked, as shown in Figure 9-26.

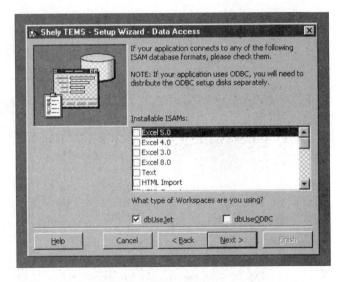

Figure 9-26: Setup Wizard – Data Access dialog box

6. The ActiveX Server Components dialog box indicates that the wizard has discovered that there are no ActiveX server components for the Shely project, which is correct. You should leave the screen as shown in Figure 9-27 and proceed to the next step.

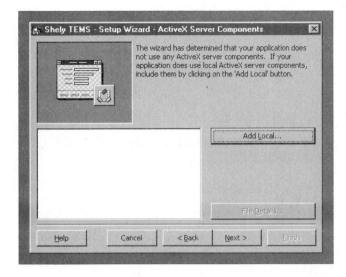

Figure 9-27: Setup Wizard – ActiveX Server Components dialog box

7. The Setup Wizard's Confirm Dependencies dialog box indicates that the application requires the use of the Crystal Reports .ocx file (Crystl32.ocx), the system common dialog file (Comdlg32.ocx), and the Microsoft Shared Dao350.dll file, which is correct. You can examine the details of these files using the File Details button. See Figure 9-28.

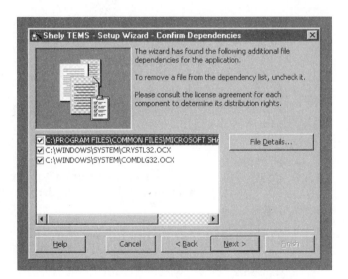

Figure 9-28: Setup Wizard – Confirm Dependencies dialog box

8. In the next step, the wizard assembles the necessary system files. After the wizard adds the necessary system files to the application, you must add the files in the C:\Program Files\Shely TEMS folder by clicking the Add button. If you choose not to add these files using the Setup Wizard, you will need to add them separately to Shely's computer before the project will function properly. Be careful not to delete any of the files selected by the wizard, and you can ignore any warning message (such as out-of-date dependency) associated with the Shely TEMS.exe file. Figure 9-29 shows the File Summary dialog box after the data files and the Shely TEMS.exe file have been added.

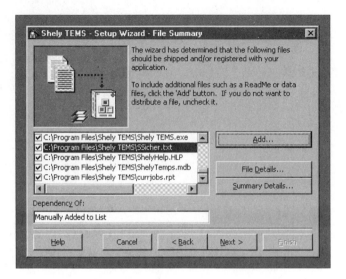

Figure 9-29: Setup Wizard – File Summary dialog box

9. Continue by completing the finish step of the Setup Wizard, and then wait while the wizard compresses all of the assembled files. You should have the number of required blank, formatted disks available based on the Setup Wizard message box shown in Figure 9-30. You can use Windows Explorer to prepare your disks if necessary prior to clicking the OK button.

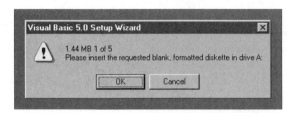

Figure 9-30: Final step of the Setup Wizard

10. The Setup Wizard finishes after you create all of the required disks. Make sure to label your disks in the order in which they were created.

Delivering the Project

The Shely TEMS system is ready for delivery to the company. To install the project on the Shely computer, you insert disk 1 in drive A, click the Start button on the taskbar, click Run, and then type "A:setup.exe" in the Open text box. The installation will prompt you for each installation disk. When the installation is complete, you should check the C:\Program Files\Shely TEMS folder to make sure that all of the files are present. Delivering the project also involves training the users and providing user documentation of the system. Normally, the client specifies user-training requirements in the project contract. Your instructor might require you to create a user manual, although this book does not include one.

A user manual accompanies the project when it is delivered to the client. The user manual is typically a step-by-step description of how to use the project. User manuals should be clearly written and include instructions for executing each component of the project. These instructions should include, where appropriate, figures and tips on how to resolve system problems. In this case, the project itself should contain messages, ToolTips, and Help files, which are part of an overall clean and attractive project with forms that are logically related and easy to navigate.

SUMMARY

After much hard work, your complete system project has been designed, created, tested, and delivered to Shely Services, Inc. You may choose at this point to print the entire project. Figure 9-31 shows the location of Event, Sub, and Function procedures for the forms and modules. You might choose to use this table and the accompanying program to review the skills implemented in this project.

If you are about to embark on completing one of the progressive projects, you have already experienced creating a substantive project. When added to your portfolio, this project could make quite an impression on a potential employer. Congratulations on your success!

Forms	Modules
frmCopyright	BackUp
Form_Load	BackUpRoutine
tmrCopyrite_Timer	HandleErrorRoutines
frmEmpeMaint	ClearEmployeeMaintenanceForm
chkPlacement_Click	ActivateButtonsAndMenus
cmdBrowse_Click	DeactivateButtonsAndMenus
Form_Load	ClearEmployeeMaintenanceFields
Form_Initialize	CrystalRpt
cmdAdd_Click	DateBaseProcessing
cmdUpdate_Click	BeSureReadOnly
cmdDelete_Click	OpendatTempEmpe
cmdClear_Click	AddEmployee
cmdReturn_Click	UpdateEmployee
cmdSearch_Click	DeleteEmployee
cmdReturn2_Click	SelectEmployee
cmdActivate_Click	ProcessRequest
mnuFileBrowse_Click	DataEditing
mnuFileClear_Click	PassWordCheck
mnuFileRefresh_Click	CheckData
mnuFileReturn_Click	GetEmployeeID
mnuMaintenanceAdd_Click	DoubleCheck
mnuMaintenanceDelete_Click	GetWordsPerMinute

Figure 9-31: Location of Event, Sub, and Function procedures

Forms	Modules
mnuMaintenanceUpdate_Click	PrintAvailableList
opt10up_Click	AvailableHeader
opt6to8_Click	AvailableDetail
opt8to10_Click	AvailableFooter
optLess6_Click	PrintJobListing
txtAddress_GotFocus	JobHeader
txtCity_GotFocus	PrintControlBreak
txtEmpeID_GotFocus	JobFooter
txtFName_GotFocus	PrintMasterList
txtLName_GotFocus	MasterHeader
txtNotes_GotFocus	MasterDetail
cboState_GotFocus	MasterFooter
txtPhone_GotFocus	RandomFileProcessing
txtOptionStorage_Change	SetUpArray
frmLogin	PrintArray
cmdCancel_Click	ScreenAvailableList
cmdOK_Click	ScreenAvailableHeader
txtPassword_GotFocus	ScreenAvailableDetail
frmMaster	ScreenAvailableFooter
cmdBackUp_Click	
cmdExit_Click	
cmdDataManagement_Click	
cmdPrintReports_Click	
Form_Initialize	
Form_Load	
Form_Unload	
mnuBackUp_Click	
mnuDataManagement_Click	
mnuExit_Click	
mnuHelp_Click	
mnuReports_Click	

Figure 9-31: Location of Event, Sub, and Function procedures (continued)

Forms	Modules

frmPrint

        cmdCurrentJobs_Click

        cmdDetailReport_Click

        cmdControlBreakReport_Click

        cmdExceptionReport_Click

        cmdSkipReport_Click

        Form_Load

frmScreen

        cmdReturn_Click

Figure 9-31: Location of Event, Sub, and Function procedures (continued)

PROGRESSIVE PROJECTS

The success of your project has been the management of the data. The reports must contain accurate data, each and every time they are generated. This aspect of the project has been emphasized throughout the various steps in the project.

Another very important aspect of completing your project is the creation and delivery of the online Help files. The ultimate success of a project is in the hands of the user, and not the programmer. Here is where Help files can play a great role in lowering a user's level of frustration. Take time and prepare ToolTips and Help files for your project. Decide where Help files are needed, and then add them to the appropriate forms.

As a final step, add a splash screen to the beginning of your project. Use a Timer object as the main screen loads. You will have to test it to get the time right. Make sure to add your name to the project.

Now you can compile the final version of the project into an executable module. If your instructor asks you to do so, use the Setup Wizard to create setup files. At any rate, be sure to transport your data files (Help, Crystal Reports, the database, and security files) with the executable module if you do not use the wizard.

Index

T